FAILED
STATE

SAM FREEDMAN

FAILED STATE

WHY NOTHING WORKS AND HOW WE FIX IT

MACMILLAN

First published 2024 by Macmillan
an imprint of Pan Macmillan
The Smithson, 6 Briset Street, London EC1M 5NR
EU representative: Macmillan Publishers Ireland Ltd, 1st Floor,
The Liffey Trust Centre, 117–126 Sheriff Street Upper,
Dublin 1, D01 YC43
Associated companies throughout the world
www.panmacmillan.com

ISBN 978-1-0350-2659-3

5 7 9 8 6 4

A CIP catalogue record for this book is available from the British Library.

Typeset in Adobe Garamond by Jouve (UK), Milton Keynes
Printed and bound by CPI Group (UK) Ltd, Croydon, CR0 4YY

Visit **www.panmacmillan.com** to read more about all our books
and to buy them. You will also find features, author interviews and
news of any author events, and you can sign up for e-newsletters
so that you're always first to hear about our new releases.

To Mum and Dad

'Nations begin by forming their institutions, but, in the end, are continuously formed by them'

LORD HAILSHAM

'A bad system will beat a good person every time'

W. EDWARDS DEMING

'If the rule you followed brought you to this, of what use was the rule?'

CORMAC McCARTHY, *NO COUNTRY FOR OLD MEN*

CONTENTS

Introduction: The Crisis Cycle   1

Part 1: Overloaded   21

1. No Ninjas   23

2. Enemies Within   59

3. Contract Killings   93

Part 2: Overpowered   125

4. Democracy Bypass   127

5. Enemies of the People   163

6. Civil War   195

Part 3: Overdrive   227

7. The Random Announcement Generator   229

8. High Speed Crash   257

Conclusion: Ending Our Crisis   291

Acknowledgements   305

Notes   309

Index   347

INTRODUCTION

The Crisis Cycle

In January 1974, Sir William Armstrong, the Head of the Home Civil Service and one of the most powerful people in the country, was found rolling around on the floor of the No. 10 waiting room babbling incoherently about the imminent end of the world.

The next day he locked all his permanent secretary colleagues, from across the civil service, in a room and told them Armageddon was coming. Then he went into the office of Victor Rothschild, a somewhat shadowy adviser to the prime minister, Edward Heath, and explained his plans for 'the Red and Blue Armies' he seemed to believe he controlled. He told another colleague that he was a reincarnation of the seer Tiresias, a blind prophet of Greek mythology.

Armstrong was quietly dispatched to Rothschild's mansion in Barbados to recover from this nervous breakdown. By the time he returned Harold Wilson had replaced Heath as prime minister and consented to Armstrong taking up a role outside the civil service as chair of Midland Bank.[1]

Sir William's breakdown was precipitated by one of the worst post-war crises to hit the British state. A combination of spectacularly misconceived economic policy and conflict in the Middle East led to a rapid increase in inflation and a brutal recession. A miners' strike left the country without enough coal. Heath was forced to implement a law that forbade non-essential companies from using electricity more than three days a week. Television stations were shut down from 10:30 p.m. to conserve energy. It got to the point where ration books were distributed to motorists and columnists wrote about a possible military coup.[2] Heath, refusing to settle with the miners, was forced into an early election, which he lost.

Armstrong, who was often called the real 'Deputy Prime Minister' due to his influence over Heath and his habit of appearing alongside him at press conferences, buckled under the pressure. He was trying to run the civil service while also acting as the prime minister's main economic policy adviser as inflation rose inexorably. The prices and incomes policy, through which the government tried to rigidly control the economy, failed. The miners' strike felt like a test of authority that the government could not back away from but also could not win. It was too much.

I asked Sir Robin Butler, who was working as Heath's private secretary at the time, and later ran No. 10 for Margaret Thatcher, John Major and Tony Blair, whether it was the worst crisis he had experienced in government.

'No,' he said, 'every crisis is a crisis in a different way . . . I don't think any of them outweigh the others.'[3]

One of the great dangers of writing a book about contemporary politics, especially when it has this title, is the declinism trap. We have a natural human tendency to focus on the problems of our times and the triumphs of the past.[4] When we look around us at the detritus of the Boris Johnson and Liz Truss premierships, an economy that has been stagnant for over fifteen years, failing public services, record levels of child poverty, overcrowded prisons, sewage in our rivers, and endless series of cancelled trains, it is hard not to think that we have never had it so bad. By contrast previous eras can be fondly imagined as ones where ministers were dedicated public servants, the cream of the crop, aided by a Rolls-Royce civil service, calmly managing challenges in the public interest.

This is, of course, not true. Modern British history is better thought of not as a story of decline but of a repeating cycle of crises that are eventually resolved, only for a new one to appear. The destruction of the Second World War ran into ongoing rationing, then Suez, the inflationary misery of the 1970s, the social decay of the 1980s and so on. Things have usually seemed bad, and sometimes terminal. As Sir Robin said, though, 'every crisis is a crisis in a different way'.

Eventually the challenges of a given era get so bad that a dam breaks and a way of doing things that has become accepted as inevitable, or too hard to change, gets washed away. These dramatic moments happen roughly every forty years and often, by resolving the biggest contemporary problems, create the conditions for the next crisis cycle.

In his book *The Death of Consensus*, the historian Phil Tinline looks at these turning points and the conditions required to trigger them: 'Democracy means that any unthinkable new idea has to go through a long trial before it can be sufficiently established for a government to win power and act on it. The dispelling of an old nightmare, the destruction of an old taboo, takes a lot of back-and-forth wrangling between the established orthodoxy and the new contender. While that is happening, things look bleak, and frightening.'[5]

My argument in this book is not that we are at the worst point in our history – we have dealt with bigger challenges in the past – but that we are reaching the end of our current cycle. Right now things look bleak and frightening, but our moment of change is due. How painful that transition will be depends on correctly diagnosing the particular crisis of our times.

The crises of the nineteenth and early twentieth centuries were dominated by questions of democracy itself. The Reform Acts and the fight for control between the House of Commons and Tory-controlled House of Lords provided the dramatic moments of resolution. In the mid-twentieth century, the demands of a newly enfranchised population combined with the grinding poverty of full industrialization, and a very limited welfare state, led to a social crisis. The key politicians of the era from Attlee to Macmillan and Heath were scarred by the social failures they had witnessed in the 1930s, and were determined to avoid another round of mass unemployment at any cost.

The society they oversaw saw steady economic growth and the rapid expansion of the state, symbolized by the creation of the NHS in 1948. But their collective embrace of what seemed like the modern innovation of economic planning through central control, alongside a complex web of exchange controls together with prices and incomes policies, led to the next wave of crisis. Industrial relations, especially with trade unions in nationally owned sectors, deteriorated. The first Wilson government was fatally undermined by its failure to limit union power. Heath, as we have seen from Sir William Armstrong's story, was brought down by it. In 1976 Britain was subject to the indignity of an International Monetary Fund bail-out after coming close to running out of money altogether.[6]

This was another dam-breaking moment that forced a dramatic moment of change, driven initially by James Callaghan's chancellor

Denis Healey and then, more forcefully, by Margaret Thatcher. The legacy of Thatcher is complex and will be a frequent focus for this book. Some of her economic reforms were unnecessary, others were needed but were not backed up with sufficient support for those who lost out. But they did end that crisis cycle.

And they helped create the cycle we are now in. The initial crises of the British state were ones of democracy; the mid-century ones were those of social conflict; and the 1970s and 1980s of economic upheaval. The one we are in now is a crisis of governance.

We have plentiful problems but they do not feel unresolvable, or terminal, as they did during some moments of these previous crises. We know at least some of the reasons we have low economic growth, such as a severe lack of investment in infrastructure, planning restrictions, a crazily incoherent tax system, and high levels of regional disparity. We know what it would take to have a well-functioning hospital system. It is easy to forget that public satisfaction with the NHS was at its highest level not much more than a decade ago. There is no fundamental threat to democracy, no imminent IMF intervention, no world war (not yet, at least).

Our problem is the total failure of our political institutions to deal with the more limited challenges we have. Britain's constitution has always been an oddity among developed countries. None of our institutions were designed but rather evolved incrementally through precedent, convention and, occasionally, crisis. Many of the core blocks of our political system have no basis in law. From the role of the prime minister, to the appointment of the cabinet, to the status of the opposition, and the powers of the speaker, it is convention all the way down.

This system has always led to difficulties caused by the lack of safeguards. It is almost fifty years since the senior Conservative politician Lord Hailsham popularized the term 'elective dictatorship' to describe the enormous power held by a government with a majority in the Commons. This is a result of having an almost entirely ceremonial head of state in the monarchy, an extremely weak and unelected second chamber in the House of Lords, a main legislature whose timetable is controlled by the government, and a judiciary that, by convention, follows the laws as laid down by that legislature. Constitutional scholars like Vernon Bogdanor and Peter Hennessy have been documenting these challenges, both real and theoretical, for many decades. As Bogdanor noted in 1995, we have 'a very peculiar constitution which no one intended . . . whereby the government of the day decides what the constitution is.'[7]

Over the last forty years, first gradually and then suddenly, these innate pressures, compounded by other factors, have caused our institutions to fail. Three trends, examined in the three main sections of this book, have caused an already troubled system to gum up completely and leave us with a crisis of governance.

The first section – Overloaded – tells the story of how the British state became one of the most centralized democracies in the world. And how, as a result, it is simply trying to do far too much through institutions, like No. 10 Downing Street and the Treasury, that do not have anywhere near the capacity or capabilities to cope.

As Rupert Harrison, who was George Osborne's most senior adviser throughout his time as chancellor, put it to me: 'The core weakness of the British state is the constant chopping and changing and the inability to stick to any long-term strategy, whether that's industrial policy, public sector reform, tax policy . . . compared to other European countries, in particular, we're just hopeless at sticking to anything . . . We're incredibly vulnerable to a new government or new minister coming in, wanting to reinvent the wheel, ripping up what came before . . . There's just this irresistible range of levers and a desire to fiddle.'[8]

This is primarily a story about England. As each of the four parts of the United Kingdom came together they kept some devolved powers and unique characteristics. The Blair government significantly extended those powers. But England, which dominates in terms of population and economy, and focus for the Westminster government, has always been highly centralized since it first came together under Anglo-Saxon monarchs. Local government has, therefore, always been weaker than in most other developed countries. And in the last forty years it has been almost destroyed by successive, highly centralizing, Whitehall administrations.

The overload trend, though, is not just about the centre taking powers away from local government but also the increasing complexity of issues they have always been responsible for. Some of this is because the world has become more complicated: digital regulation, for instance, was a lot simpler before the internet took off. Changing technology increases expectations. When Spanish Flu broke out at the end of the First World War the government did not, and were not expected to, have a pandemic preparedness strategy. There were no vaccines, not any possibility of them, nor would lockdowns communicated quickly at national scale have been plausible.

Better awareness of risk and a greater desire to stop problems before they happen has led to a vast array of new public bodies and regulators overseen by ministers. The so-called 'regulatory state', monitoring everything from school and hospital performance, to environmental standards and adherence to equality law, has exploded in size over the past forty years. Concentrating power at the centre of government, and destroying state capacity outside of it, while at the same time massively increasing the scope of what government covers, is a core reason for our policy paralysis.

The loss of capacity has also meant an increasing reliance on outsourcing and the use of private companies to provide taxpayer-funded services. This is reasonable enough for services that are easy to measure and for which there is a proper competitive market, like cleaning or rubbish collection. But we now routinely use it for exceptionally complex services with no existing providers. As a result a handful of outsourcing companies have become inordinately powerful, despite repeated scandalous failures. Likewise some of our most important services like children's homes and social care are delivered largely by private companies, many of whom are owned by private-equity firms extracting enormous profits from stricken councils unable to challenge them.

Section two – Overpowered – tells the story of how the British government became the most dominant of any Western democracy at the expense of both Parliament and, ultimately, the British people Parliament is supposed to represent.

Executive dominance is not a new phenomenon. As we have seen, Lord Hailsham was worrying about it in the 1970s. It is a function of the way British democracy evolved. By the early twentieth century the monarch's role had become almost entirely ceremonial, with full executive power shifting to his or her ministers. Then with the passing of the Parliament Act in 1911, the Commons achieved dominance over the Lords.

From then on, a prime minister with a majority in Parliament, who could keep their own party on board, was one of the most powerful elected officials in the world. Most democracies have a network of inbuilt checks and balances. This can be a head of state with meaningful powers; a second chamber that can block legislation;

and/or a judiciary with independent responsibility for safeguarding a written constitution. We have none of these things. In addition, the executive are nearly all appointed from within the Commons, so only three quarters of MPs are primarily focused on their parliamentary role.

Checks and balances can create their own problems. At the other end of the spectrum to us, the United States has so many that stalemate between different branches of government has become the norm. Watching the President and Congress spend months trying to reach agreement on raising the debt ceiling, which allows the country to function, does not seem a good advert for constitutional complexity.

But Britain is a real outlier in having very few real checks at all and that puts an unusual amount of pressure on the government to behave appropriately – and on the Commons to scrutinize their performance and any laws they put forward. As William Gladstone famously put it, the British constitution 'presumes more boldly than any other the good sense and the good faith of those who work it'.

That good sense and good faith has always been lacking. David Lloyd George's government was more openly corrupt than any in recent years and avoided censure. Anthony Eden outright lied to Parliament about collusion with the Israelis in advance of the Suez crisis but was never sanctioned. Since the formation of the modern party system, whipping MPs to vote for government legislation regardless of their own doubts about its merits has been standard. Indeed, rebellions against the whips have actually become more frequent over the past few decades, and Parliament more willing to challenge government.

But governments have reacted to this challenge by trying to shut it down, through a whole series of parliamentary rule changes and inappropriate use of existing powers. In doing so they have made House of Commons scrutiny of a majority government exceptionally difficult. As a result the Lords have had to spend more time trying to unravel poorly constructed laws, but as they are both relatively weak and conscious of being unelected, they have not been able to act as much of a defence. Instead we have seen the courts get more involved in politics, quite explicitly as a defence against an over-powerful executive. But judges are often not best placed to make decisions about inherently political topics, nor does our constitution make the balance of power between them and the government clear.

Ultimately lack of scrutiny leads to worse laws and governments failing to achieve their own goals. It is easy for ministers, even if they are acting in good faith, to think they are better off taking short cuts but the reality is that problems just emerge when it is too late. In recent years many ministers have not seemed interested in trying to achieve concrete real-world goals at all.

Likewise the civil service is supposed to take forward government policy, regardless of whether individual officials agree with it, but they are also supposed to challenge bad ideas and present alternatives for ministers to decide on. But here, again, we have seen govern-ments try to shut down scrutiny, and take a paranoid approach to any pushback. As a result, scrutiny has weakened, and an ever more centralized government has taken advice from ever fewer people. Governments have also taken to appointing partisans to key public bodies like the Charity Commission and Ofcom, to insulate them-selves from independent thought.

In the final section we turn to how the pace of politics has gone into overdrive, creating a terrible environment in which to make good decisions and a destructive set of incentives for politicians.

At the heart of this story is the media and, as with the other two trends, the often baleful presence of powerful and unaccountable press barons is hardly new. Partisan and scurrilous pamphlets appeared alongside the early glimmerings of democracy in the seventeenth century. Richard Littlejohn and Sarah Vine are tame compared to Jonathan Swift and Daniel Defoe. As media became big business in the late nineteenth century, ownership of newspapers fell to wealthy businessmen who wanted to exert influence over politicians.

But if these rows aren't new, the frequency and intensity of the relationship between media and politics shifted dramatically in 1989 when Parliament was televised for the first time and Sky launched 24-hour rolling news. This was followed by another revolution with the arrival of social media in the late noughties. The consequences have not all been negative. Higher levels of transparency have improved the behaviour and work rate of politicians, on average. Conspiracies of silence, such as when Churchill's team covered up a serious stroke he suffered in 1953, would be much harder these days.

Most of the changes, though, have been harmful to good government. Firstly, decisions need to be taken much faster under a lot more pressure, which rarely ends well. Secondly, managing the insatiable appetite of modern media leads to terrible incentives to make far too many announcements, which are often poorly thought through. Given the already severely limited capacity of central government, the time spent on media management crowds out space for good policy-making. As Camilla Cavendish, who ran David Cameron's Policy Unit in No. 10, put it: 'Walk into No. 10 and the ground floor is essentially the cabinet room, the prime minister's office and an enormous comms operation. And that tells you the priorities of any government.'[9]

Social media has accelerated these trends and perpetuated an 'always online' culture across Westminster. Everyone in politics is now constantly bombarded with information, judgements and requests. It is rare to have a conversation with a politician or adviser that is not punctuated with regular looks down at the phone. It is a bad habit I learned as a government adviser and have never quite been able to drop.

Beyond the news, the rise of social media abuse has, more than any of the other trends explored in this book, led to making politics a deeply unpleasant job with high rates of burnout. It is particularly true for women and people of colour who are on the receiving end of regular misogynistic and racist abuse, but it applies across the board. It also adds to the feeling politicians have always had of being under constant attack, which again leads to worse decision-making, and an obstructive and defensive mentality.

We can see the malign effects in the growing number of younger MPs standing down in preference for less miserable and more lucrative careers. Likewise, of the many potential MPs I have spoken to who have decided against running, fear of relentless abuse is the biggest reason given for choosing to stay out of elected politics.

These three trends – hyper-centralization; executive dominance of an ever bigger and more complex state; and a superfast media cycle – are bad enough in themselves but combined together they are a brutally toxic mix. We have seen power over everything captured by a handful of people who can't cope with what they've taken on, while at the same time scrutiny has been deteriorating and the incentives for those people have been skewed ever more towards communications rather than policy.

Each trend exacerbates the others. Centralization in government has not only overwhelmed ministers and civil servants, but also Parliament, which now has to deal with far more legislation than ever before. The intense pressure for announcements has made this even worse as governments now regularly introduce unnecessary legislation, which has no other purpose but to make news, to keep the media beast well fed. The consequent lack of scrutiny makes centralizing more powers both easier to do and more attractive. The rapidity of decision-making in a world where the news cycle is essentially operating in real-time leads to even more instability in services that have been centralized. It is a horrible mess.

A common problem with books like this one is that they spend a lot of time focusing on problems and have a thin chapter at the end with a few anaemic suggestions for improvements. I have tried to avoid this by focusing throughout the book on positive counter-trends that might be developed. The final chapter pulls together these approaches into a plan for reform. It is a more radical plan than I imagined proposing when I started research on this book, but through doing so I have come to the conclusion that incremental improvements are not enough. We do need change on the scale of universal suffrage; the post-war expansion of the welfare state; or the economic revolution of the Thatcher years.

It has to start with a wholesale restructuring of the state to shift power down from Whitehall to regional government. Without doing this we will never see our cities outside London achieve their potential. Nor will central government ever be able to cope with the status quo. Fiddling around with central government machinery – by, for instance, strengthening No. 10 and providing better support to the prime minister – could certainly help but it would not solve the underlying problem of them simply having too much day-to-day responsibility.

Devolution of power would also mean devolving scrutiny down

to the level of local democracy too, rather than local elections just being an opportunity to punish the national government of the day. Just as it would give the government more breathing space to think about big strategic issues, it would give Parliament the space to scrutinize the areas left under national control. There would also be genuine local representation so MPs could focus less on constituency issues and more on the big picture.

Devolution needs to be accompanied by a constitutional over-haul to strengthen Parliament and close loopholes exploited by the worst of our political class. MPs should be legislators above all else, and selected for their ability to scrutinize government decisions and behaviours. Doing this means making the MP role itself more attractive so that people do not see ministerial office as the main purpose of a political career. A stronger Commons would take the pressure off the Lords, which could also be strengthened, while main-taining its role as an expert scrutiny body.

There is no way to reverse the pace of modern politics, though governments could make their lives easier by constructing a polit-ical calendar that put less stress on set-piece events, from which the media have come to expect a slew of announcements. But a gov-ernment with fewer responsibilities, and subject to more oversight, would have more space, and more incentives, to make good deci-sions. Stronger local government would lead to more local media, especially if national government did more to siphon advertising funds towards it, more likely to cover issues that are actually relevant to people's lives rather than the latest bit of Westminster gossip. And while there are, rightly, strict limits to how much government should interfere with the press, there are ways to increase transparency and limit bad incentives.

*

INTRODUCTION

I have spoken to a huge number of people for this book. This includes dozens who have spent time at the top of politics in the institutions I focus on: cabinet ministers, senior civil servants, special advisers, local government leaders, policy experts and political correspondents. But in the course of my day job writing about policy I've also heard from numerous doctors, nurses, teachers and others struggling on the frontline of our failing state, and lots of ordinary people let down by it too.

One question that repeatedly came up is whether we are in a unique situation. Many of those who needed the most convincing were experts from other countries. To us, Britain looks in a bad way and is underperforming other developed states. But citizens of every country have a much better view of their own problems, while imagining things work better elsewhere. Indeed, elements of the UK system that I am criticizing can look attractive from abroad.

If you are an American watching another deadlocked Congress fighting with the President then executive dominance does not seem too bad an idea (until you ask them about the consequences of a completely untrammelled Trump administration). A German politician in national government frustrated at their inability to reform public services without getting states on board might welcome the prospect of centralization. And someone living in an actual failed state like Somalia or Syria would be entitled to wonder what on earth we are all complaining about.

But these things are all relative. When I talk about the British state failing I mean institutions that did once broadly work no longer do so. That is very different from never having functioning institutions to start with. Our standards of living may be slipping down the global rankings, but we are, for now, still a rich country, with the ability to rapidly improve things if there is the will to do so. As the great economist Adam Smith calmly replied to the news of a British army defeat during the American War of Independence, 'there is a great deal of ruin in a nation'.

As for the US, the Netherlands, Germany or anywhere else, I do not want to pretend that they are utopian paradises that we should be attempting to copy. Every country has its own problems, its own historical context, its own crisis cycle. But ours do seem particularly bad. Taking purchasing power into account, the average Brit is considerably poorer than their Western European counterparts, let alone Americans. On current trends this will be true of Slovenia soon and Poland by the end of the 2020s.[10] While many of the problems I talk about are true across rich countries, we are outliers in having a government so powerful and with control over so much. While we might not want to swing too far in the other direction, and find ourselves with the problems other countries complain about, we do need to rebalance.

Fellow Brits I have spoken to had less difficulty in accepting our system was broken. But some told me that in blaming our problems on institutional failure I am letting our current crop of politicians off the hook. The Tory-leaning version of this blames our woes on the last Labour government for increasing indebtedness in the run-up to the financial crash, allowing house prices to shoot up, and encouraging unprecedented levels of immigration that drove an inevitable populist backlash.

The Labour version argues responsibility lies with reckless Tory austerity, compounded by the self-inflicted injury of Brexit and the breathtaking incompetence of Boris Johnson and Liz Truss. The far left think all the mainstream parties are to blame for their embrace of neoliberal economics; the radical right that we are overrun by a 'new elite' obsessed with wokery and identity politics.

I am certainly not claiming that the individuals in charge, the ideologies they hold, and the decisions they take, do not matter. But I do argue that we have the politicians we do because of the system we have. We have an entire incentive structure that selects for qualities unrelated to the ability to govern well. No doubt many MPs, of all parties, are genuinely motivated by a sense of public service, but they are not the ones who will necessarily get to the top. Sometimes people who do have the ability to govern well will find themselves in positions of power but this is, too often, a matter of luck.

Even when more talented people find themselves in power, they are trapped in institutions that do not work, and bad systems beat good people every time. Every prime minister, after a short period in Downing Street, realizes how few effective levers they have. Departmental ministers nearly all feel trapped in a battle for resources and status with their cabinet colleagues, even when they are well aware that collaborating on issues would help. They usually appreciate the efforts of their civil service teams but feel like they lack policy advice, and often *know* they are not being effective.

As Helen MacNamara, who was one of the most senior civil servants in government before leaving in 2021, put it: '[There is a huge] gap between what people think government is and what it actually has become in practice. It's really easy to say, it's this useless minister or that bad SPAD. You can have, rightly or wrongly, as many opinions as you'd like about them as individuals. But actually the structural foundation, the underpinning of the way our government operates, has become so different to what people imagine it to be.'[11]

Senior officials are profoundly frustrated by this. At the highest levels they have, like Helen, left in droves, with dozens of people lined up by previous cabinet secretaries to be the next generation of leaders now working in the private or voluntary sectors. The ones who remain are increasingly despondent that things will get better. Leaders of organizations that work with government – pressure groups, charities, think-tanks – share war stories of the incompetence and absurdities they have to endure daily. As do all of us who are unable to get a hospital appointment or see another list of cancelled trains when we arrive at the station.

In short, absolutely nobody is happy with the current state of affairs. No ideological grouping feels like it is getting its way. Libertarian Tories have seen the tax burden rise to record levels and the planning system grind to a halt. Fiscal hawks have seen debt levels increase to peaks unimaginable a few decades ago. Social conservatives have watched on as net migration has hit numbers well beyond previous records. The centre-left has seen public services weaken, in some cases to the point of collapse, and basic standards of government overturned. Child poverty is at record levels, and homelessness is on the rise again.[12]

The one thing everyone does seem to be able to agree on is that the system is broken. Even Prime Minister Rishi Sunak said as much in his 2023 party conference speech: 'Politics doesn't work the way it should. We've had thirty years of a political system which incentivizes the easy decision, not the right one. Thirty years of vested interests standing in the way of change. Thirty years of rhetorical ambition which achieves little more than a short-term headline. And why? Because our political system is too focused on short-term advantage, not long-term success. Politicians spend more time campaigning for change than actually delivering it.'[13]

This is from the leader of the party that had been in charge for most of that period. Sadly, he did not make any attempt to change the culture he criticized in any meaningful way. In that very speech he announced an extremely short-termist decision to cancel the second leg of the HS2 rail project with no proper consultation or plan.

But a prime minister who wanted to could make a big difference. Politics does not work the way it should. But it could. It would just take focus on the real problems and a genuine sense of long-term perspective given much of what is required involves giving away power and control, the opposite of what Sunak did. The opportunity to be the next Lloyd George, Attlee or Thatcher is there for the taking, and our recent set of prime ministers have clearly fallen well short.

Beyond personal qualities, though, beyond even the distorted incentives which drive political success, there is another reason why fixing our system of governance is ignored: it is seen as something for nerdy Westminster obsessives.

You see this attitude all the time, even from knowledgeable commentators who are well aware, on one level, of all the problems I have described. And, of course, there is truth to this. A focus group will get far more animated talking about issues like immigration or capital punishment than the role of Parliament or local government structures. A radio phone-in producer looking for callers will get more joy with a request for views on the state of the NHS or schools than the role of statutory instruments or judicial oversight. But that just means these issues are complex, hard to decode, and hidden from most people. The average level of interest in national politics is, not unreasonably given everything I've said, extremely low. But this does not mean these issues are unimportant. In fact, they are often the root cause of all the other problems that people *do* get exercised about.

Issues of governance and constitutional failure are inherently abstract and, to most of the population, impenetrable. Persuading people that the structure of government, or the way ministers timetable legislation, is the ultimate cause of their pay packet not increasing in a decade, or their inability to get a GP appointment, or sewage spewing out onto the local beach, is a hard sell. That makes the crisis self-reinforcing in a way previous ones were not. As things get worse, the more likely it is that the very suggestion of focusing on what can seem like arcane 'Westminster bubble' issues is dismissed. MPs will not even vote to repair the building they are sitting in for fear it would seem self-indulgent.

But as in 1911, 1945 and 1979, the crisis has reached breaking point. Faith in politicians and our political institutions has collapsed to record lows. The pollster Ipsos have been measuring levels of trust in different professions for forty years. Politicians are now at 9 per cent. Even estate agents get 28 per cent.[14] People have no faith in our institutions' ability to fix anything – and they are right. They may blame the individuals rather than the system, but it is within those individuals' power to change the system.

No doubt many of the people who work in and around Westminster will be shaking their heads at the thought of trying to make progress on some of these issues, thinking 'it'll never happen'. The assumption is that governments, even if they hint at reforms like the ones discussed in this book in opposition, will never give away power in practice, and never strengthen the ability of others to hold them to account. But resolving a crisis cycle requires overturning a previously fixed orthodoxy. Whether it takes two years, ten or twenty, eventually a government will realize they cannot achieve much with broken institutions. And we do not have twenty years.

PART I

OVERLOADED

I

NO NINJAS

How No. 10 and the Treasury ate
the rest of government

*'You might think somewhere there must be a quiet calm centre,
like in a James Bond movie, where you open the door and there
is where the ninjas are who actually know what they're doing.
There are no ninjas. There is no door.'*

DOMINIC CUMMINGS[1]

*'To reform the Treasury is like trying to reform the Kremlin or
the Vatican. These institutions are apt to have the last laugh.'*

HAROLD MACMILLAN[2]

For anyone interested in politics, walking through the door of No. 10
Downing Street is a somewhat mystical experience. There's the cabinet table at which Winston Churchill sat. The famous staircase with
portraits of every prime minister ascending up the wall (even Liz
Truss). The huge globe at the bottom of the stairs gifted to Margaret
Thatcher by French President François Mitterrand, which almost
caused a diplomatic incident when, to her consternation, she realized the Falkland Islands were labelled as the Malvinas. As Thatcher's
speechwriter Ronnie Millar wrote: 'you're a dull stick if you are not

stirred and humbled by the experience, for you are standing in the engine room of our country's history.'[3]

It's also an absolutely ridiculous place from which to try and run a modern advanced economy. While bigger inside than it appears from the street, as it is actually three houses mashed crookedly into one, it's still tiny. It is full of cubbyholes and corridors that don't go anywhere. The only place you can get any food, outside of formal dinners, is a miniature greasy spoon cafe in the basement. Down the years, prime ministers have worked in different parts of the building but these days, they tend to use a small office just off the cabinet room. Given the importance of proximity to the boss, several of the most important people in the country are scattered around nearby, crammed into rooms that were originally built as walk-in closets and waiting areas. (Tony Blair's chief of staff Jonathan Powell once recorded in his diary that trying to negotiate who had which office in Downing Street was 'much harder than trying to sort out Northern Ireland'.)[4]

It is obvious to anyone who tries to work there that the building is not suitable. The general consensus among the staff I spoke to was, in the words of one former adviser, that it should be used 'for ceremonial purposes but put the prime minister somewhere else. It definitely makes a material difference; people are in weird rooms and pokey places. I hated it there. Horrible place.'[5]

There have been several attempts to escape and create a modern open-plan office. Powell, who described No. 10 as 'extraordinarily ill-suited to be the headquarters of a modern government',[6] wanted to co-opt the Queen Elizabeth II Centre in Westminster for a new prime ministerial base. Gordon Brown kicked the press team out of their large room in No. 12 Downing Street and used that as a bigger office with his key advisers and officials arranged around him in a horseshoe. Theresa May's team briefly set up an open-plan centre in the Cabinet Office, while she was campaigning for her Brexit deal around the country. Dominic Cummings had plans to do the same permanently, but Boris Johnson refused to countenance moving.

None of these plans have stuck due to a curious mix of nostalgia, convention and inertia. The small group of people who get to be prime minister tend to have been dreaming of it all their life; they are very attached to the history. Nor is moving ever a priority given the sea of daily troubles in which prime ministers swim. Focusing on your own workspace might seem self-indulgent to voters who want action on the economy, housing or healthcare.

These things, though, make a much bigger difference than people realize and not just because it is inconvenient. The geography of the building changes the way the government is run. The Policy Unit, for instance, is usually hidden away on the third floor in the top corner ('they feel like teenagers in the spare room' says Theresa May's first chief of staff Nick Timothy)[7] with the political secretary and press team much closer to hand. Naturally, this makes it harder for them to be present at key moments and to push their case. It helps politics dominate policy.

The main issue is that there's just nowhere near enough space for the number of people needed to run the country effectively. Ferdinand Mount, who ran Thatcher's Policy Unit in the early 1980s, noted she had a 'tiny staff, considerably less than the staff at the disposal of the mayor of a major German city'.[8] The prime minister's team has grown somewhat since those days, from around a hundred to nearer double that, and is now scattered across parts of No. 11 and No. 12 as well. However, it still doesn't bear comparison with other world leaders, especially when you consider that most of those staff are focused on administration, logistics and communications.

When it comes to policy prime ministers will typically have a unit of ten to twelve people, mostly made up of special advisers that cover one or two departments each. Sometimes fewer. Truss had one 25-year-old adviser covering education, health and welfare, which between them account for around half a trillion pounds of public spending each year. They also have a private office of six or seven civil servants who cover a group of departments each and manage the flow of information to and from the prime minister. Not surprisingly these people are overwhelmed, leaving little space for strategic thinking or, often, any thinking at all.

This mattered less until a few decades ago because prime ministers were not responsible for as much. Without any formal constitutional definition, the role has ballooned as the responsibilities of the state have both grown and centralized.

By the late nineteenth century, the job of prime minister had evolved into broadly its current form but the state's footprint was a fraction of what it is now. The two world wars triggered rapid central expansion to cope with the demands of running an all-consuming national military effort. They also brought to power two presidential politicians in David Lloyd George and Winston Churchill, neither of whom operated comfortably within traditional party machinery and who tended to appeal over the heads of MPs to the public directly via close relationships with media barons.

Both oversaw an expansion of the prime minister's role. The Cabinet Office – the central government department that's supposed to coordinate all the other ones – emerged under Lloyd George as a way of supporting his growing team of advisers. Churchill built a formidable war machine that went well beyond the normal functions of the job.

But after the war there was a return to a more conventional model, with prime ministers supported by little more than a small private office and one press secretary. The idea, and often the reality, was that prime ministers were supposed to be the chair of cabinet, setting the overall strategic direction of government but not getting involved with the day-to-day except on matters of national security. Even during this period, though, as the state grew, so did the range of material over which the prime minister needed to pay attention.

Churchill complained to Harold Macmillan during his second, peacetime, administration that 'at every cabinet today there are discussed at least two or three problems which would have filled a whole session before the first war'.[9] The historian Peter Hennessy looked at the volume of prime ministerial files relating to different areas of business collected in 1948, 1952, 1958 and 1965 and found a steady increase, particularly on economic and domestic policy.[10]

The arrival of regular Prime Minister's Questions (PMQs) in Parliament also forced premiers to take a wider interest in every aspect of government activity. Twice-weekly slots were first introduced in 1961 but they were reasonably sedate affairs. It was quite normal for prime ministers to refer questions to cabinet colleagues, until Thatcher ended that convention. Likewise, Labour's Neil Kinnock was the first opposition leader to consistently make use of all his questions.

To cope with this expanding remit, prime ministers started to build up their personal team. Heath introduced the 'think-tank', a group of civil servants, albeit unconventionally recruited, who sat in the Cabinet Office. They were supposed to support the whole cabinet with briefings on topics under discussion, but in practice supported Heath in developing policy ideas. Harold Wilson, when he returned for his second stint, having beaten Heath, decided he wanted a proper Policy Unit, staffed with political appointees, within No. 10, which Thatcher retained.

Heath, Wilson and Callaghan had all been more engaged in the minutiae of government than the prime ministers that immediately followed the Second World War. But their attention had been heavily targeted on the ongoing challenge of a turbulent economy. They spent inordinate amounts of time, with senior advisers and chancellors, trying to manage prices, incomes, exchange controls and so forth, while also negotiating with powerful trade union leaders. Thatcher and her first two chancellors, Geoffrey Howe and Nigel Lawson, abandoned these approaches.

Their haphazard deregulation of the economy caused plenty of problems, as we will see over coming chapters, but it also released the prime minister from spending so much time directly managing it, freeing her up to roam more widely. Thatcher, a more ideological and revolutionary leader than those who had come before her, also had an extraordinary capacity for detail and involved herself in many more policy areas. Thus, she became the first to feel confident answering questions on any topic that might come her way at PMQs.

This was a step change. Her predecessor Callaghan commented on the 'relative idleness' of the premiership compared to the other senior cabinet roles he had held. A prime minister, he felt, 'need not be the hardest worked member of his Government . . . Ideally he should keep enough time to stand back a little from the Cabinet's day-to-day work, to keep touch with Parliamentary and outside opinion.'[11]

This was not Thatcher's approach. She dominated her cabinet, even more so from her second term onwards, which was reflected by the press who presented her in vivid and primary colours to the electorate. She was well aware of the benefits of her profile and rewarded key media barons and editors with honours, as well as interfering in supposedly independent government decisions about monopoly ownership. Her determination to apply her ideology to every part of the British state that couldn't be privatized led to a dramatic increase in centralization as more powers were taken from local government (see chapter two). This in turn led to a big increase in central government contracting private companies to deliver services (see chapter three).

While she managed for many years with a remarkably small team, partly due to her immense capacity for work, she was eventually overwhelmed by the weight of additional responsibility she had brought onto herself. She fell out with her chancellor and other senior ministers and persisted with the spectacularly misconceived (and deeply unpopular) poll tax, while failing to spend time with her MPs – the one group, apart from the electorate, who could remove her.

When John Major replaced Thatcher, he made an effort to reassert the principles of cabinet government. His premiership represents the last time there was a sustained attempt, outside moments of crisis, to have serious and genuine debate in cabinet meetings. He also dispersed power more across trusted (and semi-trusted) colleagues. For instance, in 1995 Michael Heseltine was made deputy prime minister, the first to be given the title officially, with extensive powers over the government agenda and its presentation.

But Major struggled to return to the old model given the expansion of the prime ministerial role under Thatcher, and the expectations she had set for personal involvement on any topic of importance. Any prime minister would have found it hard to cope with a party at war with itself over Europe, a tiny majority in Parliament, and a relentless series of 'sleaze' scandals, but the lack of support within Downing Street made it harder still. His team were unable to deal with the increasingly rapid media cycle. Major's use of non-partisan civil servants as press secretaries exemplified his perhaps admirable, if doomed, attempt to turn back the clock. As a result, he got crushed, despite a rapidly growing economy, under the 1997 Labour landslide.

Watching on were Tony Blair and his team. They realized that a new approach was needed to survive the demands now associated with being prime minister, and the media environment in which they would be operating. Within the tight confines of the available physical space, Blair tried to build a machine that would give him the ability to directly drive government activity in a way no previous prime minister had attempted. Initially he expanded the political side, with Alastair Campbell building a bigger and more partisan communications team, designed for the age of 24-hour rolling news, and Jonathan Powell becoming the first proper chief of staff. Both were given the formal power to direct civil servants.

With the Tories in disarray this new political operation was extremely effective, at least initially, securing a second huge major-ity. But the policy side was a different story. During his first term Blair became increasingly unhappy at his inability to drive reform of public services from the centre.

As his political secretary Sally Morgan told me: 'We were not getting what we needed. Tony was increasingly frustrated. He was also starting to get groups of people in . . . and asking what's stop-ping you? What do you need? And we didn't know how to get that translated.'[12]

Campbell, while he felt Blair underplayed what had been achieved in the first term, agrees: '[Tony] felt that people assumed that you had your hands on the levers, and you pulled the levers and stuff moved. And sometimes it did but often it didn't. And we were surprised when we went in at what seemed to be the lack of genuine, intellectual assessment of whether policy was working or not, it was all very . . . haphazard.'[13]

In 2001, Blair asked the former BBC director-general John Birt to rethink how the centre of government worked. This is the only time a prime minister has made a meaningful effort while in office to consider the question strategically (as opposed to the usual poorly thought through tweaks and reorganizations). Birt proposed a new prime minister's department created via rationalizing the existing No. 10 staffing with the bloated Cabinet Office. It was to be based in a large open-plan office, with Downing Street retained for events.[14]

It was entirely logical but came up against sustained opposition from the Treasury and the cabinet secretary, Richard Wilson, for whom, like cabinet secretaries before him, the distinction between the Cabinet Office and No. 10 was sacrosanct. The former was supposed to represent the cabinet as a whole, facilitating disputes between departments and managing collective decision-making. Jeremy Heywood, Blair's principal private secretary, who would go on to be the dominant official in No. 10 for most of the next seventeen years, until his untimely death from cancer, did not see such a clear distinction.

In the memoir written by his wife Suzanne she notes: 'What Richard meant, it emerged, was that, since – at least in Richard's view – the Prime Minister had virtually no executive powers, with these instead being vested in his secretaries of state or other ministers, the split of accountabilities between Downing Street and the Cabinet Office made sense.'[15]

But of course the prime minister does, in practice, have extensive executive powers that are exercised through his or her ability to remove any minister who goes against their wishes. And critically, they are seen as having that power by the media and voters. From Thatcher onwards, apart from the brief renaissance under Major, cabinet government has been largely an illusion, yet the systems of central government remain anchored to this illusion.

Wilson and Heywood reached a compromise whereby the Cabinet Office/No. 10 split would remain but the latter would be strengthened with two new teams. A Delivery Unit, based on the one that a highly effective civil servant named Michael Barber had set up in the Department for Education, and a Strategy Unit that would be able to provide the long-term policy analysis that the Policy Unit were unable to do as they were putting out day-to-day fires.

For the rest of Blair's time as prime minister, No. 10 got as close to being a functional centre of government as we have seen before or since. The Strategy Unit produced a long series of detailed reports, packed with data, mixing outside expertise with insights from those who understood the inner workings of government. Some of these reports, for instance those on childcare, had a big impact on policy direction. The work was often genuinely analytic and long-term.

As a civil servant who worked there at the time and now has a senior role in Whitehall told me: 'One report on crime was the first time we'd identified that there's an incredibly small number of people in the country who commit a massive percentage of the crime. And if you look at the transport one . . . It basically identifies all of the big transport problems that we're dealing with now. So there's loads of incredibly good stuff from it. And subsequently nobody ever takes the time to do pieces of work like that.'[16]

The Delivery Unit, which Michael Barber ended up running, focused on four Blair priorities: school attainment; NHS waiting lists; improving transport; and Home Office effectiveness, particularly around anti-social behaviour and immigration. In each of these areas, the government made significant progress, in a way no subsequent prime minister has been able to achieve. Much has been written about the approach, including by Barber in his book *Instruction to Deliver*, but essentially it involved relentless focus on a small number of targets combined with regular 'stocktakes' with Blair, where departments would be expected to justify their progress against these targets.[17]

These targets were a subset of the 'public service agreements' (PSAs) which departments signed up to in return for the money they received from the Treasury in spending reviews that took place every three years.[18] Meeting them was critical for a department's standing with both No. 10 and the Treasury and so became the number-one priority for the cabinet ministers and permanent secretaries in question. If they found themselves struggling, they were able to make use of Barber's small but carefully selected central team.[19]

Both units stayed in place after Brown replaced Blair but lost effectiveness given the new prime minister's struggles to master the transition from chancellor to PM, followed by the all-consuming intensity of the financial crisis. When Cameron arrived in No. 10 the whole machinery was dismantled, much to the dismay of senior officials, by a political team who had convinced themselves that Blair's tendency to manage everything from the centre was the problem. However, at the same time, Cameron's team had grand plans for rethinking the state and no interest in local government. Steve Hilton, Cameron's senior adviser, was indicative of this contradiction, airily dismissing the need for a strong centre while at the same time arguing for enormously ambitious policy goals.

Cameron made Oliver Letwin his lead Cabinet Office minister. He had been a special adviser in Thatcher's Policy Unit and sought to turn back the clock – 'Maggie ran things with only five people. If it worked then there's no reason why it won't work now.'[20] Letwin was much liked and respected across the Coalition but on this he had completely missed the transformation in the prime minister's burden, and the overall responsibilities of central government, since Thatcher had been in charge.

It quickly became apparent that this much-slimmed-down No. 10 was woefully inadequate. Across government, ministers were able to operate with largely unfettered authority, leading to all sorts of policies that didn't fit into any overall strategic approach. Health Secretary Andrew Lansley's plans for the NHS, for instance, grew well beyond anything previously envisaged. By the end of 2010 a string of negative press stories had been triggered by departments acting without No. 10's knowledge, including DEFRA (Department for Environment, Food, and Rural Affairs) proposing to sell vast tracts of woodland and the Department for Education writing to a children's book charity removing their funding. The latter led to a Christmas Day broadside from a who's who of the nation's most beloved authors.[21]

Cameron, realizing his mistake, added more advisers to the Policy Unit to man-mark departments. But the damage had been done and No. 10 remained a shadow of what it was during the Blair years. In 2012 Heywood, and a chastened Letwin, managed to convince the prime minister to create an 'Implementation Unit', which bore suspicious similarities to Blair's Delivery Unit.[22] With occasional tweaks, this is more or less the structure that has held to this day. Notably no Conservative prime minister has tried to recreate Blair's Strategy Unit, which is indicative of an almost total loss of focus on the long term.

These various incarnations of Policy and Delivery Units, despite containing many smart and dedicated people over the years, have never come close to recapturing the intensity and focus of the 2001–07 period. This is partly because the benign domestic conditions of that period – a growing economy and an absence of major crises at home – have never been recreated. But it is also because we have never had another prime minister prepared to dedicate so much time to either the long term or delivery of promises. Neither have they had leadership teams with the cross-Whitehall stature of Michael Barber running the Delivery Unit, or David Miliband and Andrew Adonis running the Policy Unit. You can tell how much this frustrates prime ministers as they keep bringing Barber back – Boris Johnson asked him to review overall government delivery, and Rishi Sunak the delivery of skills reform.[23]

Reviews of the centre of government typically revert back to that period too, as the most effective it has ever been and something that future prime ministers should aspire to. But this misses the point. The Blair years demonstrated that even with the most talented people, stable conditions and a prime minister who was both engaged and strategically minded, the ability of the centre to manage the responsibilities of a modern government are very limited. Indeed, by managing as well as they did, even for a short time, Heywood, Barber and others set expectations at a level that is almost impossible to match, and have led people to ignore the real problem. Which is that central government is simply trying to do far too much, under too much pressure. This has got significantly worse in the sixteen years since Blair left Downing Street.

After all, despite their successes, the Blair units were still highly constrained. For a start neither the Strategy nor Delivery Units were physically based in No. 10, due to the lack of space, which meant the former lost influence over time and the latter was dependent for prime ministerial time and input on Barber himself, who retained a desk in Downing Street and a close relationship with Blair. This is where the limitations of the building itself really make a difference.

Moreover, despite Blair being more prepared to give time and energy to this work than subsequent prime ministers, and despite not being overwhelmed with crises like bank collapses, post-Brexit turmoil or Covid, he still struggled to invest enough time to drive the changes he wanted. (He did, of course, spend a large proportion of his second term focused on the Iraq War and its messy aftermath – one of the many tragedies of the decision to join the US invasion was the opportunity cost.)

The Strategy Unit did do some impressive work that made a real difference to policy areas like childcare and transport but it also did a lot of work that went nowhere. As one of the senior officials involved told me: 'The trouble is . . . that sort of work is really interesting, but even with a Labour government with a massive majority, the inability to think beyond the five years is just extraordinary. I mean, there's complete election-cycle mania. So even with a prime minister, who actually was a bit of a long-termist, we couldn't really get those projects off the ground.'[24]

Barber ensured the Delivery Unit was effective by focusing energy on a limited number of priorities because he knew that the prime minister and his core team had little available time for his work. On these priorities, good progress was usually made, and compared to the near absence of prioritization in recent years, it looks impressive. But it was narrow. For instance, A&E waiting times were improved dramatically but preventative health, social care and mental health were not given the same focus, storing up problems for the future. Whole departments were left out, covering key topics like housing, the environment and energy.

Barber was absolutely right to prioritize but it is a real problem when progress requires such intensive focus from the centre as there is so little capacity available to provide this focus. Moreover, the approach was built entirely around targets as there is no other way to drive change in huge and complex systems from a small centre. This was not a popular approach at the time, and for understandable reasons. Targets require simplifying difficult and complicated problems into crude measures. They create perverse incentives that can harm quality. Two examples often cited at the time were hospitals admitting patients close to the four-hour A&E waiting-time target when they didn't need to be admitted at all. Or schools encouraging pupils to take easier exams to boost results.

A parliamentary select committee reporting in 2003, at the height of the Delivery Unit's powers, collated these complaints from across the public sector. Their summary can be taken for a widely held view: 'Targets can never be substitutes for a proper and clearly expressed strategy and set of priorities, and we found that witnesses identified a significant risk that the target setting process had subverted this relationship, with targets becoming almost an end in themselves rather than providing an accurate measure of progress towards the organization's goals and objectives. Targets can be good servants, but they are poor masters.'[25]

The government was well aware of the criticism and tried to respond by releasing a report, partially authored by the Delivery Unit, on devolving more decision-making, but it didn't make much difference to the approach in practice.[26] This was why Cameron's team were so against the Blair approach to running No. 10 and why they thought that not only was it unnecessary, but an active impediment to running government effectively. They really did want to devolve power, at least initially.

Unfortunately, they had no one to devolve it to, which left an empty hole where Barber and Co had stood. It did not occur to them that local or regional government might be the delivery mechanism they were lacking. The historical memory of Thatcherism meant councils were still perceived as the enemy, targeted for cuts by Chancellor George Osborne, and new levels of intensive interference by Eric Pickles, secretary of state at the Department of Communities and Local Government. Indeed, the education reform programme was predicated on ending the role of local government altogether.

Rhetorically they filled the gap with the concept of 'the Big Society', but this never really meant much in practice. Their 2010 manifesto explained the idea: 'Our alternative to big government is the Big Society: a society with much higher levels of personal, professional, civic and corporate responsibility; a society where people come together to solve problems and improve life for themselves and their communities; a society where the leading force for progress is social responsibility, not state control . . . These plans involve redistributing power from the state to society; from the centre to local communities, giving people the opportunity to take more control over their lives.'[27]

Even if people had the time, and were willing, to engage in civic duty to this extent there is no plausible way complex and interconnected public services can be run by local communities in the absence of significant oversight, funding and support. None of which was forthcoming.

As the Big Society petered out, Cameron was left without an approach to delivery. It turned out that in a highly centralized system it's either targets backed up by prime ministerial focus or it's nothing. Targets never went away exactly but without any link to spending reviews, and without being backed by central authority, their application became haphazard. Some ministers, like Nick Gibb at the Department for Education, continued to use them in a New Labour-ish way; others like Andrew Lansley and Jeremy Hunt at the Department for Health saw them as a negative and watered them down, one reason NHS waiting lists were getting so much worse even before Covid-19 hit.

In the absence of any alternative, No. 10 drifted back towards Blair's structure but without the conviction or grip such an approach required. This was even more true under Cameron's successors. Initially Theresa May's team had grand plans for rethinking the role of the centre. But after their disastrous 2017 election the original team was largely replaced and May's focus was on survival in the face of opposition to her Brexit deal from all sides. Boris Johnson, following the 2019 election, had the majority May wanted and a deal with the EU, but none of the attributes required to do the job effectively. His No. 10 turned into a battleground of competing courts and stopped functioning as a government at all.

Rishi Sunak, picking up after the painfully inept Truss interregnum, returned No. 10 to the late Cameron structure, with Policy and Delivery Units. And he probably came as close as anyone to the Blair approach, using occasional stocktakes to focus on his key priorities like reducing immigration and record NHS waiting lists. But it didn't work. There was no sign Blair's machine could be resurrected following years of additional damage and attrition to the capabilities of the British state. While the attempts to do so are understandable, they are not desirable, because they allow politicians to ignore the real problem.

I asked Gus O'Donnell, who was the cabinet secretary from 2005 to 2011 and oversaw Cameron's transition, why successive governments had struggled so much to make No. 10 effective: 'This goes to a fundamental point: the prime minister's role is huge and therefore any prime minister needs a lot of help. And it's probably too big a role, as well as being a very unhealthy one'.[28]

I would go further. It *is* much too big. There is a longstanding debate among political scientists as to whether Britain has drifted into a presidential system. This was exemplified by Boris Johnson and his supporters claiming it was undemocratic for Tory MPs to remove him as prime minister because he had a personal mandate. But we've gone well past this point. As long as prime ministers can retain the support of their party, which, as we have seen in recent years, is a big 'if', they have substantially more de facto power than presidents in democratic countries. In the US, for instance, the President is subject to the Supreme Court and Congress, with at least one of the chambers usually held by the other party, and most public services are devolved to states. They cannot, like our prime minister, decide to simply reorganize the health service or instruct a change in the national curriculum for schools.

We have the worst of both worlds. Prime ministers have, in practice, enormous executive power over every aspect of policy, domestic and international, but a support system designed for someone with 'virtually no executive powers'. They have more responsibility than an American president but with a team smaller than a German city mayor. It is hardly surprising that prime ministers struggle to set strategic direction and get so overwhelmed by events. They are drawn into numerous detailed discussions about policy minutiae that should sit far below their level, while at the same time they are supposed to do the duties of other world leaders like spend dozens of days each year at global summits and evenings gladhanding at receptions for the great and good. They spend between half a day and a day a week preparing for parliamentary questions, which could be on any topic. It is neither sustainable nor desirable.

The Treasury takeover

Walking into the Treasury is a very different experience to No. 10. It was built in the early twentieth century off seventeenth-century designs for a new Whitehall Palace, and is as imposing as that sounds. A refurbishment completed in 2002 only made it even more palatial, with vast glass atriums mixing in with the baroque style of the original building. Unlike the winding corridors and pokey rooms of Downing Street, it is a land of wide walkways and large offices with high ceilings. Everything about it is designed to cow ministers visiting from other departments – and they always have to go to the Treasury – into accepting whatever demands are made on them.

Again the geography matters. From the time of the first prime minister, Robert Walpole, to the Second World War, the Treasury was based where the Cabinet Office is now: right next to Downing Street. This reflected the historic role of the prime minister as 'First Lord of the Treasury'. It was, in many ways, his department, and the secretary to the Treasury one of his key aides. Even in the late nineteenth century, prime ministers like Benjamin Disraeli and William Gladstone were, for periods, also their own chancellors.

It was Gladstone who began the Treasury's transition into its modern incarnation, using the huge cost of the Crimean War as an opportunity to introduce better ways to control spending. He also introduced the practice of an annual Budget collecting together all financial policy measures.[29] Because of these additional powers, by the early twentieth century, the chancellor had emerged as the second most powerful man in government. As public spending rose rapidly as a proportion of the economy, and as the welfare state started to emerge, the importance of the role was further magnified.

Both Herbert Asquith and David Lloyd George used control of the Treasury as a platform from which to secure the premiership, the latter in a hostile manoeuvre during the First World War. Meanwhile the Cabinet Office, established by Lloyd George, became the prime minister's support department instead. During the Second World War the Treasury moved into their current home, on an ostensibly temporary basis, to make way for the expanded wartime requirements of No. 10. They never moved back.

In 1958, when No. 10 and surrounding buildings underwent a major refurbishment, Harold Macmillan used the opportunity to permanently switch the Cabinet Office and Treasury. As Robert Armstrong, Thatcher's first cabinet secretary, has said, this was a critical moment in the creation of the modern centre of government: 'It is crucially important in the history of the Cabinet Office, and to some extent the history of No. 10, that the arrival of the Cabinet Office in that building, and the immediacy of the connection, really meant that the Prime Minister looked first of all, apart from his private office, to the Secretary of the Cabinet next door . . . It's more than symbolic. It was practically – hugely – significant.'[30]

It also cemented the place of the Treasury as an alternative power base, now physically separate, and in a palace. Increasingly it developed its own culture, biases and ideologies, as well as a reputation for recruiting the brightest, the best – and the haughtiest – of officials. Already by this point, the idea of a 'Treasury view' – essentially that spending money was to be avoided whenever possible – was well established. John Maynard Keynes criticized this fixation during the great depression when officials refused to entertain his proposals for increasing spending to create employment and jump-start the economy.[31]

After the Second World War, governments adopted more Keynesian approaches, determined to avoid high unemployment again, and often went well beyond Keynes's proposals in trying to centrally manage the economy. But the Treasury retained a residual scepticism to what its former permanent secretary Nicholas Macpherson, in a 2016 speech, called 'naïve Keynesianism'.[32] This tended to create friction with prime ministers who were keener on spending money. Harold Wilson commented, 'the only thing we need to nationalize in this country is the Treasury, but no one has ever succeeded'.[33] He did try to challenge its authority by creating a separate economics ministry – the Department of Economic Affairs in 1964 – in an attempt to boost growth. But its quixotic attempts at economic planning, under the initial leadership of the unstable George Brown, were unsupported by an unimpressed Treasury and it was closed in 1969.

The rapid rise in inflation from 1972 onwards, followed by the humiliation of relying on an IMF bailout in 1976, led to a renewed focus on spending control across government, which very much suited the Treasury, and increased its power. Prior to this point, departmental budgets were agreed in advance but spending always tended to end up higher than estimated. Over the subsequent few years, the Treasury managed to fix cash limits on these budgets with serious consequences for permanent secretaries if they exceeded them. It also managed, when the Civil Service Department was abolished in 1981, to get control of pay and promotion for senior civil servants. Unsurprisingly, this meant most new permanent secretaries appointed across government had spent some time in the Treasury. There was also more man-marking of other departments, with spending teams for each established.[34]

Many of the key Thatcher reforms like weakening local government and mass privatizations were strongly supported by the Treasury as it made the job of managing public spending easier. As Macpherson told me, when he joined in 1985: 'It's hard to remember, but it was still a world where local government had considerable freedom to determine tax rates paid by local businesses and by individuals. On top of which there was a large nationalized industry sector whose deficits were difficult to control. So the Treasury I joined was still in Dead Hand mode – it was about bearing down on public spending, trying to make controls more rigorous.'[35]

Its biggest victory was in 1993, the year after the Black Wednesday fiasco saw Britain forced out of the European Exchange Rate Mechanism. This again meant there was a need to bear down on public spending and led to the introduction of top-down spending reviews based on a single overall spending target for the whole of government. Previously each department had negotiated separately with the Treasury, leading to what Macpherson calls 'the aggregation of a series of compromises', so the total amount was always higher than the Treasury would have wanted. An overall total, agreed in advance by the prime minister and cabinet, and set at a lower level than economic growth, was, from their perspective, a major improvement. Spending departments were less keen and public services suffered in the mid-1990s, contributing to Labour's landslide win.

At the same time there was a big shift in the Treasury's approach to growth. From the post-war period to the late 1970s macroeconomics – tools designed to direct the economy like interest rates, exchange rates, price controls and so on – had been the main ones used in attempts to boost growth. But from the 1980s, Nigel Lawson, who had more influence than probably any other chancellor since Gladstone, had won them round to his point of view that, as

Macpherson explains, 'macroeconomics wasn't about growth, it was about creating stability. And it was microeconomic reform which would do what needed to be done for growth.'[36]

Ken Clarke, who became chancellor in 1993, not only had more control over spending than any of his predecessors, but also managed to find, largely by luck, the route to this macroeconomic stability. He did this by setting an inflation target – initially a range of 1–4 per cent – and working more transparently with the Bank of England to adjust interest rates to keep in that range.[37] Clarke, having had experience of many other government departments, also started to expand the Treasury's role in trying to boost productivity and growth through microeconomic means – policies designed to correct market failures, such as investing in skills, innovation and reform of public services, rather than setting the overall direction of the economy.

This created an ideal platform for the most powerful chancellor of the modern era, Gordon Brown. In his mind, at least, he had agreed a deal with Tony Blair that he would be responsible for large chunks of social policy, as well the economy, and he grew the Treasury's empire accordingly. So not only was Blair far more interventionist as a prime minister than any that had come before him, but the Treasury also started getting far more involved in directing other departments' activity, as well as trying to control their spending. This was because of the switch to a microeconomic approach to growth begun under Clarke, but also to achieve Brown's domestic policy objectives.

Ed Balls, who was Brown's unusually influential special adviser, in effect his deputy, explained this change in philosophy to me. He and his boss set much more far-reaching objectives for the Treasury than the department was used to: 'We said it would be an object-ive to raise trend growth and reduce child poverty. And that was another challenge that we had to think about . . . Do we have a welfare-to-work team as opposed to a social security spending team? How did the Treasury think about raising the trend rate of growth as a policy objective? . . . Could defence procurement be used as a way of raising growth? . . . [so for that Treasury team] their main role in life has been reducing defence spending. But actually, we now care about something as well, which is whether we are using defence spending strategically.'[38]

Naturally the Ministry of Defence were not delighted by this shift. Nor were other departments. It also led to persistent tension between No. 10 and the Treasury, personified in the increasingly toxic relationship between Blair and Brown. Things just about held together as processes designed to increase the control of both prime minister and chancellor were melded together during the course of Blair's second term by their teams.

As we have seen, the Delivery Unit was a critical part of the infrastructure No. 10 built to manage key priorities, with Michael Barber located near the prime minister in Downing Street. But his team were based in the Treasury, so as to keep the chancellor engaged and on board. And the targets they used, the Public Service Agreements (PSAs), were the ones negotiated between departments and the Treasury during the most recent spending review.

Clarke had introduced top-down spending reviews but Brown and Balls took the idea to the next level. First they decided to have them every two years, from 1998, with three-year rolling budgets, to create more of an opportunity to shape departments' agendas. And they did this by setting the PSAs, which allowed them to direct departments' priorities.

Over the next two cycles both No. 10 and then individual departments got more involved in drawing up the targets and they became tied in with the Delivery Unit. This reflected the fact that while there was considerable personal animus between Blair and Brown's teams, and their own relationship was fractious, they nevertheless had similar priorities.

As Dame Helen Ghosh, a permanent secretary during these years, told me, this clear sense of prioritization, directed via the Downing Street and Treasury machinery, was powerful because '[across all] departments – Treasury, social security, education, health – there was a real sense that we should all join up. It gave the lie to departments refusing to work with each other being the inevitable way government works.'[39]

In many of the discussions I had with ministers, advisers and senior officials from the Blair/Brown era there was a sense that their psychodramas, and the briefing wars between their teams, had obscured an underlying strength in their relationship that underpinned the relative success of this machinery.

As Macpherson put it: 'The only person who Blair ever treated as a grown-up was Brown. And it kind of worked . . . because of the strength of the relationships . . . between No. 10 and the Treasury which ensured that decisions were made. And there was a true belief both in the Cabinet Office and the Treasury that actually performance did matter, and that the PSA regime mattered.'[40]

Nevertheless, this machinery had serious limitations. The Treasury had more capacity than No. 10 but still, on any given topic, significantly less than the department responsible for running it. By taking so much control, they enabled much better prioritization than before or since, but the price was emasculated departments whose ability to think for themselves diminished, and a heavily targets-based regime that was, at times, extremely crude.

Balls saw the problem for himself when he became a secretary of state: 'When I went to education, to begin with, it'd be just really hard to get them to say anything to me. Because I would say: "So, what do we think about this?" And they go, "Well . . . what do No. 10 think?" . . . My view was having been in the Treasury all those years, you know, well, once we've decided what we want to do we'll tell No. 10 . . . They had got used to being in the room while the Policy Unit person [from Downing Street] and the minister argued [it] out. They all sat there and, when the conclusion was reached, they went off to do it.'[41]

Balls was an unusually confident minister and a close ally of Gordon Brown, who was by that point prime minister, so he felt able to challenge this approach. However, he was an exception, leaving the direction of policy far too dependent on a low-capacity centre of government.

When the Conservatives arrived, George Osborne applied the same initial approach as Cameron in No. 10, scrapping the whole infrastructure of central management via PSAs that he had inherited. Osborne, though, was never as naïve as Cameron. He was not of the view that departments could happily run themselves with only minimal central oversight. Nor did he ever invest much attention or capital in the Big Society idea. Instead he used the battery of spending control powers, built up over the previous decades, to control the strategy of other departments.

Because Cameron's No. 10 had thrown out most of the levers of control Blair had carefully constructed, and because Osborne was much more interested in the day-to-day business of government than his boss, this seriously unbalanced the centre of government.

The tools Osborne used to exert control were the ones created by his predecessors: Clarke's internal spending control limit; Brown's spending reviews. And another Brown innovation: fiscal rules. The idea was that by publicly committing to rules that would determine a ceiling on government spending, financial markets would be given confidence in the UK's fiscal credibility, creating more benign economic conditions. Brown's rule, which he called, in a classic bit of New Labour theatre, 'the golden rule', stated that government wouldn't spend more on 'day-to-day' spending than it received in revenue 'over the economic cycle'.[42]

In practice this gave Brown quite a lot of leeway. One-off spending on infrastructure like roads or hospitals was excluded from the definition, and what counted as the 'economic cycle' was open to creative interpretation. It only marginally constrained spending. By 2009, though, the economic cycle had been blown to pieces by the global financial crisis and the ensuing recession. Government borrowing shot up. Alistair Darling replaced Brown's rule with a much more precise one about falls in deficit and the debt to reassure markets that Labour would respond to this challenge.

This gave the Treasury, which had by this point already dramatically increased its power, yet another tool with which to manage the rest of government, something Osborne would enthusiastically embrace. He even created a new independent organization – the Office of Budget Responsibility – to oversee adherence to the rules so neither he nor any future chancellor could fiddle the figures. At least not explicitly.

In the absence of any coherent strategy from No. 10 from 2010 onwards these, largely arbitrary, fiscal rules have become the primary driver of government policy. Osborne initially set an eye-wateringly aggressive rule to create the justification for the largest cuts to government spending since the early 1980s. When it turned out this was too ambitious the rules were relaxed to a new set of made-up numbers. Then after Brexit, and Covid, they were relaxed again. Every time there was a problem it was immediately accepted the rules no longer made sense, and yet during brief periods of calm they were clung to as if they held biblical significance. By 2024 the government were gaming the rules so openly that the OBR called them out, with its chair criticizing the unrealistic spending figures plugged into the model as not even fiction, since 'someone has bothered to write a work of fiction and the government hasn't even bothered to write down its departmental spending plans.'[43]

And yet these plans were all the rest of government, and every hospital trust or local council, had to go on when thinking about future strategy.

Unbalanced government

Government by spreadsheet has become the norm, with Treasury officials now commanding the centre of government, their position usually unchallengeable. This leads to all sorts of absurdities. The most recent incarnation of the rules, as of 2022, that debt should be falling as a share of GDP (Gross Domestic Product) in five years' time is particularly ludicrous.[44] It means government policy is being set in order that a distant forecast, that will definitely be wrong, falls just the right side of an arbitrary line.

This isn't just some arcane Westminster nonsense, it has serious real-world effects. For instance, a whole load of critical infrastructure projects, like high-speed rail, have been paused or stopped in order that this target can be met. This will reduce future economic growth and make it harder, in practice, to actually bring the debt down, or travel around the country.

It is not a bad idea in principle to have a transparent target for spending; Brown was right that they could build confidence in a government's credibility. But the problem with the way they are now used is twofold. Firstly, they have become rigid, unlike Brown's which provided some constraint, and comfort to market, while still allowing for flexibility to pursue other objectives, like reducing child poverty. Secondly, they are overseen by a Treasury which has become all-powerful within Westminster due to a steady accretion of controls and personnel, the weakening of other departments, and the failure of No. 10 to offer a serious institutional counterweight post-Blair.

This hugely distorts government behaviour, especially given the very high centralization of British policy-making. It builds in a deep instability as any decision involving spending is, by definition, short-term to fit with the Treasury's needs. Giles Wilkes, who worked as a special adviser to ministers in the business department during the Coalition years and then in No. 10 under Theresa May, explained the problem: 'This asymmetry of power is just a very, very real thing. It's very hard for departments to plan . . . with confidence. They're thinking every year, "I'm going to have to go back and make the case to the Treasury." So I do think the fact that so much power sits there means, effectively, the Treasury feels like the only place where they can make a long-term plan.'

This dominant position within the Whitehall hierarchy inevitably breeds a culture unlike any other department. As Wilkes says: 'It means there is this culture of superiority . . . They [see themselves as] the smartest people, but they are also the least biased people. Everyone else has got some special interest they're trying to deal with . . . And only they have the bloodless logic to understand.'[45]

To some degree this is true. They do often recruit very smart people. And, though they do have a lot of turnover among junior staff, there is a lot of stability at senior levels, which is rare elsewhere. Treasury officials are right that much departmental, and prime ministerial, policy is poorly thought through and would be a bad use of public money. To some degree, finance ministries need to think like this.

The global instability of recent years, combined with a self-manufactured insecurity from Brexit, has only strengthened the need for oversight. The Truss/Kwarteng debacle offered a reminder of what happens when you give the markets the impression you don't have any interest in controls at all. Many in the Treasury, having seen their permanent secretary, Tom Scholar, thrown out by Truss on day one as a symbol of her determination to undermine their power, felt thoroughly vindicated once the crisis hit.

The problem is that there's no counterweight. No one checks the Treasury's work. No one can overrule them and say, 'On this one you're wrong.' And because their pursuit of spending control is nearly always at the top of their mind their perspective is inevitably short-termist. They have a rule that has to be hit at all costs.

Paul Kissack worked in a range of senior civil service roles, but started in the Treasury. He explained their mentality as follows: 'If you're on the productivity side of the Treasury, you think investment in public infrastructure is a good thing. And if you're on the spending controls side you think it's going to be a bad thing, because it's money going in the wrong direction. And sometimes it plays out as crudely as that. And when chancellors have to pick a winner, or senior officials in the Treasury are picking a winner, they will invariably pick spending control. This is partly because we're good at controlling spending compared to other countries. We didn't used to be so there is this angst about losing control.'

If this culture was in balance with other, equally powerful, forces across government that were making the case for long-term investment then it would be fine. But it isn't. No doubt Treasury officials have stopped much waste over the years but they've also blocked necessary expenditure.

One former senior official gave me a sobering example from when he worked in the public spending directorate: 'There was a weekly meeting where the deputy directors would all come together. And we'd get these back-slapping moments like, "We have knocked back the Department of Health's latest mad plan to stockpile flu vaccines." At the time, somebody did say, what if there's a major flu outbreak, and everyone looked at their shoes. Because that was just like, well, you know, that's the sort of nonsense the DH [Department for Health] would say, our job is to knock this down. And so there was often a culture on the public spending side which was quite crude.'[46]

This mentality – a fixation on short-term spending control to the exclusion of all other considerations including long-term fiscal prudence – is now widely known across Whitehall as 'Treasury brain'.

As John Kingman, who was second permanent secretary at the Treasury under Osborne, explained to me, this often ends up handicapping its own objectives to save money: 'The most frustrating cases of Treasury brain are when the Treasury instincts actually stand in the way of getting the best value on public expenditure. To give you the most extreme example, the Treasury's agenda on HMRC [the tax collection agency] has usually been to reduce its budget. And yet we know that marginal additional spend on HMRC pays for itself many times over. And I've literally never understood that.'[47]

I have my own memories of spending hours, during my time at the Department for Education, fruitlessly trying to convince spending teams to spend more on the crumbling school estate (at a time when borrowing was essentially interest-free for government). A decade later, the Department for Education had to publish a report saying it was very likely a school building would collapse putting lives at risk, and in September 2023 a number of schools had to be closed due to the risk of crumbling concrete.[48] There is a maintenance backlog of at least £11.5 billion, which will now be much more expensive to fix than if it had been tackled in a timely manner.[49]

No strategy and no capacity

This, then, is the state of our centre of government.

We have a No. 10 that has accumulated much more power over recent decades, but does not have the means to use it, partly supported by a Cabinet Office whose original purpose has been superseded due to the demise of cabinet government. As a consequence, the Treasury, which has also been accumulating power, has become the dominant institution, unbalancing the whole of government towards a fixation on short-term spending at the expense of any long-term strategic thinking. This has not led to better public finances. Ultimately growth is critical to managing national debt and the commitment to hit arbitrary rules has meant many opportunities to help boost the economy, by investing in infrastructure or skills, have been overlooked and rejected.

No one is happy about the situation, except, perhaps, Chancellors. Other departments feel deeply frustrated and unable to engage in any proper long-term policy or planning, even if they have a minister interested in doing so. If they get out of line they are quickly slapped down. For instance, the local government department, under one of the more active and impatient ministers of recent years, Michael Gove, announced £30 million of spending to improve substandard housing following the death of two-year-old

Awaab Ishak from prolonged exposure to mould. It was within the departmental budget but the Treasury had not signed off the spending so they immediately banned any capital spending without their approval.[50]

Prime ministers too have been repeatedly frustrated. While they can, in theory, dismiss their chancellor if they refuse to act in line with their instructions it is, in practice, perilous to do so. We have already seen how Blair was unable to go ahead with a 2001 plan by John Birt to consolidate the Cabinet Office into a Prime Minister's Department, but a few years later Birt proposed an even more radical plan: to split the Treasury, bringing its spending control responsibilities into No. 10.[51] This plan was kept secret to a few people within No. 10 and, rather incongruously, called 'Project Teddy Bear'. Following through with the plan would have required removing Brown, and Blair wasn't prepared to take the political risk.

Brown as prime minister had a torrid relationship with his chancellor Alistair Darling. Having done the job himself he wanted to control the response to the financial crisis. In the immediate aftermath of the Lehman Brothers collapse in 2008, they did work together effectively to come up with a plan to save the banks. But by 2009 they had increasingly divergent views on the need to rein in public spending as debt shot up. Brown wanted a more Keynesian approach, with ongoing fiscal stimulus to contrast with the threat of Tory cuts. He considered replacing Darling with his loyal adviser Balls, but again concluded he didn't have the political capital. The chancellor, strongly backed by Treasury officials, was determined to regain control of spending. He won the argument, introducing new fiscal rules in 2009 before Osborne got near the building.

Cameron was happy to outsource much of the day-to-day thinking about governing to Osborne, and thus the Treasury, but the return of a more controlling prime minister in Theresa May led to another round of conversations about breaking up the Treasury. As her adviser Nick Timothy told me: 'I had a conversation reasonably early on with Jeremy Heywood [who was, by this point, cabinet secretary]. And I said, I find the role of the Treasury hugely problematic. For example, its role in oversight of spending and second-guessing departments that are much more expert in what they're doing is wrong. What if decisions over spending were made in the Cabinet Office? It is much more closely aligned with the PM than the chancellor. Because then we're going to be much more focused in terms of policy goals.'[52]

Had May won the 2017 election with the handsome majority that was initially expected then Timothy might have pursued this further. But she didn't and, despite a very difficult relationship with chancellor Philip Hammond, she was unable to move him. Johnson rarely had a coherent plan around anything but he was also frustrated with Sunak at the Treasury, particularly when the latter refused to allow him to announce his social care plan without a tax rise. However, by the time he decided he would like a different chancellor, he was in political difficulties over Partygate and other scandals.

One of the main reasons Truss made such a hash of things was her determination not to be stifled by the Treasury, which led to the damaging decision to fire its permanent secretary on day one. His former colleagues were not unhappy to see her and Kwasi Kwarteng quickly dispatched, with a much more conventional chancellor, Jeremy Hunt, taking over. But while the Truss approach of, essentially, scrapping controls altogether in favour of splurging on tax cuts made no sense, returning to the status quo was not satisfactory either.

So what could a more effective centre of government look like? There have been a number of proposals from the Institute for

Government, the think-tank Nesta, and the Commission for Smart Government, all comprising numerous former senior civil servants and ministers from across the political spectrum.[53] All highlight the same problems. This, from the Commission, can be taken as a summary: 'The divided centre and under-powered Prime Minister's office do not produce a clear, focused, set of priorities for the government as a whole, against which plans for resources and performance could be drawn up . . . Processes have tended to operate separately, or even competitively, between the Treasury and the Cabinet Office, with the Treasury focusing on allocating public spending.'[54]

They propose different solutions. The Institute for Government suggests a beefed-up Prime Minister's Office, a small executive cabinet to support the prime minister, and a new approach to setting a cross-government strategy. Nesta advocates splitting the Treasury, with spending control powers going to No. 10, much like Blair and May considered. The Commission recommends a slightly clunky hybrid model whereby the prime minister and chancellor would jointly oversee an 'Office of Strategy, Delivery and Resources'. In each case there is a goal of moving away from a weak and unstrategic court-like No. 10, to a coherent and coordinated body capable of creating a unified strategy for government.

It's undoubtedly true that the centre is badly designed, or rather, not designed at all. The Blair years demonstrated that some thought around design can improve delivery. But this is missing the real problem, which means these technical solutions, while they would likely be an improvement on the status quo, would only help at the margins.

The real issue is that the prime minister and chancellor are simply responsible for far too much. The jobs have ballooned out of control due to the overwhelming concentration of responsibility for nearly all aspects of the national economy and public services to Whitehall; and then, on top of that, the overwhelming concentration of power within Whitehall to the centre. It is not possible to be strategic – even with a much stronger and more capable team – if you are having to take decisions about every aspect of national life from the tiny to the immensely consequential.

The response to Covid was a vivid example of how bad this has become. As Helen MacNamara set out in her testimony to the Covid Inquiry: 'It was striking at the time and is more so in retrospect how No. 10 and the Cabinet Office operated as a separate island from the rest of Whitehall. The centre felt very much alone . . . disempowered . . . departments had become over-reliant on direction from the centre. The political culture was not to jump unless No. 10 had told you how high.'[55]

Fixing it requires not just tinkering around with Whitehall structures but dramatically reducing the number of decisions that the centre of government needs to be involved in. Which in turn means undoing another baleful trend of the past forty years: the destruction of local government.

2

ENEMIES WITHIN

How local government was destroyed

'Margaret did not have much time for local councils, which she expected to be the agents of central government. She once said to me with a resigned sigh, "I suppose we need them."'

KEN BAKER[1]

Back in 2010 I was working in the Department for Education (DfE) as an adviser to the new secretary of state, Michael Gove. One of our big ideas was to 'supercharge' the academies programme, a policy begun under the previous Labour government, which itself was a copy of a scheme begun under Thatcher's administration.

The aim was to 'free' schools from council control and allow them to work with each other by joining trusts that would report directly to the DfE. It was voluntary but there were strong financial incentives to shift. Three quarters of state secondary schools were academies within five years and, in many areas, local government involvement in schools was reduced to almost nothing.

Looking back almost fifteen years later, there have been benefits to the policy. Some academy trusts have become expert at transforming previously underperforming schools. For many of those schools, their council had been adding little value, which is one reason so many took advantage of the policy so quickly.

Overall, though, the policy hasn't been as transformative as hoped. While we have no gold standard studies, schools that didn't become academies perform roughly as well. There is as much variation between academy trusts as there was between local authorities when they controlled all schools. No doubt the policy could have been designed and implemented better, and could still be improved, but for now, all we can say is a lot of time and money has gone into something that's probably made less difference to pupils than other policies.

The biggest cost has been in what it's done to the DfE itself. Like most government departments it was not designed for operational management and yet it has found itself in direct charge of thousands of schools. My first pangs of doubt were felt during weekly meetings with ministers trying to deal with a load of minutiae about school sites – renegotiating leases or deciding whether small parcels of overgrown land could be sold to finance a new sports hall. We were literally and metaphorically being sucked into the weeds. Over the past few years the DfE has almost entirely lost the ability to think strategically because its own role has become so confused. Ministers' time has been consumed on issues that would be nowhere near the desks of their counterparts in other countries.

We made a common conceptual error that I now realize has contributed, perhaps more than anything else, to the crisis of governance we now face. We could see, correctly, that many local-council-controlled schools were underperforming and were not being given the right support. This led to the conclusion that schools should be directly responsible to the centre instead – after all, we knew what good looked like.

Instead, we should have asked *why* council support was so variable and what could be done to make it better – both in terms of money and guidance but also accountability. By jumping to more centralization as the answer, we made a mistake that governments have been making for many decades. The consequence is a central government completely overwhelmed by the responsibilities it has taken onto itself, and entirely unable to discharge them successfully.

One of the most centralized countries in the world

What's happened at the DfE has happened across government. We have become one of the most centralized countries in the world. In recent years this has reached farcical levels. In 2014, the Coalition government trumpeted 'the first ever guidance on weekly bin collections' from central government, replete with a £250 million 'weekly collection support scheme', that councils could bid for.[2] Today, we have rules preventing councils from: putting up road signs warning of hedgehogs crossing roads; installing a cattle grid; publishing more than four newsletters a year; or holding meetings online.[3] Even when they still retain nominal responsibility for services, like ensuring adequate childcare provision in their area, they are heavily constrained to the point of impotence. They can't, for instance, set up their own nurseries or make their own assessments of quality.

Not only does central government dictate their actions to the smallest detail but it also controls spending to the point where, even if councils do find a way to innovate, they have no money to do so. Increasingly local government is funded via grants dispersed via competitive bids – like that weekly bin collection one – which apart from anything else makes long-term planning impossible. Council tax is the only lever they have available and that is tightly capped. No other country allows so little devolution of taxation. All this means councils have become (barely) glorified service providers in hock to the whims of government ministers. It is a recipe for instability and low productivity.

The absence of any regional or sub-regional tier of government with the ability or incentives to develop local economies is a major cause of Britain's economic weakness compared to our competitors. It is well known that the UK's productivity is lower than other large developed countries and has been for some time – it's a common concern aired by politicians and commentators as a leading cause of our woes. It is less well known that the south-east of England is *more* productive than most other countries, but the rest of Britain is far less so. In 2015 a worker in the south-east was 7 per cent more productive than the average German, but elsewhere they were 22 per cent less productive.[4]

As John Kingman, who was the senior civil servant responsible for growth policy under Gordon Brown, Alistair Darling and George Osborne, put it to me: 'It is hard to believe that you can do something serious about the performance of the British economy without doing something about the colossal weakness of Britain's big cities outside of London. If you look at any international comparisons, it is very, very stark.'[5]

To illustrate this, in 2011 Manchester was 30 per cent less productive than Marseille, and 63 per cent less productive than Munich.[6] The Centre for Cities think-tank has calculated that if all cities were as productive as those in the south-east, the economy would be £203 billion larger.[7] After the Brexit referendum result there was much discussion about 'left behind' towns in northern and coastal England, who voted heavily to leave the EU. But ultimately these places are dependent on their nearest cities. Bolton cannot succeed without Manchester succeeding, nor Doncaster without Sheffield.

There are many elements to these regional disparities, including: lower levels of skilled workers outside the south-east; worse infrastructure, particularly transport; and not enough of the right kind of housing in the right places. But it all links back to centralization. With local government given so little room for manoeuvre, highly unstable funding and little incentive to grow, due to their inability to create local taxes, they can't do much to grow their economy. Nor can they improve their public services, which can draw investment and people to their area.

None of this analysis is new. We have known this growing centralization is a problem for decades even as it has become more embedded. Government-commissioned reports have been clear on this. The Layfield Committee in 1976 argued 'the only way to sustain a vital local democracy is to enlarge the share of local taxation in total local revenue'. Over thirty years later, in 2007, the Lyons Committee said the same thing: 'a link between health of the economy and the size of local tax base would be a key motivation for local communities to take growth seriously.'[8] But rather than respond to these critiques, successive governments have just kept going in the opposite direction, making things worse and worse.

Not only have these trends made it impossible for councils to boost growth and reduce regional inequalities; they've also made life far harder for central government. Cabinet ministers often like the idea of more power and responsibility in the abstract. In practice, they are increasingly overwhelmed by problems they barely have time to understand. The sheer weight of minor decisions crushes any ability to think strategically, especially as ministers are rarely in post long enough to get to grips with their subject area. Highly centralized public services are subject to whims, U-turns, and last-minute decisions of a central government that cannot cope. This drastically reduces efficiency and is powerfully demotivating for those on the frontline.

It's also demoralizing for those in Whitehall. I was struck when talking to recently departed senior civil servants about how frustrated they were by the relentless, operational, nature of modern central government. Paul Kissack, who held senior roles at the DfE and Cabinet Office before leaving to run the Joseph Rowntree Foundation, told me: 'I've gone somewhere where I can start thinking about policy in a way that I wouldn't be encouraged to in Whitehall. I wasn't able to think about it there because the requirements of policy-making in Whitehall are that you too often think quickly, tactically, shallowly, and you move on to the next issue.'[9]

Any kind of deeper thinking can't happen much in local government either, because they are constantly having to respond to the consequences of the shallow thinking at the centre. Local government has become so hollowed out that even if a government wanted to – and both main parties often claim to want to – they would struggle to devolve much because there is no one left to devolve to.

So how did we end up in this mess and how do we get out of it?

The centre seizes control

The structures of nations, and the relationship between centre and local, are largely a result of their origins. Countries that emerged in the modern era, built out of pre-existing states, like the USA and Germany, are federal countries with strong powers held at the regional level, protected by a constitution. Others like Italy and

Spain have seen regional powers strengthened in more recent rounds of constitutional reform.

The UK replicates this in the relationships between its constituent nations – England, Scotland, Wales and Northern Ireland. But it is a highly unusual set-up because England is so dominant, representing 84 per cent of the population and 87 per cent of its GDP. This is why we have the strange situation where England doesn't have its own parliament, as the UK one is so predominantly focused on it.

The Blair government devolved significant powers to the other nations of the UK, with additional tax-raising powers granted to Scotland in 2012. England, though, which is the focus of this chapter, is highly centralized with no protection for the rights of local government, who have no real revenue-raising powers. It became a national state under a single monarch very early on in its history and, while counties have a historic identity, they have always operated under central authority. France is most similar to England in this respect, and indeed is also highly centralized, though decentralization laws in 1982 created elected regional administrations, and some local government powers are embedded in their constitution. Whereas we have gone in the other direction.

English local government briefly flourished in the nineteenth century after the industrial revolution. Urbanization created the need and demand for state provision beyond the limited justice and welfare responsibilities that had been initially established under the Tudors. The need for sanitation, health, transport and housing investment led to local councils levying taxes – primarily 'rates' on domestic and business property – while providing services, in a haphazard and inadequate way, largely outside the control of central government.

However, ministers gradually started to build up their own powers in response to this inadequacy of provision in most of the country, initially over law and order, and then in other services like education later in the century. As they did so, they made various attempts to rationalize local government, with something looking recognizable to ours emerging by the end of Queen Victoria's reign. Central government also started to take more control of local government financing, with dozens of grants emerging to pay for specific services.

The early twentieth century saw the emergence of the Labour Party and a surge in popular demand for welfare support, partly alleviated by David Lloyd George's introduction of National Insurance. But councils still played a major role in poverty relief and the increase in the number of Labour-run authorities led to a backlash from middle-class 'ratepayers'. As a result, Conservative central government took control of rates with a uniform national level set in 1925.[10] There was also growing demand for services of consistently higher quality across the nation. The provision of medical care pre-war was, for instance, hopelessly unequal, with well-run local authority hospitals supplementing voluntary provision in London. However, those who lived in poorer towns were left with appalling care and few medical specialists.

After the war, Attlee's government looked to nationalize not just key industries, like coal and steel, but also services that had historically been provided at the local level. Prior to this point, while central government had become more involved in what local government had to do, and how it was funded, it had largely stayed out of actually delivering services. But by the 1950s Whitehall had taken over operational control of electricity, gas, major roads and, most symbolically, hospitals, via the creation of the NHS in 1948.

There was a major cabinet debate about whether hospitals, which had previously been run by a mix of local authorities and charities, should be centralized. Herbert Morrison, Lord President of the Council (and Peter Mandelson's grandfather), had run London County Council and warned of the dangers of weakening local government. He also cautioned that hospital boards directly responsible to the Ministry of Health would be 'creatures . . . with little vitality of their own'. Health Secretary Aneurin Bevan won out, though, with an argument that would feature repeatedly as more and more services were centralized over the decades: 'any scheme which leaves responsibility for the hospital services with local authorities must be unequal in its operation. This would be unjust to the public who will pay equal contributions.'[11]

By the 1970s this argument was increasingly prevailing over those who fought, like Morrison, for the importance of local democracy. Water, sewerage and other healthcare services had all been centralized. As the Thatcher era began, local government was weakened but still played a major role in the provision of housing, schools, adult education, childcare, social services and other services. They were agents of central government, and the majority of funding already came via grants rather than local taxes, but they were agents with considerable responsibility and autonomy.[12]

All of that changed in the 1980s. Thatcher took a hostile attitude towards local government from the start, a feeling that was reciprocated. The relationship only deteriorated during her time in power. She was content to devolve control of many economic levers to the markets, quickly removing exchange controls, and privatizing anything that could be viably delivered commercially. Most controversially, this included utilities – water, gas, and electricity – that could not easily be delivered competitively and were core public services. When it came to services that remained public, her natural instinct was to centralize. Her view of society was not one that celebrated political pluralism.

The shift towards a much looser approach to managing the economy and the substantial reduction in state-owned assets created the space for central government to focus more on the delivery of public services. And here Thatcher, and most of her colleagues, felt local government was doing a bad job at high cost to the taxpayer.

This view was coloured by the increasing politicization of local government. In 1965, only 50 per cent of councils were controlled by a party, or a coalition of parties, and independent councillors were commonplace. By the mid-1980s it was 84 per cent.[13] In urban areas, those councils tended to be controlled by Labour, and many cities, including London, were controlled by the left of Labour. These authorities were explicitly included on her list of the 'enemy within' in a speech made to party colleagues in 1984.[14] The comparison was with the Argentinians defeated during the Falklands War who were 'the enemy without'. She made it clear she intended to achieve the same result with their domestic counterparts.

The previous Labour government, under pressure to cut costs following the 1976 IMF bailout, had cut central grants to councils. This had led councillors to raise rates to cope with rising costs. In 1980 the Conservatives had passed a law allowing them to remove grants from higher-spending councils, but a number of high-profile Labour councils had continued to push rates higher to avoid cuts, even as their central funding was stripped away.

When Thatcher made her 'enemy within' speech, a bill was passing through Parliament that allowed the government to cap rates, removing any meaningful financial autonomy. She also abolished the most aggressive of her opponents – the metropolitan county councils, including the Greater London Council run, noisily, by Ken Livingstone.

Not content with setting council budgets, over her tenure Thatcher also increased control over how they were spent. In 1980 her government brought in compulsory competitive tendering – i.e. outsourcing to the private sector – for council building projects and road maintenance. When, despite prodding, Labour councils refused to outsource beyond this mandated list, it was updated in 1988 to include a far longer list of services.[15]

On top of this she significantly reduced local autonomy over many of the services they continued to deliver, most notably housing and education. By 1980 over 5 million households lived in council housing, around a third of the total.[16] Local authorities had built millions of homes since the war and were spending over £20 billion a year, in today's money.[17] Thatcher gave council tenants the right to buy their homes at a large discount, one of her most totemic policies and still regularly referenced as a triumph by Conservative politicians today. It certainly helped create a pool of loyal voters, grateful for their home, and was a key reason why the number of households owning their own property shot up from around half to over 70 per cent at the time of the 2008 financial crash.[18] In terms of revenue it was the single biggest privatization of the Thatcher era.

But it also led to a collapse in council housing that has never been replaced, leading to enormous shortages, and long waiting lists across the country today. Critically the government prevented councils from spending the receipts of sales on new housing, tightening the rules several times, until in 1990 just 25 per cent could be used. In practice councils had to use much of the rest to pay down the debt incurred in building homes that were now being sold off cheaply. With no money and little incentive to build more housing, the share of property run by councils collapsed to just 6 per cent by 2022. Many councils now own no homes at all.[19] Most social housing is run by private housing associations.

The loss of local control over schools was more protracted. Concern about 'progressive' left-wing councils controlling classroom content, and applying overly lax approaches to behaviour, had been building since the 1960s with the publication of the 'Black Papers', a series of essays urging that traditional standards were reimposed, from luminaries like Kingsley Amis and Iris Murdoch. In the mid-70s there was an enormous and prolonged row about William Tyndale Junior School in Islington, which introduced a set of 'child-centred' policies. Pupils were given an unusually high level of freedom, which led to entirely predictable breakdowns in behaviour. Bizarrely, in retrospect, the upset at this one school led to a parliamentary inquiry, extensive press coverage, and even a change in government policy. Previously central government had stayed out of education but in 1976 James Callaghan, for the first time, suggested that there might need to be a national curriculum.[20]

Some measures were taken in the early days of the Thatcher government to increase parental control over school governance and ensure their preferences were being considered in the admissions process.[21] But, while the press continued to push the case for change, it wasn't until 1988 that major reforms were introduced. That 1988 Act – nicknamed GERBIL (Great Education Reform Bill) – essentially created the modern schools system, hollowing out council control in two directions. Power over budgets and staffing were devolved down to individual schools, making them some of the most autonomous in the developed world. Regulation of standards was centralized, with the creation of a new national curriculum, followed a few years later by the introduction of Ofsted, and annual testing with published league tables.

The Act also allowed schools to remove themselves from local authority control by going 'grant-maintained' and created 'City Technology Colleges', which were new schools sponsored by businesses. These were the precursors to academy schools developed under New Labour.

Ultimately it was frustration with (what Thatcher saw as) poor-value local government that led to her downfall via the poll tax fiasco. Her ministers realized that repeated waves of centralization, combined with a lack of financial autonomy, had reduced local government accountability. The more they became mere delivery agents the more they would simply blame central government for their lack of funding. To the Conservative mind, allowing councils to raise 'rates' without a cap was no answer because the bill fell on those with property, whereas more council services were consumed by poorer families.

As the most comprehensive academic analysis of the poll tax explains: 'For Thatcherites, much of the appeal of the poll tax lay in the conviction it would reduce local spending. It would, it was hoped, prove unpopular for councils to seek to levy a poll tax at a high level; and because it was a nominal, not a percentage, tax it would neither benefit from "fiscal drag" [automatically increasing as inflation went up], nor would it prove easy for councils to increase year on year.'[22]

The original plan was to leave the tax uncapped and reduce grants, putting pressure on councils to take unpopular decisions in order to increase spending. As everyone would have to pay the same rate (beyond a small list of exemptions) it could not be used by Labour councils to force the rich to subsidize the poor. Of course, in practice, this was not how it played out. The furore around the perceived unfairness of the tax meant the higher amounts most people were paying were blamed squarely on central government. Its unpopularity doomed it from the start and was a contributing factor to Thatcher being forced out of office in November 1990.

Not only did it fail, it had the opposite effect to that intended: Labour won more councils due to unhappiness over the tax and, in order to clean up the mess, the government ended up increasing central grants as a proportion of local spending from 60 per cent to 80 per cent, and capping the new 'community charge' (our current property-based council tax) more tightly than ever. The whole farrago cemented councils' place as outposts of central government with very limited autonomy over spending or activity.

Little changed after the Conservatives finally ceded office in 1997. While New Labour did devolve power to Scotland and Wales, they did nothing to change the picture in England. Indeed, Blair's government took much the same attitude towards the weaknesses of local democracy as Thatcher's had done. As one overview of their policy towards councils puts it: 'One of the most remarkable features of local government since 1997 is the extent to which these flawed Conservative policies, aiming to privatize local services and shift delivery away from local authorities, were made to work by a Labour administration . . . New Labour policies after 1997 breathed new life into ailing Thatcherite policies.'[23]

The shift of social housing stock from councils to housing associations rapidly increased under Labour; the stock of public housing declined more quickly than it had done under the Conservatives. Grant-maintained schools were abolished – something Blair said he regretted doing in his memoirs – but the principle was quickly restored in the form of academy schools, which were also 'free' of local authority control. Because switching a school to academy status did not require a parental ballot, unlike grant-maintained schools, it was much easier to do.

Likewise Labour initially abolished compulsory competitive tendering, but replaced it with something called 'Best Value'. This gave councils more theoretical control over how they delivered services but was accompanied by an immensely complex set of ninety performance indicators, against which councils were inspected and audited. Some of these targets did drive New Labour success stories, like a major reduction in rough sleeping, but they also extended centralization beyond anything Thatcher imagined.[24]

Neither did New Labour do anything to tackle the fundamental problem of local government finance. Gordon Brown's Treasury had no intention of handing away powers over taxation, so the system of central grants continued, ensuring that councils had little autonomy or accountability. It left councils extremely vulnerable to what came next.

The death blow

In opposition both the Conservatives, under David Cameron, and the Liberal Democrats had strongly criticized Labour's centralizing and bureaucratic tendencies. But they then discovered that central control suited them quite nicely when in government. If anything, their shift from proclaiming localism to yet more centralization was more rapid and shameless than usual.

In 2011 the secretary of state responsible for local government, Eric Pickles, trumpeted his new Localism Act, which would 'reverse 100 years of creeping centralization and restore a gaping local democratic deficit'.[25] But from the start his approach was schizo-phrenic. On the one hand he gave councils a 'general power of competence' – creating the presumption that they could do anything that wasn't explicitly prevented.[26] But on the other hand he imple-mented a whole raft of petty new restrictions on councils around things like bin collections; the amount they could pay staff; and what they could do with data.

These things were typically preoccupations of his powerful spe-cial adviser Sheridan Westlake – the only one to have served under all prime ministers from Cameron to Sunak – who used them to get reams of press coverage about crackdowns on local fat-cat bureaucrats and so forth. Pickles and Westlake abolished the Audit Commission, who had managed Labour's web of targets, but then maintained controls, in a messier and more sporadic way, through their own department. While the Audit Commission's inspections had got out of hand, the loss of a proper audit function caused immense problems, with several councils having got into serious and avoidable financial difficulties in recent years.

The other part of the 'localism' agenda was inspired by Cameron's adviser Steve Hilton and his conception of the 'Big Society', which was exactly the sort of amorphous and ill-thought-through idea you'd expect from someone who's ended up as a talking head on Fox News. The Localism Act contained provisions to allow community groups to bid for local authority land and the right to challenge to run local council services. In reality people want good public services, but they rarely want to run them themselves. In the first flush of Hiltonian enthusiasm, money was assigned to appoint hundreds of community organizers for unclear purposes. After 2012 Hilton was no longer a force in government and this agenda disappeared.

By far and away the most important aspect of Coalition policy towards local government was the heavy cuts imposed by George Osborne as part of his austerity measures. During the 2010 election the Tories had made the decision to 'protect' budgets for the NHS and schools, the most politically salient public services, and also made commitments around defence and overseas aid. That left other Whitehall departments having to soak up one of the biggest reductions in public spending ever attempted in the UK. Welfare payments took a big hit, but when it came to public services the easiest target was local government, as so much of what it is now responsible for, outside of bin collection and road maintenance, is hidden to most voters. Osborne even handed control over public health spending, which covers things like anti-obesity programmes, to councils – a rare example of actual decentralization – but largely so he could cut it while keeping his promise to maintain NHS budgets.

Between 2010 and 2020 local authority 'spending power' fell by 24 per cent, and that doesn't tell the whole story.[27] Central government grants were slashed by 40 per cent, from £46.5 billion to £28 billion. To recover some ground councils were forced to raise council tax by 30 per cent over the period.[28] The government continued to cap the tax but allowed the cap to rise enough to replace some of the grant losses. In perhaps the most cynical play of their 'localism' agenda the Coalition 'allowed' councils to hold a local referendum if they wanted to raise tax above the cap set by the government. Unsurprisingly this option was not widely taken up. There has been one referendum, in Bedfordshire in 2015, and voters decided not to raise their own taxes.[29]

All this has taken the core historic problem of accountability and autonomy to new levels. Councils have been caught in a pincer, with funding falling and yet statutory duties remaining in place. This has squeezed out discretionary spending on projects that might benefit all citizens, because they have had to retain spending on these legal responsibilities like adult social care, children's homes and special educational needs, all of which are of crucial importance but affect a very small percentage of the population. Indeed it's even worse than this, as demand for these services has risen well beyond inflationary levels, as the population ages, child abuse cases rise, and more young people are diagnosed with conditions like autism.

At the same time council tax has been rising, for the whole population, with little obvious benefit for most – reducing legitimacy. When I spoke to council CEOs, this was a huge shared frustration. They are being forced to increase tax but it all has to go on a small range of services invisible to their citizens. As one told me: 'When I became CEO [in 2017], 49 pence in the pound of council tax was spent on children, adult social care and public health. This year, it's 72 pence. There are places where it's at 87 pence. So, particularly for upper tier councils, we are effectively a social care funding agency.'[30]

Central government income is mostly tied into a complex mesh of grants – the largest of which are for things like schools and the police. These have to be passed through to the relevant institutions. Most of the rest of the money comes in small pots, attached to the pet projects of one or other minister or agency, and have to be patched together by councils to create any opportunity for autonomous activity. Moreover, they are constantly changing, making long-term planning a nightmare.

One report found 448 different grants between 2015 and 2018 from 14 different Whitehall departments and 24 different quangos. And that was not a comprehensive list. They also found huge churn, with a quarter to a third of grants not being paid from one year to the next, while new ones were added in. Central government is dealing with so many issues directly and does not have the space to engage with any properly, so the response is often a short-term grant or initiative so they have something to say.[31]

The council CEOs I spoke to confirmed how much harder this made it for them to manage their budgets. Joanne Roney, the CEO of Manchester City Council, told me: 'We've got 130 different funding pots, or grants, different grants. And we've got thirty-five capital funding pots . . . So for me the cost of doing that, as opposed to being given significant long-term certainty of funding on revenue and capital, is a real distraction.'[32]

What's worse is that many of these grants – around a third of the total – require competitive bidding, including for many of the bigger capital grants for things like regeneration projects.[33] This is a horribly inefficient way to hand out money as councils spend tens of millions a year on consultants and bid teams preparing applications, many of which fail. It also prevents planning, as most of these bid pots are one-off and may not offer any opportunity for councils to bid again.

One 2022 study of competitive bidding for economic regeneration found '53 funds, all with different criteria and varying timescales and eligibilities being offered by 10 government departments and agencies. Five levels of government are eligible to bid for or receive funding, with another 19 other types of organizations eligible.'[34]

Councils had spent £63 million bidding for just three of the larger pots – and that's without taking into account the staff time that could have been used for other things. What makes this even more frustrating is that bidding processes tend to be extremely opaque, with last-minute rule changes and what appear to be high levels of political interference.

Roney told me about her experience bidding for 'levelling up' funding: 'We were successful in levelling up round one – we got £20 million for Manchester [to develop a creative and digital hub in the city]. We bid again for levelling up round two, which was for Wythenshawe town centre, near the airport, that is one of the most deprived areas in the north, and we want to completely kick-start regeneration there. And we didn't get that. After the announcements were made, we were then told you couldn't get it in round two if you'd got it in round one. But there was nothing that said there would be a limit to how many rounds you could bid for, or what the criteria were.'[35]

Other councils found themselves caught out by this unknown rule too. So, they spent millions of precious cash on bids they had no chance of winning and may have chosen to prioritize in round one if they'd known.[36] A parliamentary select committee even found that civil servants were 'encouraging applicants who were successful in the first round to submit bids again for the second round' before later ruling these bids ineligible.[37] Perhaps as a result of this embarrassment Manchester did get their project funded in round three.

There is also a widespread belief, despite government denials, that money has been targeted at certain areas for political reasons rather than due to need. The same select committee noted, with eyebrows arched, that Rishi Sunak's Richmondshire constituency had received £19 million of Levelling Up Fund money, despite being one of the richest in the country.[38] A different committee – Public Accounts – eviscerated the process for choosing towns for another large pot, the 'Towns Fund', which was supposed to be for the kind of struggling towns 'left behind' by deindustrialization.

They noted the process lacked transparency and was designed to allow ministers to pick towns based on no meaningful criteria, which inevitably looked like political bias, and said: 'The selection process was not impartial. Ministers chose most of the towns from a large group deemed eligible, based on assumptions around broad criteria. Although departmental officials scored and ranked all towns across England against a set of criteria, such as income deprivation, the selection process gave Ministers discretion to choose which individual towns would be eligible to bid ... the rationales given for the selection of towns from the medium-priority group are scant and appear based on sweeping assumptions.'[39]

The twelve towns that had been classed as 'low priority' by officials, but were nevertheless picked by ministers to receive funding, were all in Conservative constituencies. They received more money per head than high-priority towns.[40] Not exactly subtle. An academic study that reviewed all the different pots of funding for levelling up together found that only three of the twenty most deprived authorities were in the twenty that received the most funding. And those three – Blackpool, Stoke and Sandwell – all had Conservative MPs.[41]

Of course, for ministers, this kind of political control may seem like a positive. But ultimately it makes central government far less effective and coherent. And it leads to completely ludicrous funds being created for things that should be nowhere near the desk of a central government minister. Perhaps the most ridiculous I've found is the 'Chewing Gum Task Force' fund, of which there have been two rounds, distributing about £3 million to almost a hundred councils to pay for the removal of chewing gum from pavements.[42] Or perhaps it was the 'installing chess tables' fund – giving one hundred lucky councils the opportunity to bid for £2,500 to place a single chess table in a local park (though they didn't get any chess pieces).[43]

The cost of all the applications for these funds, the time needed to assess them, the press releases and glossy annual reports is unknown. There are plenty of other examples, another favourite is the Changing

Places toilet fund.[44] What better way to spend the time of Whitehall civil servants that deciding which councils most need funding for a disabled toilet?

All these forms of control – the pettifogging rules, the tax caps, the ever-lengthening list of statutory duties, the endless pots of short-term uncoordinated money – serve to weaken both local and central government. The former because it is so highly constrained, the latter because it is spending so much time on this activity. Accountability is minimal.

The worse things get, the harder it is to escape the pattern, because local capacity is degraded and the little trust the centre has in councils diminishes further. Which leads them to centralize more; which exacerbates the problem.

The level of disdain for local government in many central departments is often unjustified, based on a kind of elitist prejudice against the operational. It is certainly the case that there are more high-flying graduates in Westminster, and that local government gives few opportunities to be truly strategic, simply because it is so constrained. But, on the flip side, those working in local government are much closer to their beneficiaries and much more aware of the reality of their lives. Central government officials, however smart, are focused on serving ministers, who are too often engaged in image management rather than the practicalities of people's lives. Few have any experience of working on the frontline of their policy area. It can be very disconnected in a way local government rarely is.

It is also the case that local government seems to be judged to a different standard to everyone else. Private firms that have ended up doing a lot of the service delivery that used to sit with councils often fail but, perhaps because they are far less accountable, or just not as useful as political targets, it doesn't seem to stick in the same way. Unsurprisingly central government tends not to highlight its own operational failures; nor draw sweeping conclusions from them.

Councils do make mistakes; they are often sclerotic, as big organizations – private or public – usually are; there is wide variation in quality and performance. But those weaknesses need to be compared to actual alternative mechanisms of delivery on offer, rather than some standard no one else can meet. Plus, the less faith is put in councils, the harder they will find it to perform well.

As the CEO of Essex County Council, Gavin Jones, told me: 'If your rhetoric is local government is no good, and you don't try to help people want to go into this sector, then it's a self-fulfilling prophecy that you won't get the quality. We've got an aging workforce so we've lost a lot of talent . . . a lot of experience. Young people are not coming into the sector. Ergo we can't compete for quality staff, ergo central government trust us less and less and less.'[45]

The rise of the mayors

Over the years, governments have periodically shown some interest in these problems – particularly on the necessity of regional engagement in economic growth. New Labour spent a lot of time fiddling around adding regional-level structures to boost business outside of London. In 1998 they introduced eight regional assemblies, which had some responsibilities for planning, and were supposed to scrutinize the strategies of Regional Development Agencies (RDAs), through which regeneration money was channelled. John Prescott, as deputy prime minister, pushed a plan to turn these assemblies into elected chambers, but a referendum on the first one in the north-east strongly rejected the idea. The 'No' campaign was run by one Dominic Cummings, during which he learned the lesson that channelling public dislike of politicians into your messaging always works wonders.

That killed that idea. Then the regional assemblies became local leaders' boards. Then the Coalition government arrived and scrapped the whole lot, setting up Local Enterprise Partnerships (LEPs) that did some of the same things as RDAs but with a lot less money.[46] All this faffing around created yet more instability and confusion. It also showed the limits of what could be done without some form of additional democratic accountability. Ultimately RDAs and LEPs were accountable to the centre and had no independent authority.

In the last year of the Labour government, though, a little noticed Local Democracy Act was passed, in the midst of the expenses scandal that claimed the scalp of Hazel Blears, the secretary of state responsible.[47] It allowed local authorities to put forward plans to create 'combined authorities' that would take on duties for economic development and transport. The idea was that bigger entities would be able to think more strategically about the needs of regions rather than (often quite small) urban councils.

In a typically British way it was this idea, that nobody noticed at the time, that would drive the biggest shift towards regional government yet seen in England, rather than all of John Prescott's grand plans. The ten councils making up Greater Manchester were the only ones to initially take advantage of the opportunity, with their plan approved by the outgoing Labour government in 2010 and backed by the new Coalition as well. The CEO of Manchester City Council, Howard Bernstein, was a champion of the idea and pushed central government to devolve more powers to the new combined authority, with a 'city deal' announced by Deputy Prime Minister Nick Clegg in March 2012.

Then, later that year, Michael Heseltine released a report into local growth commissioned by David Cameron. He had been one of the very few Thatcher-era Tories who had tried to decentralize and push local regeneration schemes, like the development of London Docklands when he was the secretary of state for the environment back in 1981. Heseltine, never one to draw away from the spotlight – he called the report overview 'One Man's Vision' – made as much as possible of the opportunity, generating more press coverage than such things usually manage. In it he pushed, like all similar government-commissioned reports over the previous few decades, for decentralization.

But Heseltine used punchier language: 'Big government does not work. Ministers and their officials are not that clever. Events are not that predictable. Yet no government can stand apart, indifferent to the results they achieve from the resources they spend on taxpayers' behalf. The challenge is to create a more balanced partnership – embracing the strengths of our cities and regions, and the resources of government. Government must now reverse the trend of the past century and unleash the dynamic potential of our local economies. The Government is committed to a local agenda. Is that policy or slogan?'[48]

Heseltine cited the Greater Manchester combined authority as a positive move and encouraged the government to devolve powers to it, and other regions to establish one. Osborne, and his senior adviser Rupert Harrison, broadly agreed with the proposals, and after the 'omnishambles' Budget of 2012 were looking around for ways to boost growth.

Osborne, ever the political tactician, also spotted an opportunity, both to create some real accountability at the regional level, and potentially create a route for the Conservative Party to gain some control over cities, by insisting that further devolution, and funding, was dependent on agreeing to elected mayors. He had London in mind, where Labour dominated central London but Boris Johnson had managed to win, and hold, the mayoralty through his appeal to the more Conservative suburbs.

As Harrison told me: 'There was a lot of resistance [by Tories to the idea of further devolution]. MPs and councillors were often quite against it in their local area. And the party often saw it as "We're just going to get a Labour mayor, why would we want to do that?" To which the political argument was always well, actually, you know, in some of these areas, that's the only way we're ever going to win.'[49]

He turned out to be right, with Conservatives Andy Street and Ben Houchen winning the mayoralties in the West Midlands (even as Birmingham moved towards Labour) and Tees Valley respectively. Osborne was also right, despite council suspicions, that mayors would give both definition and accountability to combined authorities. Manchester agreed to one in 2014, in return for significant additional powers over things like housing, policing and transport and an extra £2 billion in funding. Others followed and the first six mayors were elected in 2017 with eleven in total by 2024 (plus the pre-existing, and differently structured, London mayoralty).

But as all of this happened in a fairly unplanned and opportunistic way it has been unnecessarily complex and confusing. Each area has a bespoke negotiated deal with different powers. Some larger single authorities, like Cornwall and Somerset, have been given their own less comprehensive devolution deals with no mayor. Many other areas, particularly more rural and provincial ones, have been unable to agree arrangements. It is extremely messy, which has meant the policy doesn't have the coherence that would drive a real shift in central/local relations.

For instance, John Kingman, who negotiated the Manchester deal from the Treasury side, told me the original intention was to give the new mayoral authority powers over planning, which could have allowed much more house-building in the city, but that was blocked due to the concerns of Trafford, the one Tory authority (at the time).[50] That meant it didn't get included in plans for any combined authorities either. This is a major lacuna, as leaving planning with local authorities is a serious block on economic development at the regional level.

It also meant that the push to devolve powers was done in a fairly arbitrary and rushed way. Kingman told me: 'We had this weird two-way negotiation, because we, the Treasury, were negotiating with Howard [Bernstein]. What freedoms are we going to give them, what money they're going to get? But actually, the tougher negotiation was back into Whitehall, you know, what powers were Whitehall going to release, that was the tougher bit . . . there's a lot of power and money out there you could give to elected mayors.'[51]

At the same time these negotiations were being done with representatives of local councils who wanted to hold on to their own power too. Manchester City Council CEO Bernstein was very unusual in the level of personal authority he had within the Manchester group. Elsewhere things were more balanced and consensus was harder to reach. As Martin Reeves, who was running Coventry City Council, told me, the need to find this balance in the West Midlands meant the mayoral role ended up quite narrow.

'We were probably our own worst enemy in terms of making

sure in the deal that there was limited power devolved to the mayor initially and that it remained balanced across the seven Mets [Metropolitan councils making up the combined authority] . . . It was very much softly, softly, keep the power of the seven leaders with a mayor that will come in and speak on behalf of the region. And . . . use more soft convening power than necessarily the hard yards of compulsory purchase order, planning control and so on.'[52]

The hope among those most keen on the mayoral model was that once trust was established these powers could be strengthened, but as Reeves says: 'What we couldn't have seen was that the conviction and commitment for devolution just started losing pace, because of all the political changes nationally . . . Those first hundred days were exciting, it felt big, it felt real. The programme felt like it could really deliver, but the devolved funding really wasn't as substantial as we needed it to be . . . and if we are honest we didn't have all the delivery mechanisms in play right from the start.'[53]

More combined authorities keep being rolled out but after Osborne left, and with the chaos of the post-Brexit years, the agenda lost some momentum. It found a later champion in Michael Gove as secretary of state for local government, but his big 'Levelling Up' white paper was ultimately stymied by a lack of Treasury support. There was a modest move in the 2023 Budget to give some combined authorities more financial autonomy and devolve a few new powers. But the control of the biggest public services like the NHS, school-aged education and welfare remain firmly in the hands of Whitehall. And the Treasury have resisted any 'fiscal devolution', insisting tax-raising powers remain with them. Half the population don't live in a combined authority anyway, which restricts what can be devolved as well.

Seizing the opportunity

The arrival of city mayors, while it has barely dented the over-centralization of the British state, has at least been the first step in the right direction for well over a century, especially given the bipartisan support. Mayors, initially an unpopular idea at local level, have now been accepted as beneficial by voters and local media. For the first time in a long while, local politicians outside London, like Manchester mayor Andy Burnham, are seen as important enough for their opinions and actions to occasionally make national news. While some are struggling the initial, limited, evidence on the effectiveness of combined authorities is positive. Greater Manchester, the only one given meaningful health powers, has seen a small bump in life expectancy versus what would otherwise have been expected, according to *The Lancet*.[54]

But as yet Whitehall has not relinquished enough power to make a significant difference. Even in Manchester, which has the most comprehensive deal, there is a real limit to what the mayor can do to drive economic improvement without the ability to raise funds, control major planning decisions or integrate public services. Progress to date has been heavily dependent on personal relationships within the city rather than formal powers.

More fundamentally there are no clear principles for what should be devolved and what needs to stay controlled by a national government. Doing everything through one-off bespoke deals is a recipe for confusion. Take education as an example. Handing oversight over schools to combined authorities would relieve pressure on the Department for Education, which has, in any case, had to set up its own regional offices to cope with directly managing all academies.

It would allow authorities to build links between schools and other services like policing and housing. This kind of integration is simply impossible in Whitehall where departments have to work to the interests of competing cabinet ministers, and with long histories of mutual mistrust. But it makes sense for central government to keep central control of the national curriculum and exams, so that there is a national standard for all children.

Rather than continue with this slow, inadequate and bespoke shift to regional government we need a proper plan for more rapid and comprehensive devolution. We need a full regional tier of government across the whole country with the responsibility, incentives and powers to grow their economic area. This would involve giving them control of more levers, including planning and transport, as well as the commissioning and oversight of public services. It would, critically, require giving them power over local taxation – council tax and business rates – as well as, ideally, some portion of income taxes. This would create a powerful incentive to develop our under-performing cities outside London. It would be accompanied by a single government grant to cover the gap between the cost of services and what could be raised through local taxation. But it would not be fragmented into hundreds of small pots, or involve any bidding, which would dramatically reduce administrative costs. In return for these additional powers, mayors would need to agree to much more stringent auditing.

The main difficulty is that different parts of the country are at different stages of devolution and have different levels of capacity, as well as different structures and leadership models. The Centre for Cities and the Resolution Foundation have produced a blueprint for how this transition could happen, with London, Manchester and the West Midlands leading the way.[55] It would then require a reorganization of local government to ensure the rest of the country could move to the same system over time. It is all doable but it would be a major project and a government would have to prioritize it.

There are three key barriers to that happening. First, a belief that local government is boring to voters, which leads governments to focus their legislative programmes on frontline issues like crime, health and education. But frankly, voters don't really engage with the technical details of *any* policy area (nor should they have to). They want better services and the benefits of more economic growth; they will reward politicians who provide that. Moreover, while voters may not be interested in the technical aspects of local government financing they do care a lot about the regeneration of their community and have responded positively to the higher profile of mayors.

The second barrier is that the centre hates giving up control. Successive governments have hoarded power, believing that they know best and that local government isn't capable or competent. The Treasury, in particular, is loath to give up economic levers. But the reality is that high levels of operational control have left the centre less powerful in practice. Politicians are so overwhelmed by the endless stream of minor decisions that they can't offer any kind of strategic leadership. Devolving would strengthen their ability to really change the country by focusing on things that matter. If every problem that happens in the country is your problem then you will always be firefighting.

As for the Treasury, even senior figures who have worked there in crucial roles and are generally supportive of its role in managing public finances are starting to accept that the centralization of powers is holding back UK growth and making it harder to pay the bills.

Osborne's adviser Harrison told me that mayors did need more control over tax: 'I think it should . . . a lot of the levers are still not available. Local income tax has always been seen as sort of a line in the sand by the Tory party, so the party might feel differently. But there are lots of interesting taxes you could localize, like vehicle excise duty, for example, that are linked to geographies. So I think you could go a lot further. And of course, fundamentally, you've got this big problem, that the council tax system isn't fit for purpose, and revaluation is impossible to do. But if you could, if you could reform local taxation, then you could shift the burden of tax on to that.'[56]

Kingman – who was the second most senior official at the Treasury for many years – told me he'd 'bet big on devolution' including tax-raising powers. We are starting to reach the critical mass of support required to get a forward-thinking government to offer some radical policy here.

The final barrier is perhaps the hardest of all to shift. As we have always been a centralized state there is a deep cultural antipathy to the idea of local differences in services or taxation – and devolution means accepting there will be differences, both ideological and in terms of quality. Some mayors will fail – some already have. Some will mismanage finances. But this has to be compared to where we are now rather than some imaginary world in which the centre of government is capable of providing uniformly high-quality national-level services. In practice, centralization has not led to equality but to extreme economic divergence between the south-east and the rest of the country. And that divergence inevitably makes it harder to run services well outside the south-east too.

That does not mean local and regional government should have carte blanche. National government should set standards against which local administrations can be measured, and they should have tools to intervene in the event of corruption or extreme failure.

Devolution would also lead to more accountability from voters towards local politicians, but that needs to be accompanied by institutions that provide accountability too.

But central government cannot do it all, and by trying to do so it has become incapable of doing anything. The core problem of the British state is a lack of capacity and that can only come from building it at regional and local level.

3

CONTRACT KILLINGS

How we became dependent on private firms to run
the state, regardless of how often they fail

'Government doesn't do anything. It's a procurement agency
that isn't very good at procurement'.

FORMER GOVERNMENT ADVISER[1]

'Carillion's rise and spectacular fall was a story of recklessness,
hubris and greed. Its business model was a relentless dash for
cash, driven by acquisitions, rising debt, expansion into new
markets and exploitation of suppliers.'

BUSINESS SELECT COMMITTEE REPORT ON THE
COLLAPSE OF CARILLION[2]

Children in care are some of the most vulnerable people in our society. They have often experienced severe trauma in the first years of
life, developed serious behavioural problems as a result, and need
intensive specialist support. In most wealthy countries this is done
by local government. Here, in at least one case, it is done by a former
OnlyFans model and reality TV star, supported financially by her
fiancée, a former pornographer.

Ampika Pickston, best known for her appearances on *The Real*

Housewives of Cheshire, registered a care home in the summer of 2023. It was financed by her partner David Sullivan, who owns West Ham United football club and made his fortune from pornographic magazines and sex shops. Nearby councils were, according to one report, charged £10,000 *per week* to place children there.[3]

In November 2023 Ofsted inspected the home and found major failings in a report that was later removed from their website. They suspended the home's registration, and the management were not allowed to look after any children until they could prove they had fixed the problems. The suspension was lifted after an initial monitoring visit in January 2024 and one child was placed in the home.[4] But then a further Ofsted visit a few weeks later found that this child had been moved out almost immediately due to the home's inability to provide adequate care. Ofsted wrote that the 'child made an allegation following a physical intervention that they had suffered bruising and a knee injury, which required hospital attendance'.[5] The home was suspended again.

It is an astonishing indictment of the British state that it no longer has the ability to provide care for those who need it most, and instead allows blatantly ill-qualified people to charge exorbitant fees to provide unacceptable levels of care. This is an extreme example but the care home market is startlingly dysfunctional. Three quarters of places are now provided by for-profit companies, many of them owned by private-equity firms who have seen an opportunity for big profits.

Councils, who have a statutory duty to provide support for children in care, are a captive market with few options. The amount they are spending on placements has risen by 72 per cent in the last five years, with an average weekly bill per child of £5,980.[6] In many cases they are sending young people miles away from where they grew up because providers set up homes in towns where property is cheaper.

In a 2023 report the Competition and Markets Authority (CMA) found that the fifteen largest providers were making annual profits of 22.6 per cent on average.[7] They also found that 'some of the largest private providers are carrying very high levels of debt, creating a risk that disorderly failure of highly leveraged firms could disrupt the placements of children in care.'[8] An investigation in 2024 found hundreds of children had been put, illegally, in unregulated homes because of a lack of places.[9]

The emergence of this care homes market is an example of one of the biggest changes in the way the British state, particularly in England, has changed over the past few decades. As state capacity has dwindled, central and local government has become ever more reliant on the private sector to cover the gap. The theory was that they could provide services more efficiently due to competitive pressure. The reality has been very different.

The state we're in

How did we end up with this unquestioned belief across Whitehall that the private sector can provide better-quality services at lower cost when, after forty years of practice, it is very clear that it often does not? The topic is often debated in simplistic left/right terms – public good and private bad, or vice versa. Critiques from the left can often ignore the weaknesses in state-run provision and make unfounded assumptions that public employees automatically have high levels of intrinsic motivation. Anyone who has worked in the public sector knows that motivation varies across the workforce, as it does in any large organization.

But defenders of the extensive use of the private sector on the right (and sometimes the centre) often seem to have completely missed that much government business with private providers no longer conforms to anything resembling a functional market with properly aligned incentives.

The core principle of contracting out is that competition will lead to innovation and lower cost than doing it yourself. This is true enough when certain conditions are met. Firstly, there needs to be many organizations, public or private, who can provide the service to generate genuine competition on both price and quality. Secondly, it needs to be relatively easy to measure whether the service you want has been delivered to an acceptable standard. Thirdly, government needs to be able to hand over most of the risk of failure – if the tax-payer is still on the hook for picking up the costs if things go wrong then the premium paid to private firms is not justified.

If all these boxes are ticked, then it can work very well. Cleaning contracts are an example of something that typically meet all these criteria. It is a well-established service that many companies offer, and for which there is already a large private market. It is easy to check cleaning is happening to an acceptable standard. If it is not then another company can be found to do it instead without too much fuss. The best evidence we have shows tendering cleaning services does save money, even if the in-house team ends up winning the tender.[10]

For more complex services, though, often none of these criteria apply. Take a specialist activity like running immigration processing. There is no existing market. That means there are few plausible bidders outside of a handful of huge multinational outsourcing firms whose sole purpose is to win new contracts, almost regardless of what they are for.

The 'big four' – who dominate the UK market – are Serco, Capita, Atos and G4S. At the time of writing, Serco are responsible for, among other things, running: detention centres for asylum seekers; facilities management for several hospitals; cycle hire schemes in various cities; ferry services to the Orkney and Shetland islands; six prisons; our warning system for incoming nuclear missiles; programmes to help unemployed people back into work; and bin collection in several councils.[11] This is a shortened list, and one that does not take into account all the things they have run in the past.

The other companies in the big four have similar lists. This is despite all of them being involved in major scandals involving failed contracts over the past decade. Successive governments have decided they do not have much choice but to keep giving them contracts – regardless of success rates – because there now aren't any alternatives.

David Laws was a Liberal Democrat minister, who worked closely with Nick Clegg during the Coalition years. In his diaries there is a revealing entry for 28 October 2013, when he was a minister in the Cabinet Office. This was just after Serco and G4S had been involved in a scandal around charging the state for electronically tagging prisoners who had left the country or even died.[12] The previous year G4S had been all over the press for messing up the Olympic security contract, and lying about it, forcing the army to step in at the last minute so the Games would go ahead.[13] Capita had just screwed up a major contract to provide court translators, causing huge delays in bringing criminals to justice.[14] Atos were in the doghouse over failures around assessing people for disability benefits.

Laws noted that, in a ministerial meeting, some cabinet ministers were worried about these companies bidding on upcoming contracts.

But George Osborne 'said it would be incredibly damaging for government outsourcing and for the engagement of government in the private sector if we stopped giving contracts to these types of companies . . . the UK market is currently highly concentrated, with four main suppliers – Atos, Capita, Serco and G4S. Three of these now have big problems . . . Osborne and Philip Hammond pointed out that these companies would still be managing extremely sensitive contracts, including being part of the consortium operating the UK's nuclear deterrent [so relations had to be maintained].'[15]

So much for a competitive market.

Accurately measuring the delivery of a contract is an even bigger problem. The more complex a service is, the harder it is to measure whether it is being delivered properly. Take school inspections, which were partially outsourced in 2009 and then brought back in-house in 2015. You can tell if the inspections have happened but how do you assess whether they have made good decisions without repeating the inspections? And, indeed, when the schools inspectorate Ofsted took it back in-house one reason was that they wanted more control over quality.[16]

If it is not possible to accurately assess quality then companies can ensure profit by cutting staff, paying them less, and providing a worse service, while staying within the rules. This happens all the time.

Then there is the question of risk. If a company fails to deliver cleaning services to an acceptable level then it is usually manageable. The contract can be cancelled and another firm brought in at short notice. But if a prison or hospital fails completely that is going to be much harder to cope with. Firstly because the level of public concern will be much higher; secondly because it will be much harder, and usually impossible, to contract someone else within an acceptable time period.

For instance, Birmingham Prison was contracted to G4S in 2011. An inspection in 2018 found it in total disarray: 'inspectors witnessed inmates being intimidated and prisoners squirting urine or throwing faeces through broken observation panels'.[17] It was taken back into public control, initially temporarily, and then, because no one else wanted to take over the contract, permanently.

Similarly, Hinchingbrooke Hospital in Cambridgeshire was handed over to a private company called Circle in 2010, as a test case. It was a complete disaster, and it failed both to provide acceptable levels of care or save money. The Care Quality Commission rated it inadequate in 2014[18] and another government report found it was the least efficient hospital in the country.[19] The management were so desperate that they launched a controversial scheme to, in effect, bribe GPs to send them patients.[20] Again the hospital had to be taken back into public ownership at great expense. The Public Accounts Committee of MPs noted that 'the total deficit incurred during the franchise will be well above the level that Circle is contractually committed to cover, leaving the taxpayer to pick up the rest'.[21]

In neither case was risk taken away from the state. Unlike a normal business, a prison or hospital cannot be allowed to fail, so ultimately the taxpayer was left holding the bill. At least, in these two examples, the state could step back in because the Ministry of Justice and the NHS still run most prisons and hospitals. If an entire service gets contracted out, and it fails, then you have the additional problem of there being no state capacity left to pick up the pieces. This means the proposed scheme just ends up being dropped altogether or, where that isn't possible, the state has to scramble to rebuild capacity, causing more delays and generating more costs.

The most horrendous example of this in recent years was the failed privatization of a large part of the probation service – which is supposed to stop people who have left prison from reoffending. Up until 2013 it had been run, in various guises, as part of the public sector. At that point there were thirty-five regional probation trusts under the supervision of the National Offender Management Service, which was also responsible for prisons. They were working reasonably well and all were rated good or exceptional by the government.[22]

Then Justice Secretary Chris Grayling, who is high up in the list of the least competent people to be given high office in British history, decided to partially outsource the service to the private sector. The idea was that low- and medium-risk offenders would be looked after by 'community rehabilitation centres' that would be run by private companies. High-risk offenders would continue to be managed by the state, as Grayling was worried about the public reaction to high-profile murderers and rapists being the responsibility of for-profit firms. The entire sector told Grayling it wouldn't work. It failed to meet all three tests of sensible outsourcing: competitiveness; ability to measure; and risk management.

The policy was not piloted, or built up carefully over time, it happened nationally and almost overnight. Probation officers were simply assigned to either the public sector, managing 'high-risk offender' teams, or the new 'rehabilitation centres', based on what they were working on at the time. Though still in the same buildings they suddenly had different bosses with very different approaches.

The lack of any preparation meant there was no opportunity to build a market of companies with any particular expertise in probation. Eleven of the twenty-one contracts went to two large outsourcing conglomerates: Sodexo, a French company best known as providers of cheap food to schools and hospitals, and Interserve, which mainly did construction work and subsequently went into administration.[23] Another winning contractor, Working Links, mainly ran programmes to get unemployed people back into work. It also went into a chaotic administration in 2019, surrounded by allegations of fraud and with one of their probation centres receiving an abysmal inspection with an 'inadequate' rating.[24]

G4S and Serco, who might have expected to win multiple contracts, did not bid due to an ongoing serious fraud investigation into their electronic tagging contracts (the ones where they had been charging to track dead people). They have, though, subsequently won numerous other Ministry of Justice contracts. This was as clear an example as you could want that competitive markets cannot be conjured out of thin air.

Probation is the definition of a complex service. Its performance is closely tied to many other parts of the public sector, most obviously policing and prisons but also health, housing and education. Grayling decided to add a 'payment by results' element to the contracts on the assumption that companies would be incentivized to reduce reoffending rates if their profits were determined by that metric. Unfortunately reoffending rates are only partly down to the actions of probation officers, and have a lot to do with all those other services private firms had no control over. They could do nothing to stop austerity cuts to housing benefits or adult education schemes from pushing up reoffending rates.

At the same time, cuts to the police meant fewer crimes were resulting in someone being charged, especially in less serious cases. That meant less business for the probation companies. A problem which had not been considered in the contract design.

It was a car crash. Some of the companies, trying to stem losses, stopped bothering trying to reduce reoffending, given how many other factors were involved, and tried to do the absolute minimum possible to meet the requirements of their contracts. They resorted to making occasional calls to offenders without any meaningful contact.[25] The chief inspector of probation wrote, in the damning inspection report on Working Links, that they were 'completing individuals' sentence plans to meet performance targets, without actually meeting the offender'. And 'the professional ethos of probation has buckled under the strain of the commercial pressures put upon it'.[26]

By this time the Ministry of Justice had acknowledged the entire programme had been a catastrophe and decided to re-nationalize probation. As a critical service, the state had never handed over any risk and it was still responsible for making probation work. So, they had to scramble around for a solution. But a huge amount of expertise had been lost, staffing shortages were severe, and the constant disruption of reorganizations had broken the service and its morale.

As of 2023 the newly unified system was still struggling badly, with the chief inspector writing of 'very inexperienced staff being handed inappropriately complex cases with minimal management oversight'. He reported that he could not honestly say the public was safe.[27] The brutal sexual assault and murder of Zara Aleena, a 35-year-old court official, in 2022 at the hands of a man who was wrongly assessed by probation officers as not high risk, is just one real-world example of this ongoing failure.

The chief inspector, in an independent review, wrote that her murderer: 'Should have been considered a high risk of serious harm offender. If he had, more urgent action would have been taken to recall him to prison, after he missed his supervision appointments on release from custody. The Probation Service failed to do so, and he was free to commit this most heinous crime on an innocent young woman. Our independent review brings into sharp focus the consequences of these missed opportunities and reveals a Probation Service, in London, under the mounting pressure of heavy workloads and high vacancy rates.'[28]

On top of this risk to public safety, the additional cost to the taxpayer from contracts having to be changed in 2017–18 and then cancelled early was almost half a billion pounds, according to the National Audit Office.[29]

This was a particularly egregious failure, even if most of the British public remain unaware of it, but these problems – lack of proper competition, the inability to write contracts that take complexity into account, and the absence of any meaningful risk-sharing – are repeated over and over again.

It is clear we have ended up with the worst of all worlds: all the costs without the benefits of competition, innovation, or risk-sharing. We have a small group of vast conglomerates, with minimal expertise in any given area, but well-practised in bidding for contracts, that the government has become entirely reliant on. But despite repeated failures they are now so embedded into the state that they are effectively part of it, except without any of the accountability or transparency that should come with that. So they cannot be jettisoned without completely rethinking the way the state works.

Calling this farrago 'a market' is a gross misnomer and criticism should not be the preserve of the political left. It should also *infuriate* any true Conservative who cares about misuse of taxpayer money. Sometimes there is a flash of recognition. In 2014, Mark Wallace, who was then editor of the Conservative Home website for the Tory party faithful wrote: 'For far too long, a small number of huge firms have won vast numbers of government contracts with huge price tags attached and delivered relatively poor value for money.'[30] Tory MPs on parliamentary committees investigating these scandals have put their names to many reports making similar points or slamming a particularly disastrous contract.

However, they can never quite take the next logical step, arguing instead that the state just needs to get better at contracting. Of course, there are plenty of examples of incompetence in contracting, though that is inevitable given large multinationals are always going to be able to pay more to the people writing the bids than the government will to those assessing them. But the bigger problem is that it is just not possible to design effective contracts for highly complex services like probation or hospitals. Nor is it desirable to put these services at such high risk, or lose state capacity to deliver them. Attempts to do so have led to many of the most dramatic examples of state failure in recent years.

To understand how we've got here, and why the principle has become so deeply embedded despite a total lack of evidence for effectiveness, we need once more to go back to the Thatcher years.

The rise of outsourcing

Initially, and contrary to the beliefs of many of her current admirers, Thatcher was cautious about managing public opinion that, she knew, was wary of involving the private sector more in running the state. In her first term privatizations were limited to entities that had only recently been nationalized, like British Aerospace. Outsourcing – where a service is contracted out rather than fully privatized – was restricted to making local authorities tender for construction and maintenance contracts, and using the NHS as a test bed for tendering cleaning contracts.

The success of these initial forays, though, plus her landslide election win in 1983, encouraged a big expansion of plans from 1984 onwards. Monopolistic utilities were privatized, starting with British Telecom in 1984, running through gas, electricity and water, and finishing with British Rail in 1994 under John Major. These privatizations were much more complex than selling off companies like British Airways into existing competitive markets as they required, and still require, extensive state regulation.

Because these services are monopolistic and essential, the government has not been able to shift the risk elsewhere, as we saw when Liz Truss was forced to announce a massive energy support package following the Russian invasion of Ukraine. Another example: in 2023, four out of sixteen rail franchises were being run by the Department for Transport due to private sector failures. Shareholders have made off with big profits but the risk still sits with the taxpayer. Indeed, staff at one rail contractor, Avanti, wrote an internal presentation called 'Roll Up, Roll Up, Get Your Free Money', exclaiming delightedly that the financial terms of their new contract sounded 'too good to be true'.[31]

Thatcher also oversaw a substantial increase in outsourcing, with compulsory tendering for local authorities expanded to cover much of their activity. Central government departments were also told they had to 'market test' discrete activities that could be either privatized completely or, in most cases, contracted out. Between 1991 and 1993 around 200 functions, worth around £1.75 billion in today's money, that had previously been run from Westminster were outsourced. These ended up being mostly peripheral services like IT, payroll and estates management, but included some more high-profile activities like the Atomic Weapons Establishment that is responsible for managing our nuclear deterrent (it was taken back in-house in 2020).[32] Increasingly, the expectation on departments was to contract out as much of the delivery of services as possible. As a result firms like Capita and Serco emerged during the 1980s and 1990s, and grew quickly.

New Labour did nothing to slow down the general growth of outsourcing, nor did they spend much time considering the long-term consequences for state capacity. They made two major contributions, neither helpful. The first was to try and improve the quality of contracts through multiple reviews and process overhauls, introducing significantly more central oversight from the Treasury – in line with its growing control under Gordon Brown. The greater complexity around bidding did allow for more nuanced tenders that went beyond simply choosing whichever provider offered the lowest price. But it also made it even harder for smaller businesses or charities to go through the arduous procurement process, and encouraged the further growth of the big specialist outsourcing conglomerates. Atos and G4S developed in the late 1990s and 2000s via mergers of smaller companies.

The second was the dramatic scaling up of 'private finance initiatives' (PFIs). These are contracts handed to companies to manage the building and maintenance of infrastructure – like hospitals and schools – so that the state pays an annual fee over several decades rather than the whole upfront cost of the project at once. Banks fund the deal and companies like Serco organize the construction and long-term management. The model was introduced by Chancellor Norman Lamont in 1992, at the peak of ideological obsession with contracting out as the route to efficiency.

It was Labour, though, who rapidly expanded their use across government. Not because they were better value for money; multiple analyses have shown they categorically were not.[33] It always costs more to borrow from banks than just fund projects directly. Labour did it because it allowed creative accounting on an epic scale. As we saw in the first chapter, Gordon Brown was the first chancellor to commit to public 'fiscal rules' which constrained spending. Until 2013, all PFI projects were 'off balance sheet' by international accounting standards, meaning that spending on them did not 'count'.

The Treasury always publicly denied they were doing this. But no one paying attention was fooled. As the Oxford professor and economist Dieter Helm told a 2011 parliamentary committee, PFI was: 'an exercise to get investment off the public balance sheet so that the debt numbers look better than they otherwise would have done'.[34] We can tell because subsequent governments largely stopped using it after it became harder to keep it off the balance sheet.

The Treasury has kept trying to create versions of PFI that would be off balance sheet, even, as the National Audit Office noted in 2018, if it has meant making them even worse value for money.[35] But so far they have not found an effective way to do so. In the meantime taxpayers will be paying for existing PFI projects well into the 2040s. As of 2018 the remaining bill was £200 billion, even if no new projects were committed to.[36] The full cost of schools built under PFI will be over £30 billion for buildings worth around £7.5 billion, though this does include ongoing maintenance.[37]

As with changes to procurement rules, PFI helped the rapid growth of the outsourcing giants as much more business came their way. It also meant that the failure of any firms running substantial numbers of PFI projects would be a huge headache for the government, increasing the incentive to avoid criticism and give them more work, even if their failures went public.

Since 2010 the government's approach to the use of outsourcing has more or less conformed to the previous pattern; most day-to-day delivery has been contracted out. However, the austerity cuts that have hit the public sector so hard have also affected outsourcing firms. Public bodies with less money to spend have had to reduce the value of contracts and limit new projects. At the same time the pipeline of PFI projects has stopped. This has had the effect of reducing the number of firms bidding to an even smaller pool of ever-larger conglomerates. And it has left departments with an extremely tricky balancing act. On the one hand they need to save money, on the other they need to keep these companies alive because they are now responsible for delivering so much of what the state does.

Thus we have arrived at a maximally dysfunctional market with minimal competition, no ability to properly monitor contracts, and no meaningful risk-sharing. As the Public Accounts Committee said in 2018: 'The Government has allowed a culture to develop in which a small number of large companies believe that they are too big to fail. [They] pursued new business with little apparent consideration of their ability to deliver the right service at the right price.'[38]

We can see this is true because the companies responsible for the most grievous and public failures continue to win contracts. One of the most widely reported failures of recent years was Atos's delivery of 'work capability assessments'. These were introduced in 2008 by Labour as a way to reduce the cost of disability benefits by identifying those who could work. It was heavily criticized by disability groups from the start and, as Atos were fronting them, their name became a by-word for the cruelty associated with the assessments.

By 2013 complaints were so widespread that MPs from across the political spectrum were raising concerns in Parliament. Iain Wright spoke of one constituent with a serious bowel complaint who was 'told that she could wear a nappy for work'; Steve Rotheram of a man declared fit for work with chronic obstructive pulmonary disease who died six weeks later; Pamela Nash of a lady who 'suffered

90% burns to her body . . . told she was ready to join the work programme'; and so on. There were multiple stories of suicides.[39]

As the journalist and author Alan White has noted, there was an element of convenience in all this for the Department for Work and Pensions (DWP), who were able to hand off a significant portion of the political blame, if not the risk: 'The assessment with which [Atos] is most closely associated – no doubt much to the frustration of the company – was drawn up not by Atos, but the DWP. Its descriptors were written by the department, which gave the company strict rules that it had to stick to.'[40]

Nevertheless, Atos made a bad situation worse through repeated incompetence, hiring assessors without knowledge of the conditions they were supposed to be assessing, failing to deal with complaints and, most importantly from the DWP's perspective, failing to complete nearly enough assessments due to 27 per cent staff turnover. By 2014 there was a backlog of 700,000 cases and the whole system was grinding to a halt.[41]

Ministers managed to get Atos to end the contract a year early and made a big political play out of how they were not obligated to pay any compensation. The political storm abated but the problems continued. There are very few companies large enough to take on the WCA contract, and even fewer who fancied the adverse publicity, so it ended up being handed to an American outsourcing giant (somewhat hubristically called Maximus), who had only just settled a lawsuit with the US government over the alleged falsification of Medicaid claims.[42] A 2016 National Audit Office report found they were performing even worse than Atos on various key indicators, and disability groups continued to raise concerns.[43]

Even more remarkably, Atos continued to hold contracts for assessments relating to another disability benefit – the Personal

Independence Payment (PIP). And they continued to win other DWP contracts, as well as many from other departments.[44] In 2023 the DWP ran a procurement process for combined disability assessments encompassing both benefits, split into five regions. Two contracts were won by Capita, who had been delivering PIP assessments alongside Atos, despite their own dreadful record including data breaches and inaccurate assessment forms. Perhaps most seriously, they were implicated in the suicide of 27-year-old mother Philippa Day by the coroner, who found failings in the PIP system were 'the predominant factor and the only acute factor' in her death.[45]

Another contract was awarded to Maximus, despite their track record, and a fourth to an Australian multinational. The fifth was awarded to Serco but was challenged by Atos. They argued the DWP had deliberately tried to avoid them winning, presumably out of embarrassment, by accepting a late and incomplete bid from Serco with bits cut and pasted from other bids.[46] This process is a perfect example of the mess Whitehall has got itself into, repeatedly rewarding the same handful of companies regardless of how badly they fail simply because there is no one else to do the work.

It is very obviously not sustainable, as was shown by the 2018 collapse of the sixth biggest outsourcing company in the UK: Carillion. Like many other fast-growing outsourcing companies Carillion grew rapidly by buying out other smaller companies. In their case, their acquisitions were for far too much money, leading to unsustainable debt, which they hid through dodgy accounting practices. They continued paying out huge dividends to shareholders, and bonuses to senior management, while desperately chasing more contracts, largely by offering to do them for less money than others, to keep enough money coming in. As one academic noted, 'this sounds suspiciously like a lawful Ponzi scheme'.[47]

When they were forced to issue a profit warning in 2017 it came out of the blue for government, though not others who had been paying closer attention. Incredibly they were awarded £2 billion of additional government work – on top of 420 existing public sector contracts – after this profit warning, 'effectively making taxpayers a kind of Ponzi scheme investor of last resort'.[48] The Cabinet Office were supposed to be monitoring Carillion on a regular basis as the large number of contracts they held made them a 'strategic supplier' but no one was assigned to this task for several months. The Cabinet Office declined to give their highest risk rating to the ailing company on the circular grounds that 'the rating would risk precipitating its financial collapse'.[49]

On 13 January 2018, a few days before the company did collapse, its chair Philip Green wrote what the Business Select Committee called a 'last minute ransom note' to the government demanding a £160 million bailout on the grounds that letting Carillion fail would 'come with enormous cost to HM Government, far exceeding the costs of continued funding for the business'.[50] Ministers refused and two days later it went into insolvency.

At this point the government had to scramble around to keep all the different services, from prison cleaning to school building maintenance, running, as well as find ways to continue contracts to build hospitals and the HS2 rail network. They spent £150 million of taxpayer money to keep services running. Other providers had to be found, some of whom demanded a 20 per cent premium to take over. The Ministry of Justice had to set up its own firm to take over the prison contracts. As we have seen over and over again, the ultimate risk remained with the state.[51]

In addition to the direct cost, several thousand people lost their jobs, many thousands more lost some of their pension entitlement, and small- and medium-sized businesses that supplied Carillion lost around £2 billion.[52] There was significant fallout with multiple inquiries by select committees and the National Audit Office. Carillion's auditors, KPMG, another big government contractor, were fined £14 million by the Financial Reporting Council for misleading the regulator and falsifying documents.[53] Carillion's CEO and two former finance directors were fined over £870,000 by the Financial Conduct Authority for making misleading statements (far less than the salary and bonus packages they'd received).[54] The finance directors were, eventually, also banned from being company directors for over a decade.[55]

While Carillion's ineptitude and dishonesty was particularly bad, the basic model of growth they adopted was standard. Multiple other companies have also got into serious trouble by buying up smaller firms to boost their position, desperately trying to win contracts to manage debts, and applying aggressive accountancy practices to make their position look stronger than it was.

We have already seen that two large providers involved in the probation outsourcing – Interserve and Working Links – ended up insolvent. But the very biggest providers are not immune either. In 2014, both G4S and Serco were in serious trouble due to public scandals like G4S's failure over Olympic security. Both companies were involved in the electronic tagging fiasco. Both also went down the familiar path of buying up too many poor-value smaller firms to boost their size, overstating their position via accountancy tricks, and underbidding for contracts. Serco ended up having to make four profit warnings in 2014 and write down £1.6 billion in their accounts.[56] They went through a 'corporate reset' with the CEO, finance director and chairman all leaving. G4S went through a similar process. Both companies survived but it was touch and go.[57]

At the time of writing, both companies, as well as Capita and Atos, are not at any immediate risk of insolvency today, but it can be hard to spot if companies are intent on covering up their true position. Their accounts are far less transparent than those provided by the public sector and contracts have commercial confidentiality clauses that make it almost impossible to understand the terms and conditions. The market keeps shrinking, putting more and more risk onto the potential collapse of these very big firms, forcing government to balance that risk against value for money for the taxpayer.

There have been dozens and dozens of official reports highlighting these problems over the past few decades from the National Audit Office, the Public Accounts Committee, and even government itself. Some deal with particular scandals like Atos's handling of disability benefits, or the probation mess. Others look at the broader picture. None of the problems highlighted in this chapter are really disputed by anyone. But these reports all conclude by arguing that the government just needs to get better at contracting and managing the market. This rather ignores that they have been trying to do that for decades and yet scandals are becoming more commonplace and risk is growing. No one seems to want to acknowledge that the model just does not work. The market cannot be functional because it does not fulfil the basic requirements of a market.

The private equity scandal

At least in central government there is an attempt to manage this highly dysfunctional market of outsourced contracts. An even bigger worry is a group of increasingly critical public services that are largely taxpayer funded but where neither central nor local government is managing – or properly tracking – what is going on. As we saw with Ampika Pickston's care home, this is creating another set of scandals.

This group of services – of which the main examples are adult social care, childcare, and children's homes – all share similar characteristics. They all used to be predominantly run by councils; have all seen demand grow dramatically due to demographic and social changes; and are all services that are not the main priority of their Whitehall department (Health for adult social care; Education for the other two). As demand has grown government deliberately designed policy to ensure the private sector would pick up the slack, with serious consequences that are only now starting to become fully clear.

Take adult social care, the most costly of the three. The state is now spending over £20 billion a year,[58] which is expected to grow to over £30 billion by 2030 as the population ages and people live longer.[59] It is already significantly more than we spend on the police or higher education. Yet almost all of it goes to for-profit companies.

This wasn't always the case. In 1979 64 per cent of social care beds were provided by the state; by 2012 it was 6 per cent. In 1993, 95 per cent of domiciliary care (i.e. being looked after in your own home) was delivered by local authorities, but by 2012 it was 11 per cent.[60] This was a direct result of the 1990 NHS and Community Care Act, which envisioned local authorities as 'commissioners' of care rather than centres of delivery, and made funding dependent on using private providers.

No subsequent government have sought to change this, finding it quite convenient that they have not had to pay to build new care homes. Essentially the shift of provision to the private sector has acted as a 'soft PFI' – private companies have paid the upfront cost of building homes – which they then get back over time in fees. That upfront cost stays off the government's balance sheet, helping them to meet fiscal rules, again showing the policy damage caused by the Treasury obsession with these arbitrary numbers.

From 2010 to 2019, council funding was, as we saw in chapter two, squeezed very hard. As providing social care is a statutory duty councils have found themselves increasingly caught between the needs of the public and the demands of companies providing services. As the fees on offer from councils have fallen, the structure of the private market has changed. Smaller and typically higher-quality independent homes have been unable to cope and sold out to big private-equity-backed firms who are able to take on very large amounts of debt for short periods.

By 2019 three of the four largest providers – representing by themselves 10 per cent of all care home beds nationally – were private-equity backed. There aren't even any statistics on the extent to which this is true across the whole sector, an indication of how little understanding the government have of the market, but we can see the average care home is run by ever-larger companies.[61]

The standard model for these private equity firms is to load up companies with debt, slash costs, and then sell on to another buyer. The five largest private-equity-backed care companies are spending a huge amount on debt repayment, around 16 per cent of their total costs.[62] In the context of an increasingly poorly funded social care sector this has meant that they have had to target parts of the country with more wealthy patients who can pay fees beyond what the state offer in order to manage their debts.

It also means paying staff as little as possible. In 2014 care workers in private homes were paid £7.23 per hour compared to £9.45 in the remaining public ones. This unsurprisingly means a much higher turnover of staff, with minimal training, and lower-quality provision. A 2022 academic study found for-profit homes fared worse in inspections and private-equity-backed ones the worst of all.[63]

As well as lowering quality this volatile market has also produced a crisis in provision. There simply aren't enough beds in many parts of the country, because homes cannot hire enough staff at rates they are willing to pay to maintain profit, given the low level of state-funded fees and their high debts. By 2023 there were over 150,000 vacancies in the social care sector, more than the total number of doctors nationally.[64] In turn this was putting huge pressure on the NHS, with precious hospital beds taken up with patients who had no medical need but for whom no care bed was available. This was one major cause of the substantial post-pandemic backlogs in the NHS – with over 7.7 million people on hospital waiting lists by the winter of 2023.

While this currently looks like a slow-puncture failure of the whole system it could quickly turn into something more rapid given the precarity of the business model. Several large providers have already collapsed. Southern Cross went under in 2011 after US private equity firm Blackstone made off with a huge profit, having bought the company, set up an unsustainable financial model that assumed ever rising property prices, and then sold it on.[65]

Then in 2019 the second largest chain at the time, Four Seasons, went into administration, unable to cope with its huge debt load. A brief history of its ownership from an article in *Fortune* magazine gives some indication of the dizzying financial complexity increasingly common in the care home market: 'From 2004 to 2017, big money came and went, with revenue at times threaded through multiple offshore vehicles. Among the groups that owned Four Seasons, in part or in its entirety: British private equity firm Alchemy

Partner; Allianz Capital Partners, a German private equity firm; Three Delta LLP, an investment fund backed by Qatar; the American hedge fund Monarch Alternative Capital; and Terra Firma, the British private equity group that wallowed in debt demands. H/2 Capital Partners, a hedge fund in Connecticut, was Four Seasons' main creditor and took over. By 2019, Four Seasons was managed by insolvency experts.'[66]

Neither local authorities nor central government have any levers to manage this market. The ownership structures are opaque, with heavy use of complex financial structures and tax havens. There is not necessarily much warning of problems. When companies collapse the homes have to find new buyers or close, as many Four Seasons institutions have, causing deserts of provision in parts of the country, and putting even more pressure on the health service. As more and more smaller independent homes are sold on, either due to financial difficulties or because their owners want to retire, and demand for social care grows, these problems will only get worse. Again there are National Audit Office and select committee reports highlighting these problems but there has been no action by government as yet.[67]

It is a similar story in childcare. Up until the mid-1990s, state provision of early years education was limited. Local authorities had the freedom to run nurseries both in schools and as separate institutions. What was available in your area depended on the level of interest at council level. Wealthier parents paid for private provision. But the rapid increase in the number of women in the labour market, and the increasing dependence on households for their income, made it a growing political priority.

In 1996 John Major introduced nursery vouchers – 12.5 free hours for every three- and four-year-old per week. Again, the explicit intention was to ensure that any state-funded growth in the sector happened in the private sector.[68] Successive governments did nothing to change this. Labour changed the voucher into an 'entitlement' but that made little difference. In 2006 they even banned local authorities from opening their own provision unless there was evidence of a lack of private places.[69] At the same time every subsequent government has increased the free entitlement as demand has kept going up. As with social care, this has led to a big expansion in the number of nurseries, initially via smaller providers and then, as the value of the entitlement reduced during the austerity years, by larger, often private-equity-backed, chains.

By 2019, 69 per cent of places were being offered by privately owned nurseries. The number of providers operating a single site fell from 85 per cent to 62 per cent of the market between 2016 and 2019 and the number of chains with more than 20 sites grew from 3 per cent to 9 per cent.[70] These trends have continued since, and are likely to have been accelerated by the pandemic.

Just as with social care, this has led to these larger groups of nurseries looking to increase revenues by targeting richer parts of the country (leaving deserts with not enough provision) and slashing costs, mainly by hiring more untrained staff, including many more apprentices who can be paid below minimum wage. Once more, there are staff shortages across the sector. And again, there is little either central government is doing, or local government can do, to remedy any of this.

The expansion of the 'free entitlement' to cover one- and two-year-old children, announced at the 2023 Budget, will reduce companies' ability to cover costs by charging richer parents of younger children, risking the collapse of more indebted chains. There are already plenty of examples of smaller chains going into administration, leaving areas without adequate places.[71] The *Financial Times* reported in

2023 that one of the biggest chains, Busy Bees, 'has been passed between private equity and corporate owners for more than two decades. Now owned by the private equity arm of Ontario Teachers' Pension Plan, its debt is about 7.5 times its earnings, according to a Moody's report last month. The rating agency has graded the debt as B3 – "speculative and subject to high credit risk".'[72]

As we saw at the start of the chapter, the children's home market is the most dysfunctional of all. Again, it was a service that used to be provided almost entirely by councils but, due to lack of available funding to build more homes, they started contracting out. At the same time the number of children requiring care has grown rapidly, by 14 per cent in England between 2016 and 2020 alone. Three quarters of places are now in the private sector, mostly for-profit.

Unlike adult social care and childcare this is a small and specialized market. The number of placements any given council will need to make will fluctuate significantly from year to year. All the funding comes from the state, so there is no wider market to provide any regulation of price or quality. As a result, local authorities are entirely at the mercy of for-profit providers.

The private equity market spotted the opportunity early and has taken full advantage. Seven of the ten largest providers, representing almost a third of the market by themselves, are now owned by private equity.[73] They are, typically, laden with debt and making frankly obscene profits in order to cover that debt. Because councils have so little money they cannot build their own provision, especially as, because numbers are small, it is difficult to predict how many children will need care in any given year. So the companies running homes can hold councils – and taxpayers – to ransom, charging more than the cost of a room at the Ritz.

Despite the fees, the quality of provision is often poor and not where it is needed. Companies are setting up homes where property is cheap, in northern towns like Blackpool and Burnley, and avoiding expensive areas, meaning councils in London and the south-east are having to send children hundreds of miles away from their existing homes and friendship networks. As one council leader told *The Observer*, this is 'blatant profiteering'.[74] The human consequences of this are devastating, with young people drifting into crime and being targeted by grooming gangs. The government have, at least, acknowledged the problem, commissioning a review which confirmed these problems and proposing a major overhaul. But as yet the money has not been found and little is happening.[75]

Rebuilding state capacity

The picture is of a government that has lost control. Over forty years, successive administrations have centralized power within Whitehall. They have undermined and underfunded local government. They have increasingly turned to for-profit companies to deliver services instead and we have ended up with highly dysfunctional markets across the public sector. A practice that worked for easy-to-manage services like cleaning and bin collection has been applied across the board. Sometimes it has led to full-blown scandals or failures, as with the probation service, or Carillion.

But the problem is much broader. Everywhere you look there is chronic failure due to the dominant position of a handful of profit-seeking conglomerates. The provision of services that have grown rapidly since the outsourcing era began – adult social care; childcare; children's homes – have been left at the mercy of unguided markets, increasingly dominated by the most rapacious organizations around. In the 1970s, labour, in the form of trade unions, was too powerful, preventing the state from operating properly. Their place has now been taken by capital.

The first step to fixing the problem is to acknowledge it. We need to accept that all the failures and scandals are not one-offs due to bad contracting, which can be fixed technocratically, but that the whole model is fundamentally broken. Then we can try to develop a more ordered approach to delivering services, while accepting things have gone too far for any quick fixes.

Of course, publicly run services can struggle too. There are plenty of examples of schools and hospitals that have been poorly run, and of scandals where management try to cover up failure. But there is a reason why ministers have never been able to hand over the most politically salient services to the private sector (with the exception of Hinchingbrooke Hospital).

This is because these services get a lot of attention and there is an expectation of accountability that only the public sector can meet. If something goes wrong it is clear whose job it is to fix it (and if they try to cover it up it is clear who is at fault there too). Ministers cannot duck responsibility by hiding behind a private company and commercial confidentiality. And while public sector staff are certainly not all angels and will often act in their own interests, they aren't pursuing an entirely contrary agenda on behalf of shareholders looking to milk the taxpayer for as big a profit as possible.

What needs to change? For a start government needs to have clear criteria for when outsourcing is the right solution. That criteria needs to assess whether there is an existing market – not just whether there will be bidders but whether they would have appropriate experience and a good track record. Critically, it needs to consider whether the service is simple enough to be measurable. If it is not, there is a high chance outsourcing will not work. Then it needs to assess the true risk to the public sector, not just of failure, but also loss of capacity and expertise.

Only if tightly drawn tests are met should new work be out-sourced, and where they are not met contracts should be run down and services taken back in-house. This would also mean they could improve procurement processes for things that do meet the criteria. At the moment they are designed in an incredibly risk-averse way due to their overuse, which makes it exceptionally hard for smaller companies or charities to win or manage contracts.

For markets like social care and childcare, the solutions lie in increasing state capacity outside of Whitehall. The proposals for devolution set out in chapter two would offer a way forward. Mayors and combined authorities need to be given powers of oversight over markets for care homes and nurseries, and be able to either set up their own provision or offer incentives for non-profit providers to open up. Individual authorities, especially in cities, are often too small to manage these markets effectively, even if they had stronger powers and more money.

As we have seen over the course of the last three chapters, successive governments have, via constant centralization and an over-reliance on the private sector, diminished state capacity to unsustainable levels. Stronger, better-funded, regional government will be critical to resolving this.

Meanwhile there is no shortage of scrutiny from organizations like the National Audit Office and parliamentary select committees regarding this lack of capacity. But all of these reports have had very little bite. Our institutions that are supposed to hold government to account and help guide its actions – be it the House of Commons, the Lords, the civil service, the courts or external regulators – have found it harder and harder to do so in recent decades. The story of why that has happened is where we turn in the next section. An overwhelmed government is bad enough. But one that's overwhelmed and has far too much power is even more dangerous.

PART 2

OVERPOWERED

4

DEMOCRACY BYPASS

How governments avoid scrutiny

'Cabinet government is cumbersome . . . difficult [and] a bit of a shambles but it has got to be as far as possible, a democratic and accountable shambles'.

JOHN HUNT (CABINET SECRETARY 1973–79)[1]

It is easy to tell the story of our Parliament as one of straightforward decline. A once great institution – the model for so many other democracies around the world – now filled with supine, low-grade nonentities, freelancing on low-rent talk shows. That the Palace of Westminster is physically collapsing, infested with rats, and perilously close to irreparable, offers a metaphor so crashingly obvious that the comedian David Mitchell was already admonishing commentators for using it a decade ago. ('The inwardly delighted wry shake of the head at that slow-news-week-political-cartoon quantity of wit and insight. Honestly, it makes me want to join Isis.'[1])

The real story is much more complex. While we can point to great statesmen and women who dominated the chamber in previous eras, the work-rate of the average MP has never been higher than in today's frantic times, and there have always been complaints about the worsening quality of parliamentarians. Nor were MPs more

127

independent in the past, or at least not for a couple of hundred years. The government has held substantial power in the British system – something known as 'executive dominance' – for a long time. This has been even more true since the rise of the party system following the Reform Acts of the nineteenth century, and procedural changes to strengthen government control of parliamentary business in the early twentieth century.[2]

As early as 1923, Winston Churchill was complaining that Parliament had been so weakened that it was 'marching silently and docilely to execution blindfold' (though, in what will become a common theme of this chapter, he was less concerned once he returned to ministerial office). The academics Matthew Flinders and Alexandra Kelso have catalogued dozens of books and articles over the twentieth century arguing that Parliament was becoming more ineffectual.[3]

Here's a particularly pungent example from a 1949 book called *Can Parliament Survive?*: 'The member is the obedient servant of the party machine. He tramps into the division lobby voting for or against he knows not what . . . As things are now, it would really be simpler and more economical to keep a flock of tame sheep and from time to time to drive them through the division lobbies in the appropriate numbers.'[4]

Most famously, in 1976, Lord Hailsham accused the government of 'elective dictatorship' and proposed constitutional reform, though he also recanted once he was back as a minister a few years later. Flinders and Kelso argue that this constant simplistic narrative of parliamentary decline has, somewhat ironically, made things worse by contributing to the increasingly dim view the public have of MPs. Both because it misrepresents the work they do to check the government behind the scenes, but also because it creates an unfair 'expectations gap' about what is possible, given our modern Parliament was explicitly constructed with the intention of allowing strong executive control.

Another academic, Philip Cowley, has done extensive work on backbench rebellions, the main way in which a government that has a majority can be blocked in Parliament, and found that, contrary to the common view, MPs have become considerably less manageable over the years.[5] Edward Heath was the first post-war prime minister to suffer a defeat at the hands of his own backbenchers, but since then it has happened at least once to all of them, even those, like Thatcher and Blair, with very substantial majorities.

In the 2005–10 Parliament, 28 per cent of votes saw at least one backbencher rebel. Post-2010 governments have also been unusually volatile. These matter not only because of the rare defeats, but because governments dislike the appearance of disunity and often back off in the face of significant backbench opposition, even if they would win the vote.[6] A good example from 2022 was when Rishi Sunak scrapped house-building targets, a hugely consequential policy decision, to avoid a backbench rebellion on a vote he would have won anyway given Labour had already said they would support the bill.[7]

Nevertheless, while we should reject the simplistic story of decline, government dominance over Parliament has become much more of an issue over the past few decades.

The first reason is that, as we have seen, governments are more involved, across more areas of activity, at greater levels of detail, than at any previous point. The complexity of material Parliament needs to scrutinize has risen, and the dangers of them not being able to do so properly has increased. The Online Safety Act, which became law in 2023, is an obvious example: 262 pages of incredibly complex and technical legislation on something that barely registered as an issue even a decade ago.

Meanwhile, the constant need to feed the media beast has led to a rapid proliferation of symbolic legislation designed not to achieve any real-world goal, but to give the impression of activity. Both of the Immigration Acts passed by the governments of Boris Johnson and Rishi Sunak fall into this category and yet had immensely serious potential consequences that consumed a vast amount of parliamentary and government effort.

The second reason executive dominance now matters more is, paradoxically, the growing difficulty party managers are having in keeping their troops in order. As backbenchers have become more assertive, helped by a more active House of Lords, successive governments have pushed back. Hard. They have used their excessive power in ways governments never used to: by finding ways of overriding Parliament in ever more damaging ways.

An unmanageable Parliament

To understand why this is happening, we need to start with the main reason why Parliament is becoming more rebellious and harder for governments to manage through conventional means.

The role of MPs has changed dramatically over the past thirty years. And in completely the opposite way to public perception. Probably the most commonly uttered phrase in focus groups is 'they're all in it for themselves' – the 2009 expenses scandal supercharged a sense that MPs were all venal and corrupt. Neither Boris Johnson's escapades, nor the succession of by-elections caused by inappropriate behaviour, have done anything to dispel this impression.

Yet, in reality, most MPs work far harder than they ever have before. Up until the 1990s, it was, for the majority, a part-time role, almost a hobby for some. Since then, it has transformed into a profession of its own, with typically extremely long and intense hours.

David Lidington, who entered the Commons in 1992, eventually rising to be Theresa May's de facto deputy prime minister, explained to me what it used to be like: 'When I first came in, I had senior colleagues who went back to the 1950s . . . They'd reminisce how there used to be a very large number of Tories who came in from their estates or their City board after lunch, or their law practice. And they'd come in to vote primarily, to do their duty by the party. And similarly on the Labour side, there were lots of experienced trade unionists who would be given a safe Labour seat as the reward for long years of trade union service. The Tory squires would sit drinking scotch or champagne in the smoking room. And the Labour trade unionists would congregate with the Federation bitter in the bar downstairs. And when the division bells rang, they'd look sharp and go and vote.'[8]

Ken Clarke, who became an MP in 1970, before taking on senior roles in successive Conservative governments, had a similar experience: 'I was a barrister when I first entered Parliament . . . and I used to practise on the circuit in the morning and then come down [to Parliament] in the afternoon. It's a totally different House of Commons now . . . It was assumed you were working doing something else, which practically every Conservative member did, those who didn't had landed interests . . . [or] family fortunes. Working class members, of whom we had more then than we do now – e.g. train drivers and coal miners – were funded to be MPs via a trade union as there were not the allowances and expenses that exist today. It was very much – to use a clichéd phrase – a part-time Parliament.'[9]

Statistics confirm these recollections. One analysis of members' declared interests found most Conservative MPs did some kind of paid outside work in 1990 and most Labour MPs had union sponsorship.[10] In 1995 70 per cent of MPs had 'financial relationships with outside bodies which directly related to their membership of the House'.[11] By 2018 just 18.5 per cent had regular paid outside commitments and that number is falling in every Parliament.[12]

A number of different factors coalesced in the mid-1990s to change the picture. A greater media presence in Parliament made the role more visible to the public and created pressure to focus on the job. Investigative journalists also uncovered a cluster of scandals around outside interests, which fitted into a wider mid-1990s narrative about 'Tory sleaze'. One of these – the 'cash for questions' affair, which saw two Conservative MPs take bribes to ask parliamentary questions on behalf of Harrods boss Mohamed Al-Fayed – forced John Major into establishing the Nolan Committee on Standards in Public Life. This led to a whole raft of rules about declarations of interests, sanctions for breaking the rules and the appointment of an independent standards commissioner. Tony Blair took the opportunity to highlight New Labour's greater distance from trade unions by banning his MPs from taking up sponsorship.[13]

At the same time, House of Commons' hours started to shift closer to the normal working day. Up to the mid-1990s business began at 2:30 in the afternoon every day, which allowed MPs to spend much of the day working in the City or at a law firm. In incremental stages between 1994 and 2012 they moved to the current model of 11:30 a.m. starts on Tuesday and Wednesday and 9:30 a.m. starts on Thursday (and Friday if the House is sitting).[14]

Alongside these internal culture shifts, the rise of the internet and readily available access to email transformed MPs' relationships with their constituents. Many MPs had always been enthusiastic about constituency engagements, with a close attachment to the area. But it had not been a requirement of the job. When Winston Churchill was MP for Dundee he only went once a year. Even MPs with seats much closer to Westminster used to spend much of their time elsewhere. Lidington told me about being shown the cup that was presented to a former MP to mark his annual visit to his Kent constituency.[15] In the 1950s and 1960s, MPs received an average of twelve to fifteen letters a week from constituents.[16]

Since then, technological change has transformed public access to MPs – they now get on average 500–1,000 letters, emails and calls a week.[17] Staffing budgets have gone up and most MPs have a constituency team of three or four, which in turn has added to responsibilities. Moreover, the rapid growth in people receiving welfare benefits, and of immigration, has added to the workload because a large proportion of correspondence relates to these issues. A survey of MPs in the 2010 Parliament found that for a third of them, constituency work was now taking up more than half their time.[18]

The job has been transformed. Substantive second jobs are almost exclusively the preserve of older backbench Conservative MPs without future ministerial ambitions, and not far off retirement.[19] Many of these MPs will leave Parliament over the next few cycles. This professionalization of the role has changed the type of person becoming an MP. The numbers coming from professions like the law and medicine fell from 45 per cent in 1979 to 31 per cent in 2015, and increasingly MPs from those professions stop practising them once they move into politics. The drop in those who worked in manual jobs is even more stark – from 16 per cent to 3 per cent – due to the changing nature of trade union membership and weakening links with the Labour Party. Meanwhile, it is becoming much more common for people already working in politics as special advisers or organizers to become MPs (3 per cent to 17 per cent).[20]

The MP role becoming a full-time job has had significant benefits for society. Constituents get a much more engaged and active service, on average, than in previous generations. MPs work harder, drink less (though still too much) and have more of a sense of vocation. There has also been a big increase in diversity when it comes to women and minorities. There are still far too many incidents of inappropriate behaviour towards younger staff. Nevertheless, things are getting better. Before the 1997 election there were more MPs called John than there were women; now 35 per cent of all MPs are women and the number is likely to keep rising.[21]

Prior to 1997, there had only been a handful of Black and minority ethnic MPs. Paul Boateng was the first Black cabinet minister as recently as 2002. Now 8 per cent of MPs are from minority ethnic backgrounds, including multiple cabinet ministers.[22] The one glaring exception to these trends is class where, due to the loss of union links on the Labour side, numbers have gone backwards.

The problem is that these professional, hard-working MPs are operating in a system designed for a strong executive and a part-time Parliament. As David Lidington says, of all those Tory squires and Labour trade unionists, 'very few of them expected or wanted to become ministers'. Now, when politics is a career choice for most MPs, how could they not want to be ministers, given how little power Parliament has compared to the government? Especially as ministers earn a lot more. But, by law, only 95 MPs can be ministers at any given time, and a government, with a majority, has at least 326.

This is a big cause of increased fractiousness among backbenchers. At the start of a government's time in power, most backbench MPs will behave because there is still a chance of realizing their ambitions.

A handful will have no interest in ministerial office, or be too old or eccentric to be in with a chance. But most will be hoping for advancement. Over time, many will realize their chance has gone, or will have some time in office only to be fired. As a result, they will be more prepared to cause trouble or even consider replacing the prime minister, as that might give them another chance at office. Combined with the fact that governments tend to become more unpopular over time, this helps explain why rebellions increased across New Labour's time in power, and why the last few years of Conservative government have been riven with internal disputes.

This has led governments to find ways of using their historic dominance in new ways to get round an increasingly assertive Parliament. It is this pushback from the executive that is undermining scrutiny and leading to a worrying drop in the quality of legislation. The fact that governments are increasingly overwhelmed makes this worse. They are even more determined to limit the amount of time spent engaged in scrutiny, which then leads to worse outcomes, which leads to government becoming more overwhelmed.

The whips fight back

As backbenchers have become more unruly, governments have found new ways to keep them loyal. Whipping MPs to vote for the party line has a long history stretching back to the seventeenth century, before recognized parties even existed (the term itself originated in the eighteenth century as a satirical reference to hunting). Over the years whips have used all sorts of tactics including bullying and bribery. In the modern Parliament there are sixteen House of Commons whips, which are ministerial positions themselves, and the parliamentary party is divided up between them. Each is assigned around twenty MPs to keep an eye on. The approach they take will depend, at least in part, on their personality.

Physical or aggressive emotional bullying is increasingly rare (memoirs of MPs who served in previous generations tend to compare the experience to being hazed by older boys at private school). In a world where workplace practices outside Westminster have changed, and where the media are poking around, it is much riskier and less culturally acceptable (which does not mean it never happens). Most whips will try to use persuasion and have a broadly positive relationship with their group. Nevertheless, dirty tricks are still used. Whips still make it their job to know the stories and rumours each MP would like to make sure stay out of the press. These can be used as retaliation if MPs persistently rebel.

They also have a new tool, and one that can be more powerful than a private-school hazing. The centralization of government spending, particularly on regeneration projects, has given whips a new way to blackmail recalcitrant MPs. Of course, these funds should be assigned according to objective criteria, but they are often used as a political tool – yet another reason why such centralization works against good governance.

Christian Wakeford, a former Tory MP who defected to Labour when Johnson was prime minister, alleged that he 'was threatened that I would not get a school for Radcliffe [in his constituency of Bury South] if I did not vote in one particular way. This is a town that has not had a high school for the best part of ten years. How would you feel when they hold back the regeneration of a town for a vote? It didn't sit comfortably. That was the start of me questioning my place, where I was and ultimately to where I am now.'[23]

Another disillusioned Tory MP, William Wragg, who stayed in the party but announced in 2022 that he would be leaving Parliament at the next election, confirmed this was happening to a parliamentary select committee: 'It is, of course, the duty of the government whips' office to secure the government's business in the House of Commons. However, it is not their function to breach the ministerial code in threatening to withdraw investment from members of parliaments' constituencies which are funded from the public purse.'[24]

Other Conservative MPs have told me off the record that this happened in either veiled or direct threats as well. Whips of previous eras would no doubt have used similar approaches had they been available to them but they didn't have such intensive centralization of infrastructure funding to work with. The loss of EU regeneration funding, replaced, to some extent, by yet more centrally controlled pots, has only increased the opportunities to use it for political control.

Another increasingly common trick used by whips has been the creation of jobs that are not formal ministerial positions but nevertheless require the recipient to vote with the government if they want to keep them. The number of 'proper' ministers has gradually grown from around 60 in 1900 to 120 (including some who sit in the House of Lords).[25] It's hard to argue that many of the more junior posts are necessary. There is much plaintive commentary in junior ministerial diaries about whether their role has any purpose, given they are often given responsibility for a small handful of low-level issues.

Former Labour MP Chris Mullin wrote about his: 'My existence is now [after four months in post] almost entirely pointless . . . with hand on heart I can say that I have less influence now over government policy than at any time in the last eight years. The only possible excuse for doing this is the hope that it will lead to something better.'[26]

But there is a hard limit of 95 ministerial posts in the Commons (and 109 paid ministers overall – there tend to be ten to fifteen unpaid ministers, mostly in the Lords, these days). So from the interwar period onwards, governments started to appoint 'parliamentary private secretaries' (PPS). These posts are unpaid assistants to ministers who are supposed to help them gauge the mood among backbenchers and build support for legislation. Some PPS's do have a genuinely significant role, especially those working for prime ministers and chancellors. But, in reality, most do very little.

Governments love appointing PPS's because they don't count towards the quotient of 95 ministers but do have to vote with them or resign their position. For new MPs, a PPS role is not seen as hugely desirable in itself but it's a step on the ladder towards ministerial position. As early as 1940, a parliamentary committee noted that: 'Your Committee cannot disregard the fact that the existence of parliamentary private secretaries is, not without reason, regarded as increasing the voting strength and influence of the Government in the House of Commons; it might (however improbably) be improperly used for this purpose.'[27]

Seventy years on Jonathan Powell, Blair's former chief of staff, was more explicit, acknowledging that: '[It] is a way of making sure you have that many votes in the House of Commons . . . If the Prime Minister had his way, he would appoint every single backbencher in his party to a ministerial job to ensure their vote.'[28]

By 1992 the number of PPS's had already reached forty-one but then Blair pushed it even further, with numbers peaking at fifty-eight during the 2001 Parliament, when he was trying to manage a large and increasingly fractious cohort of MPs.[29] This meant some junior ministers, with little to do themselves, now had an assistant with nothing to do either.

Conservative prime ministers have recently taken this approach to the next level. Having exhausted the possibilities of the PPS role, they have invented whole swathes of jobs with no precedent, and no pay or ministerial responsibilities, creating a 'wider payroll' vote. Cameron created 'big society ambassadors'; Theresa May added 'trade envoys' to various countries which also offered the promise of exotic junkets; Boris Johnson threw in multiple 'vice-chairs' of the Conservative party.

This trick doesn't always work. The former Tory MP Charlotte Leslie told me about the whips' attempt to use her 'big society ambassadorship' to stop her voting against the government: 'I remember once when I was rebelling on Lords reform, my whip phoned me up, and I said, "I'm just not doing this. It's just nuts." And he said, "Charlotte, if you don't vote for this, we will revoke your big society ambassadorship." And I hooted with laughter and said, "Do you honestly think that matters?" . . . My problem with politics is that I was completely, catastrophically, unable to see this thing, other than for what it was, which was some ridiculous hat, that someone gives you to wear . . . because they think you're going to vote for them.'[30]

Charlotte was unusual. By her own admission, despite widespread expectation that she would attain ministerial office, she failed to play the game and ended up stranded on the backbenches before losing her seat in 2017. Most of her colleagues, and those on the Labour benches too, are more prepared to compromise to keep moving up the ladder. It is hard to keep track of exactly how big this 'wider payroll', including all these non-jobs that don't actually get paid, actually is because details aren't published anywhere. As of March 2023 the Institute for Government estimated it included as many as 160 MPs, out of 360 on the Conservative side.[31]

All these tricks can, though, only go so far. There are always MPs who cannot be bought off with jobs or bribed with projects for their constituencies. This is often because they are deeply committed to a particular issue. Britain's place in the EU is an obvious example. Indeed it was votes on this topic from the 1970s onwards that started the trend towards more rebellions – initially on both sides but over time more so from the Conservatives. Despite having only been in power for a year, forty-six Tory MPs were, in 2011, already prepared to rebel on a vote indicating a desire for a referendum on EU membership. By the time May's proposed Brexit deal was under consideration in 2018 and 2019, MPs, knowing her leadership was not going to survive much longer, rebelled in the largest numbers ever seen. Rishi Sunak, despite working hard to maintain party unity, often at the cost of his desired agenda, faced regular rebellions simply because so many MPs knew their shot at ministerial office had gone.

Such unruliness led party leaderships to get increasingly creative in their uses of parliamentary procedure to avoid scrutiny altogether. Which represents a fundamental system failure for the British state.

Avoiding scrutiny

The most extreme example of this new approach was Boris Johnson's attempt to prorogue Parliament in 2019, to avoid MPs undermining his Brexit strategy. Prorogations are normally an uncontroversial means to end a session of Parliament. But Johnson tried to use one, in September 2019, to shut down Parliament for five weeks in the run-up to the deadline for a Brexit deal. Parliament has no ability to stop it, so initially it went ahead.[32]

This was so brazen as to attract the notice of the media and wider

British public, who are usually happy to ignore procedural disputes. Ultimately the Supreme Court decided to invalidate the prorogation on the grounds that the government had given the Queen incorrect advice. But the decision could easily have gone the other way. After all, the High Court had declared the issue to be 'non-justiciable' – i.e. a political matter that was outside the remit of judges.[33]

The Supreme Court unanimously disagreed with this verdict, but there were plenty of experts who expected them to give their assent given the lack of any clear legal restrictions on the monarch's prerogative power to prorogue. Had it done so, a precedent would have been set that Parliament could be closed down for weeks whenever it suited the government.

While the attempted prorogation was unusual in its sheer arrogance and constitutional disdain for parliamentary sovereignty, it was not substantially different in intent from all the other ways that governments have tried to reduce the ability of MPs to scrutinize their actions. Boris Johnson and his senior adviser, Dominic Cummings, neither of whom had the slightest interest in the spirit of the rules, were just so aggressively blatant as to attract more attention than normal.

Theresa May, even before she lost her majority in the ill-judged 2017 election, had also tried to keep Parliament's role in the Brexit process to an absolute minimum. One former Cabinet minister told Meg Russell and Lisa James, the authors of a major study into the process of leaving the EU, that: 'the truth is the government is never that keen on Parliament having a big role in anything'.[34] This was an attitude held by civil servants as much as ministers. A senior official told them that it was 'a sort of rule of thumb throughout all of this [Brexit], the less done with Parliament the better'.[35]

May was initially unprepared to accept that Parliament should even have a vote on the final Brexit deal, though that position was unsustainable, given the determination of MPs to have one. She also went to court to challenge Parliament's right to vote on triggering Article 50, the EU treaty clause that started the process of leaving the union. There was never any serious doubt that Parliament would vote to trigger, which made it all the more surprising that May insisted on fighting. Russell and James argue that, again, officials wanted to protect prerogative powers for the executive but also that the political side of No. 10 saw the opportunity to, in the words of one pro-Brexit government insider, 'set up the narrative of the Remainers trying to undermine the result and all that'.[36]

Ultimately this failure to engage Parliament and seek to work with MPs across all parties to find a way through led to three chaotic years of turmoil, with Johnson's attempts to prorogue coming at the end of a bitter war with MPs, who were determined to constrain a minority government. This was, in part, a reaction to the Speaker, John Bercow, engaging in his own constitutional innovations, against the wishes of his clerks, which enabled rebel MPs to briefly seize control of parliamentary business from the government and pass their own legislation.

The chaos of the Brexit years was an intense example of a general phenomenon – the increasing desire of ministers, and to some degree officials, to avoid scrutiny, especially when that scrutiny might have meaningful consequences. This is closely linked to the professionalization of politics in the mid-1990s, with a seemingly small change made by the New Labour government in 1997 that created a mechanism for governments to avoid debate.

When Tony Blair's Labour took power, they introduced a series of changes notionally designed to make the Commons more family-friendly, given a big increase in the number of women MPs (men seeing their children had apparently not been considered much of an issue). One of these was to introduce 'programme motions'. Until this point there had been no time limit on debates about government bills as they made their way through Parliament. Governments could draw a debate to a close using a so-called 'guillotine motion', but they rarely did. On the whole MPs got to exhaust all their concerns about any bill.[37] This was annoying to ministers, who were often kept awake into the early morning as MPs waffled on, but it ensured all aspects of a bill could be subject to scrutiny.

Programme motions, for the first time, created a timetable for bills with hard cut-off points when time ran out, regardless of how many issues were left to debate. Initially these programme motions were supposed to be agreed between the parties, but that quickly broke down as opposition Conservatives were repeatedly unhappy with the paucity of time allocated.[38] Since 2000 they have been determined by the government at the point a bill has its 'second reading' – which, rather confusingly, is the first time it is properly debated. In practice this has meant many amendments to bills – either by opposition MPs or even more problematically from the government – get no debate time at all. They are simply voted through, or knocked down, with no discussion.

Overs the years governments have become increasingly adept at manipulating the flow of amendments to avoid discussing awkward ones, and at wasting as much time as possible giving windy speeches about nothing, helped by planted backbench questions. They have also become cavalier about offering very limited amounts of time in their programme motions, even on extremely controversial issues. To pick one example, the Illegal Migration Bill, which proposed to remove basic rights of migrants to claim asylum, was highly contentious. It was only given four hours in the Commons for its final stage, with dozens of government amendments voted through without discussion.[39] The full Brexit agreement – a 1,200-page treaty – was pushed through Parliament in a single day in December 2021.

As David Lidington said in a 2022 speech: 'The combination of a reliable Commons majority and automatic timetabling tempted Labour and then Conservative governments to introduce inadequately prepared and poorly drafted legislation, large chunks of which were never debated at all by the House of Commons and ended up having to be substantially redrafted by government amendment in the House of Lords.'[40]

There are two critical points here. Firstly, by removing the need to spend much time discussing bills, it has allowed the government to be far more lax about the quality of legislation, as it will be subjected to minimal scrutiny by MPs. This matters because drafting good bills requires thinking through knotty policy problems properly. Bad thinking gets turned into confusing laws full of fudges, that then have to be resolved later. As it takes less time and effort to force bills through the Commons, it has also created the space for much more 'performative' or symbolic legislation the only purpose of which is to create newspaper headlines and appease party factions.

Secondly, bad laws getting rushed through the Commons has put far more pressure on the House of Lords, where there are no automatic limits on how long they can spend discussing bills. The Lords is not designed to be the primary scrutiny chamber but rather to check detail, and yet it is increasingly being sent half-formed bills that need to be completely rebuilt.

Putting the Lords in this position is invidious for several reasons. While there are experts on different policy areas among the membership they are thinly spread, as the parties now stuff the chamber with loyal former MPs, advisers and donors. A Lords Appointments

Commission was introduced in 2000 to vet new peers, in a very light-touch way, but even then, the prime minister can overrule them.

Boris Johnson did so in 2021 when he appointed Peter Cruddas, a major Tory donor. Cruddas had been forced to resign as party treasurer in 2012 over allegations he offered access to David Cameron and George Osborne in return for cash. Just days after Johnson confirmed his Lords appointment Cruddas made a further £500,000 payment to the party.[41] Johnson also pushed through the peerage of his supporter, Russian businessman Evgeny Lebedev, despite concerns from the security services.[42] He became Lord Lebedev of Hampton and Siberia in 2020.

By the time Johnson's 'resignation honours' list was published in the summer of 2023 his abuse of the system had become farcical. The Appointments Committee blocked eight of his proposed peers, which Rishi Sunak declined to overturn, but they let through supporters who it seems had no reasonable claim to a lifetime position in the legislature. These included 29-year-old Charlotte Owen, who had spent eighteen months as a junior special adviser in Downing Street under Truss and Johnson, and Ross Kempsell, a 31-year-old former writer for the Guido Fawkes gossip website, who worked as the ex-PM's media adviser. Liz Truss also appointed several peers in her 'resignation honours' despite only being prime minister for seven weeks.

While Johnson and Truss were more brazen than previous prime ministers, what they did was not a substantial deviation from the norm. Since Labour's reform of the Lords in 1999, which saw all but ninety-two of the hereditary peers lose their right to participate, the number of politically appointed peers has kept going up. There are now almost 800 peers in total, making it one of the biggest legislative chambers in the world. Blair appointed numerous political supporters and donors himself, getting embroiled in his own honours for cash scandal, and eventually making Labour the largest party in the Lords by 2006.

Cameron and Clegg did their own rebalancing in 2014, securing a majority between them, with plenty of political appointees. Seventeen of the eighteen Tory party treasurers between 1993 and 2020 – mostly big donors too – have been given peerages. The eighteenth (Sir Mick Davis) was offered one but turned it down. There are no rules or process around any of this and nothing, bar the King's willingness to sign it off, to stop a future prime minister packing the Lords with hundreds more supporters.

Peers are well aware of the problem. The Lords' Speaker, Norman Fowler, has written that the chamber's numbers are 'far in excess of what is needed to transact its business'. And that 'the present powers of the House of Lords Appointments Commission are fundamentally deficient. The commission has a strong and independent membership. It is absurd that its powers are only advisory.'[43] A Lords Committee in 2017 proposed a fixed membership of 600 peers and a formula for balancing political appointments but, unsurprisingly, this was ignored by a government who value patronage.[44]

The ongoing drift towards more and more political appointments to the Lords has had several baleful effects. Firstly, the expertise of the chamber has been diluted. Donors and hangers-on have little to offer when it comes to detailed scrutiny of complex legislation. The more independently minded experts that are still there have to do the bulk of the work, and that workload is increasing as more and more half-baked bills find their way into the Lords. With no restrictions on hours, this can be punishing. In the first four months of 2023, the Upper House sat beyond 10 p.m. sixteen times – roughly once every four sitting days.[45] Given many peers are elderly this is not conducive to high-quality debate.

It also means the Lords is gradually becoming more like the Commons, and less independent. There are about 180 cross-bench peers not affiliated to any party, and political appointees can rebel without worrying so much about their long-term political future. However, there are increasing numbers of younger lords who do actively want ministerial roles in order to supplement their income and status. They have as much reason to be loyal as MPs. Others are keen to demonstrate loyalty in return for their patronage and will nearly always take the whip on votes.

As David Cameron's former head of policy, now Baroness Camilla Cavendish, told me: 'The Lords works best when it's not just a mirror of the Commons. You sometimes go to vote, and there are people going in different directions. And you say something like, "Oh, is this amendment 64?" And some look like they have no idea. The former MPs often just go with their tribe. Independent scrutiny is at its best when people from all sides come together to propose amendments, and people vote with their consciences.'[46]

The reason Conservative governments have struggled so much in the Lords since 2016 is partly because a number of bills have been so bad that even normally loyal supporters have refused to back them (particularly around Brexit, given that many older Tories are more attached to the idea of European integration). But it is mainly because they do not have a majority. In the eighteen years of Conservative government between 1979 and 1997 they lost an average of thirteen votes in the Lords a year, and had a large majority throughout due to the dominance of hereditary peers. Labour, who did not have a majority in their newly reformed House of Lords for a decade, lost forty-one a year. Under the Coalition, the government

147

lost twenty-five per year as they did have a majority when both parties voted together. Between 2015 and 2022, with the Conservatives governing alone, losses shot up to sixty a year (increasing to eighty since 2019).[47]

This illustrates the increase in legislative workload as the Lords has been increasingly dragged into scrutinizing bills the Commons has barely glanced at. And also that the independence of the Lords is bolstered by the balance of power between the parties. If the Lords ever became too troublesome to a government they could simply appoint as many peers as required to give themselves a majority.

This takes us to the other big reason why the Lords is not an appropriate place for picking apart badly prepared legislation. While peers can push back on bad laws, they cannot actually stop them if the government do not want to compromise. Most of those lost votes were, in the end, overturned. Peers can never push too hard because they know that the elected government has to take precedence over an unelected chamber.

The trend towards less scrutiny in the Commons has, by forcing the Lords to take a much bigger role, exacerbated the tension between its legislative role and its undemocratic make-up. The dominance of the elected Commons was established by the 1911 and 1949 Parliament Acts that ensure the Lords cannot, with a handful of exceptions, block legislation from the Commons. There are many bills they cannot vote against at all – ones related to finance (by law), and ones that appeared in the government's manifesto (by convention).

They can vote against other legislation and by doing so delay it by a year but, as long as the government reintroduce it in the following session in the same form, they must then pass it. In practice the Lords is very reluctant to push things that far, given the democratic imbalance between the chambers. Governments have only made use of the Parliament Act seven times, and not at all since 2004.[48] Usually the Lords will give way.

Governments will sometimes accept the Lords' advice that a bill has been so badly designed as to be unworkable. In May 2022, a Schools Bill was introduced into the Lords. It was ripped to shreds by peers who noted that in the government's rush to introduce it they had designed clauses that would give them extraordinary powers to interfere directly in the running of schools. It was an indication of how little care is now given to the preparation of bills that the Lords Minister, Baroness Diana Barran, who had to present the bill, had not even seen a final draft, and similar concerns she had raised earlier in the process had been ignored.[49]

In this case the bill was widely criticized by peers of all parties; those concerns were also held by some Conservative MPs and even ministers. This meant that, despite the embarrassment, they were prepared to delete a large section of the bill, and then, amid the chaos of the Truss administration that autumn, to scrap it completely. But it is more often the case that ministers are determined to push incoherent legislation through because once they have started it is seen as a failure to back off. Either that or the purpose is primarily to indicate symbolic commitment on an issue.

Many Lords were highly critical of the Illegal Migration Bill, and passed multiple amendments that would have softened its most extreme effects. One related to the ability to detain children indefinitely, another that adults could not be detained beyond six months. The government made a few minor changes but voted down these amendments in the Commons. Unusually, many cross-bench Lords, including the Archbishop of Canterbury, fought back and the bill ended up in 'ping-pong', going back and forth between the two houses (they really do call it 'ping-pong'). Eventually the government managed to persuade enough Tory Lords to turn up, and forced the bill through. This is despite the fact it will likely be found to run contrary to human rights law.

Skeleton bills and Henry VIII powers

Laws passed with minimal debate are one thing. But increasingly governments aren't bothering with proper legislation at all, instead creating more and more powers that give them the freedom to make decisions without bothering Parliament. The Delegated Powers and Regulatory Reform Committee of the House of the Lords – not a group known for scintillating rhetoric or hyperbole – described this trend in 2022 as 'an abuse of Parliament and an abuse of democracy'.[50]

The equally thrillingly named Secondary Legislation Scrutiny Committee of the House of Lords published a report at the same time called 'Government by Diktat' in which they issued a 'stark warning': 'The balance of power between Parliament and government has for some time been shifting away from Parliament, a trend accentuated by the twin challenges of Brexit and the COVID-19 pandemic. A critical moment has now been reached when that balance must be re-set: not restored to how things were.'[51]

This is coming not from some lefty activists but committees containing former Conservative and Labour cabinet ministers as well as luminaries like Robin Janvrin, Queen Elizabeth's former private secretary (played by Roger Allam in *The Queen*), and John Thomas, the former Lord Chief Justice.

Governments have been able to do this because the rules about what can go into a bill are very limited. They can be designed to award huge powers to ministers that come with very minimal scrutiny. Bills that create these wide and unspecified powers are called 'skeleton bills' and they are becoming increasingly common. In part this is because governments are overwhelmed and are rushing into legislation before they have a clear policy objective in mind. But it is also a deliberate way for the executive, supported by a civil service keen to make their own lives easier, to strengthen its own position.

A good example of how wide these powers can be is the Childcare Act of 2016. It is a few pages long and was hurried through to meet the 2015 Conservative manifesto promise to increase free childcare hours but 'contains virtually nothing of substance'.[52] Instead it grants the secretary of state an enormous array of powers – including to fine and imprison people – via regulation. Even more egregiously it allows unspecified regulations to give any person the power to 'make different provisions for different purposes'; and 'amend, repeal or revoke any provision made by or under an Act (whenever passed or made)'. This last line – allowing any other Act to be changed via regulation – is known as a 'Henry VIII' power in reference to the 1539 Statute of Proclamations that gave the King the power to make laws without reference to Parliament.

In a speech called 'Ceding Power to the Executive: The Resurrection of Henry VIII', the former Lord Chief Justice, Lord Judge (yes, that is really his surname), was heavily critical of this Act: '[The ability to give] "any" person: I emphasise, "any" person, presumably someone identified by, and agreeable to, the executive: power to repeal any existing, or indeed any statute even one not yet enacted. What on earth do you think the Commons of 1539 would have called such a provision? I think their language would have been unprintable, and the Speaker might have wondered why he had risked incarceration in the tower.'[53]

There are multiple other examples of skeleton bills, with the numbers rising rapidly over the past decade. There was a raft of them around Brexit, given how rushed the process ended up being. The powers provided in these bills are typically then made use of via secondary legislation, usually in the form of statutory instruments (SIs), one of those phrases where the innate dullness hides an almighty impact on people's lives.

In theory these SIs allow for some scrutiny, but far less than with a normal bill. They cannot be amended and are only subject to debate at all if one is requested. Even then the government can choose when to hold it. In practice they are almost never rejected. Most MPs will fully acknowledge they do not really understand all the different types of SI with their different rules. The Commons has not rejected one since 1979. The Lords pay more attention to them and can reject them, but very rarely use this power, because if they do the Commons cannot revive them, again highlighting the problem caused by their lack of democratic legitimacy.

Statutory instruments were introduced after the Second World War to help governments manage the big expansion of the state and the concomitant increase in their responsibilities. No one disputes they are necessary – there have been over 170,000 now, most of which are minor and technical. But increasingly they are being used to implement big policy changes while avoiding scrutiny. This is not a phenomenon restricted to Conservative governments. There was a substantial increase in their use during the New Labour years too and some were so poorly drafted as to cause serious problems.

For instance, in 2004, an SI was used to set out a long list of criminal offences for which immigrants could be deported. In 2009 it was overturned by the courts as being incompatible with European law.

The government had been illegally locking people up and deporting them, but the law was never even discussed by Parliament.[54]

It was, though, under the Conservative governments from 2015 onwards that misuse of this type of legislation increased dramatically. After the 2015 election, a bunch of contentious austerity cuts were pushed through via SI, including the abolition of maintenance grants for students from poorer families. Even more controversially, the government tried to make a nearly £5 billion cut to tax credits via SI, which led to a rare rejection by the Lords. Ministers responded by establishing a review into whether the Lords should lose this power, which did not end up going anywhere but had the desired effect of preventing further rejections.[55] Remarkably the contentious net-zero target was created, in 2019, through an SI, due to the wide powers granted in the Climate Change Act 2008, despite the very significant financial commitment required to meet it.[56]

The barrister Tom de la Mare KC has, in a helpful metaphor, noted that the use of SI to make laws is a kind of addiction for the executive, which developed over time, but that 'Brexit is that coca leaf refined into cocaine'. The government were able to use the speed and complexity of the Brexit discussions to justify delegating powers to the executive on a level not seen before.[57] One database has over a thousand Brexit-related SIs. Many of them were simply transcribing EU law into UK law, but in doing so significant changes were introduced, especially in areas like agriculture and food standards, which were heavily regulated by the EU.[58] These changes were never debated in Parliament or even flagged to MPs. Only now are journalists and MPs realizing the substantive changes they've wrought, including, for instance, the weakening of rules on pesticides and on air quality.[59]

That the addiction triggered by Brexit had stuck became clear when the emergency nature of a pandemic was used to justify the most draconian measures ever introduced in peacetime by a British government, with barely any oversight. In the initial weeks of the pandemic it was undoubtedly necessary to use emergency powers to deal with a rapidly emerging crisis.

But even at this stage the government were thinking about how best to avoid scrutiny. They chose to push through in only a few days a new law, called the Coronavirus Act, which granted powers to pass a vast number of different regulations without debate. They could have used the existing Civil Contingencies Act (CCA) but, as the lawyer Adam Wagner has written: 'The CCA gives ministers very significant powers to make new regulations and could have been used to do nearly all the things the Coronavirus Act ultimately did. However, it also contained strong democratic safeguards, such as Parliament having to approve any emergency regulations within seven days of them being "laid", giving Parliament the opportunity to amend regulations, and regulations lapsing thirty days after they were made.'[60] Even if ministers felt a new law was necessary they could have replicated these safeguards but chose not to.

The new Act gave far more power. But because it was written before the government realized lockdowns would be necessary, it did not create the powers required to implement them. For this they used the Public Health Act of 1984, which had been significantly strengthened in 2008, again with minimal debate. Statutory instruments laid under this Act were used for the next two years to regulate every aspect of our lives. The first arrived three days after Boris Johnson announced the initial lockdown. Things were so chaotic that no one had started writing them yet when he made the speech, and they became law two hours before they were even published. Parliament didn't even discuss them for six weeks.[61]

154

As the pandemic progressed, the dangers of making law in this way became more and more apparent. In other countries Parliament played a much bigger role. Sweden and New Zealand took very different approaches to the pandemic but in both countries plans were overseen by cross-party committees, which ensured coherence.[62] In the UK, the government had carte blanche. If Parliament had voted down any regulations it would have meant scrapping all the rules, as they were not amendable, so it wasn't really a viable option. Overmighty executive power led, as we have seen throughout this chapter, to laziness, confusion and performative lawmaking.

Because they could, the government fiddled with the rules constantly. From the start politicians were saying the rules were different to what was actually set out in the law, but as the regulations got longer and more complex they became impossible to follow. The police were unable to keep up, repeatedly making mistakes on social media, such as when Cambridgeshire Police memorably suggested supermarkets should close aisles containing non-essential products. A review of prosecutions by the Crown Prosecution Service (CPS) found that every single prosecution under the Coronavirus Act was incorrect.[63]

As Helen MacNamara – who, as deputy cabinet secretary, was at the heart of Covid policy-making – put it in her witness statement to the Covid Inquiry: 'It felt as if once ministers and civil servants had realized that they did not have to go through anything like the normal processes of government then they had no appetite to go back . . . It's this short fuse between hurried policy discussion and regulation that gave us the somewhat surreal craze for serving Scotch eggs in pubs in December 2020 along with a bewildering pace of regulatory changes (in London we were subject to four different sets of regulations in December 2020 to January 2021).'[64]

This is not the place to discuss the medical merits of lockdowns, but what is indisputable is that badly drawn regulations – leading to many thousands of incorrect prosecutions – and a public who were entirely unclear on what they were allowed to do, was highly damaging. As the barrister Tom Hickman KC put it, the pandemic showed 'how fragile Parliament's constitutional role is in relation to delegated legislation and how easily the government can turn down the accountability dial to something approaching zero'.[65]

The ability to do this, while using a crisis as justification, undoubtedly intensified the addiction to executive power. As Hannah White, director of the Institute for Government, has written: 'The temptation for ministers to minimise the role of parliament was well established before the pandemic. But there is now a danger that this period of exception has reinforced ministers' existing tendency . . . The risk is that Covid-19, like Brexit, has reinforced the vicious cycle of decline in Westminster – in which executive disregard for parliament undermines public trust in its role, and in turn further emboldens ministers to side-line the legislature.'[66]

As the pandemic recedes into the past it is becoming increasingly apparent that the addiction formed during Brexit and Covid has not been kicked. For instance, in 2020, a whole raft of new planning law was created via statutory instruments. Dominic Cummings, being uninterested in subtlety, told everyone that this was done specifically to avoid scrutiny in a tweet after leaving government: 'important SECONDARY legislation changes pushed thro last year, which we barely discussed publicly so MPs wdn't get overexcited [sic]'.[67] And it continued after Johnson and Cummings were gone, particularly with regards to Home Office legislation, given the overtly populist agenda of Suella Braverman.

Most egregious was the unprecedented use of an SI to introduce law that Parliament had previously rejected. During the passage of the Public Order Act 2023, the government tried to add an amendment in the Lords, after it had already passed the Commons, that would make it easier for the police to shut down protests. The Lords defeated it, and it could not be put back in by the Commons, because it had been introduced so late. Instead, the government laid an SI under the Public Order Act 2003 that had almost the same effect.

This was unamendable and the Lords chose not to vote it down – presumably with previous threats from the government over the 2015 tax credits dispute in mind. Labour refused to whip against it on the grounds that the Lords should not overturn the will of the elected Commons.

But, as the constitutional lawyer David Allen Green noted, this was a serious misuse of executive power: 'A government, using wide enabling legislation, can put legislation into place that it cannot achieve by passing primary legislation. This cannot be the right way of doing things . . . and the increasing use (and abuse) by the government of secondary legislation to do things they cannot (or will not) get otherwise enacted in primary legislation is worrying. A government casually and/or cynically using (and abusing) wide enabling powers is not a story that usually ends well.'[68]

Building a Parliament fit for our times

Executive dominance is not new but it is now being abused in novel and troubling ways. What worked, most of the time, in a part-time Parliament operating under less pressure, with more institutional norms, does not work now. The government uses its control over Parliament's agenda to push through bills without proper scrutiny. It has further debased the Lords, filling it with partisan cheerleaders. And it has used delegated powers to make massive changes to our lives without even consulting MPs. Boris Johnson tried to shut Parliament down altogether and was only foiled by the courts. Successive governments have made it clear they consider Parliament an unhelpful nuisance, to be avoided as much as possible. In doing so they are too often supported by civil servants looking for an easier life.

This is not just a pedantic complaint. The absence of scrutiny leads to worse laws because it allows lazy governments or, worse, arrogant ones to ram through incoherent and unworkable legislation. It is a core element of our crisis of governance. Supporters of an unencumbered executive point to the value of strong government. But bad law weakens government too.

The rush of Brexit regulations have thrown up all sorts of problems that ministers have had to spend large amounts of time resolving. The overcomplicated and fussy Covid rules led to tens of thousands of people being wrongly convicted at great expense, and ultimately reduced the legitimacy of the rules. Many liberals disagree with government policy around immigration on principle but the weaknesses in legislation has meant the government have not been able to achieve their stated goals, and find themselves repeatedly frustrated in the courts.

A government enlightened enough to realize the benefits of scrutiny would not be short of guidance to improve the situation. Organizations like the Hansard Society, the Constitution Unit at University College London, and the Institute for Government have proposed myriad changes that would bolster Parliament. Ideas include giving MPs more control over parliamentary time; introducing new ways to review legislation in advance to ensure it is ready; and severely limiting powers to use secondary or delegated legislation.[69]

If the Commons were so strengthened, it would mean radical reform of the Lords was less necessary. There are ways of electing second chambers to avoid the careerism that prevails in the Commons – for instance, having long terms with a one-term limit. But it would bring the risk of more clashes between the two houses. As long as the Commons has the ability to scrutinize, and actually does so, this is not needed.

But the Lords could be significantly improved without shifting to elected members. For instance, there could be fixed limits on numbers with a bolstered appointments committee and more non-partisan appointments. The remaining hereditary peers, a pure anachronism, should be removed. None of this would be objected to by the Lords. Indeed, many of these proposals have been made by them (they tried to introduce a cap on numbers as early as 1719 but were fought off by Robert Walpole, who wanted to retain the power of his patron the Prince of Wales to appoint peers once he became King).

To make any or all of these technical fixes work we would need a broader acknowledgement that the purpose of Parliament needs to change. There has never been a golden age of parliamentary power to restore. Instead it needs to be created for a modern world in which government does much more at much greater speed. Critically, we need MPs who want to be legislators. At the moment most come into Parliament – understandably – wanting to be ministers with the real power to make things happen. Those who don't are often most interested in the constituency aspect of their work, which has become more dominant in recent years. If Parliament had the ability to consistently make a difference too, then interest in being true legislators would increase. If we want better MPs, we need to make it a better job.

We have seen glimpses of how this could improve things in the rise of select committees – groups of MPs who monitor the work of each government department and who conduct inquiries in that policy area. The modern system began in 1980 and they have become increasingly influential, with recommendations often being adopted by departments and wide press coverage for critical reports. The chairing role, in particular, has become an attractive option for MPs. Since 2003 it has come with additional pay, currently set at £16,422, albeit this is only a quarter of the extra pay a cabinet minister gets.

A critical change in 2010 saw chairs appointed via a secret ballot of the whole House of Commons, and committee members by a secret ballot of their own MPs, which has made it much harder for the whips to use these positions for patronage. During the Johnson premiership many senior Tory MPs who disliked his approach – like Jeremy Hunt and Tom Tugendhat – ended up chairing committees and used them to scrutinize poor government behaviour.

As Hansard Society analysis shows, it is not yet an alternative career choice. Most are held as either launchpads to a ministerial career, a postscript to resignation or losing out in a reshuffle, or as an interlude for those with ambitions to get back into office, as it was for many of those who stepped up during the Johnson years.[70] However, it would only take a few changes to help make 'legislator' a real alternative career to 'minister'. Pay should be equalized with ministerial salaries and, more importantly, committees given significant additional powers to direct Commons time. They should be able to scrutinize legislation in advance of it being introduced, and direct ministers to give evidence.

It is this kind of cultural change that is needed if Parliament is going to be recreated as a body that can support better government through scrutiny. Future ministers will inevitably be concerned that such changes will reduce their freedom for manoeuvre, but any government with a majority will still be able to secure its core agenda. A stronger Parliament would mean, though, that governments actually had to focus on what would achieve that agenda, with fewer, better and more-focused bills. It is crucial to resolving our crisis of governance.

5

ENEMIES OF THE PEOPLE

Why our biggest political rows now end up being fought in the courts

'Executive support for the judiciary is not an optional extra within a democracy governed by the rule of law. It is a necessary means of securing it.'
LORD BURNETT, LORD CHIEF JUSTICE (2022)[1]

In the absence of a stronger Parliament, judges have ended up stepping into the breach. The extent of judicial oversight over government decisions has grown over many decades, but in recent years court battles have become a standard feature in most important political debates. This is widely viewed as a response to the growing power of the government, and the inability of Parliament to apply proper scrutiny. Judicial review is now used by political campaigners to achieve their aims where conventional democratic routes have failed.

Government's determination to bypass Parliament at key points during the Brexit negotiations led to several high-profile cases. In 2016, judges ruled that the government needed Parliament's permission to trigger the Article 50 exit process (known as Miller 1, after the activist Gina Miller who instigated the process). This is the case that led the *Daily Mail* to denounce three High Court judges as 'enemies of the people' on their front page. The second case, in 2019, saw Supreme Court judges rule unanimously that Boris Johnson's attempt to prorogue Parliament was unconstitutional (Miller 2).

During the pandemic, as government again did their best to sideline Parliament, there were a series of major court cases relating to all aspects of the response. Courts rejected a judicial review application into the general principle of lockdown laws, and another case brought against rules requiring people to be detained at hotels when arriving in the UK.[2] But campaigners won several other cases, including one against restrictions on protests after the Met used lockdown laws to break up a vigil for Sarah Everard, who had been murdered by a police officer.[3] Courts also found the emergency process the government set up to buy protective equipment (PPE) for the NHS to be unlawful.[4] And judges ruled that the government had to hand over documents, including Boris Johnson's notebooks and diaries, to the Covid Inquiry.[5]

In 2023, the Supreme Court blocked the government's plan to deport asylum seekers to Rwanda, a measure intended to act as a deterrent to others who might seek to make the Channel crossing by small boat.[6] This was the most politically explosive ruling yet, but many aspects of government asylum policy have been found unlawful over the past few decades, under successive governments.[7] Governments have also lost multiple judicial reviews on welfare policy decisions considered to be unfair on recipients.[8]

In recent decades, the tension between the government and judiciary has ratcheted up to levels not previously seen in modern political discourse, perhaps not since the Glorious Revolution settled the constitutional (and actual) battles that dominated the seventeenth century. Under New Labour, ministers angrily expressed their frustrations with the courts too. In 2003 David Blunkett, then home secretary, gave an interview to *The Daily Telegraph*, after losing an asylum case, in which he said: 'If public policy can always be overridden by individual challenge through the courts, *then democracy itself is under threat* [author italics]. We must be careful that it does not snowball. If it does, people will believe that they turn to the courts for satisfaction, not to MPs and to democracy.'[9]

A few years later, John Reid, now in Blunkett's job, repeatedly attacked judges for, in his view, failing to understand the magnitude of terrorist threats. After the Court of Appeal ruled that government 'control orders' to restrain the movement of terror suspects violated their human rights, he suggested judges 'just don't get' that 'we may have to modify our freedoms to prevent their use and abuse'. Some months later he said he was prepared to declare a 'state of emergency' to suspend parts of human rights law.[10]

Under the subsequent Conservative governments, the rhetoric continued whenever they lost a case. 'Liberal lefty' judges and lawyers became a prime target to blame for the country's problems. The deputy chairman of the Conservative Party even proposed 'ignoring the laws' after the Rwanda judgment and going ahead with the policy anyway.[11] Long before this clash, the government had sought ways to undermine the courts. In 2015 the Coalition passed a law to restrict access to judicial review.[12] Then, after Brexit inflamed tensions further, the attacks got even stronger, with menacing briefings suggesting potential changes to limit judges' power further.

The 2019 Conservative manifesto promised to: 'Ensure that judicial review is available to protect the rights of the individuals against an overbearing state, *while ensuring that it is not abused to conduct politics by another means* [author italics] or to create needless delays.

In our first year we will . . . come up with proposals to restore trust in our institutions and in how our democracy operates.'[13]

Actual changes as a result of this promise have been limited. But press briefings on potential future changes – such as annual legislation to strike out court rulings ministers don't like – have continued to increase in prevalence and vociferousness.[14] A review of judicial independence by the All-Party Parliamentary Group on Democracy and the Constitution in 2022 argued that these constant briefings by government were intended to create pressure on judges to conform, arguing: 'Since 2020 the judiciary has been subjected to two separate inquiries touching on its decision-making in cases in which the executive is a litigant and the prospect of at least two major reform bills (not to mention speculation about more aggressive reforms such as empowering the executive to overturn judicial decisions with which it disagrees or the political vetting of Supreme Court judges). This may create a context in which it would be understandable for the judiciary to feel pressurised by the executive.'[15]

In a 2020 survey of judges, 94 per cent said they were concerned by loss of respect from government and 70 per cent over the loss of judicial independence.[16]

Just as with Parliament, governments have responded to judicial attempts to hold them to account by trying to overpower that accountability, rather than question the decisions they are taking, or consider why they are losing so many important cases. While there is legitimate criticism of the ways in which some activists seek to use judicial review, crude attempts to dismiss the judiciary as a 'liberal elite' trying to undermine the 'will of the people' are deeply damaging. Genuine attempts to reform judicial review would have to consider the wider context of a larger and more powerful state, alongside the problems of executive dominance and a weakened Parliament.

The current approach, whereby the government finds itself spending a huge amount of time, and taxpayer money, fighting in the courts is another symptom of a crisis of governance in our failed state. And then, in light of the Supreme Court's Rwanda decision, the government risked a full-blown constitutional crisis. They attempted to overturn the Court's decision by passing a bill through Parliament that required the courts to ignore international law, as well as their own previous assessment, by finding that Rwanda is a safe country for asylum seekers. In doing so they were taking us into very murky waters.

The rise of judicial power

Since the Second World War there has been a global expansion of judicial power. In many countries this shift has been easy to explain as, following the horrors of that war, they adopted new constitutions giving a greater role to judges to protect them. In doing so they typically copied countries like America, which has a judiciary with clear powers that are independent of the legislature or executive.[17] Further waves of democratization around the world (now under threat in many places) gave momentum to this growth of judicial power.[18]

This expansion has happened in the UK too, but here it is harder to explain. We remain one of a dwindling handful of countries not to have a written constitution – or more precisely a codified one, given there are many different documents that feed into our constitutional settlement. Not having one offers a level of flexibility that codified constitutions do not have. But the downside is that the basis for decisions, and who gets to make them, often lacks clarity.

The UK operates under a system of parliamentary sovereignty, where Parliament is the supreme decision-making body. This still gives the courts considerable scope to interpret their purpose and give judgments that expand their role, as long as there is no legislation that explicitly forbids them from doing so. In more recent years Parliament has actively encouraged them to do so by passing the Human Rights Act (HRA) in 1998, which incorporated into UK law the rights contained in the European Convention on Human Rights.

Section three of this Act required judges 'so far as it is possible to do so . . . to read and give effect' to all other legislation 'in a way which is compatible with the Convention rights'.[19] When it is impossible to read primary legislation in a way that is compatible, courts make a 'declaration of incompatibility', which has no effect on the implementation of the legislation that breaches rights, but is seen as a request to Parliament to resolve that incompatibility.

In practice the HRA has significantly extended the role of the courts. As Lord Neuberger put it in a 2014 lecture, when he was President of the Supreme Court: 'Given that we have a set of rules which governs our approach to law and protects individuals, it is almost as if we have a constitution.'[20]

Judges have used section three of the Human Rights Act to interpret the meaning of legislation creatively. In doing so they have built on a pre-existing trend towards a so-called 'principle of legality' – essentially that some rights, such as the right to justice, are so important that they can only be overridden by Parliament if it is absolutely clear that it was their intention to do so.

Lord Hoffman, in a 1999 decision to protect a prisoner's

free-speech rights to give interviews, expanded on this idea: 'Fundamental rights cannot be overridden by general or ambiguous words. This is because there is too great a risk that the full implications of their unqualified meaning may have passed unnoticed in the democratic process . . . In this way the courts of the United Kingdom, though acknowledging the sovereignty of Parliament, apply principles of constitutionality little different from those which exist in countries where the power of the legislature is expressly limited by a constitutional document.'[21]

While judges have been restrained in using this principle it clearly expands the scope of their role and brings them further into policy-making territory as interpreters of the purpose of legislation.[22]

The 'principle of legality' became established in the 1980s and early 1990s, meaning the scope of judicial review had already grown significantly well before the Human Rights Act.[23] The first major change was in the 1960s when a series of cases saw judges challenge a previously highly deferential approach to government decision-making.[24] Some of this was down to the character of individual and influential judges. But the broader shift was triggered by the growth in government responsibilities generally, and the changing role of the executive relative to Parliament.

As another senior judge, Lord Dyson, explained in 2015: 'There is no doubt that . . . in the past few decades there has been a massive increase in the number of applications for judicial review . . . This may in part be because our judges are no longer as executive-minded as they once were. Secondly, there has been an explosion of legislation, much of it rushed through without sufficient consideration. This has given rise to uncertainty which generates litigation. Thirdly, under the pressure of major national and international challenges, executive public bodies take risks and make decisions which are, at least arguably, of doubtful legality.'[25]

We can see here a critical interaction between the growth of judicial review and the trends discussed in the previous chapter around executive dominance. Some judges have been explicit about this as a justification for thinking differently about their constitutional role. In *R (Jackson) v Attorney General*, 2005, a case brought by the Countryside Alliance to challenge the Labour government's decision to force through an Act banning hunting with dogs, Lord Steyn said: 'The dominance of a government elected with a large majority over Parliament has progressively become greater. This process *has continued and strengthened inexorably* [author italics] since Lord Hailsham warned of its dangers.'[26]

Steyn had left South Africa as a young lawyer due to his opposition to apartheid so was, perhaps, more aware than most of the risks of undiluted executive power. He even went on to question whether parliamentary sovereignty is actually absolute: 'The classic account . . . of the doctrine of the supremacy of Parliament, pure and absolute as It was, can now be seen to be out of place in the modern United Kingdom . . . It is a construct of the common law. The judges created this principle. If that is so, it is not unthinkable that circumstances could arise where the courts may have to qualify a principle established on a different hypothesis of constitutionalism.'[27]

In other words he argued that the limits of parliamentary sovereignty, and thus the power of the executive with a large majority, were ultimately guarded by the courts. This was supported by two of the other House of Lords judges: Lord Hope and Baroness Hale. The former said: 'It is no longer right to say that [Parliament's] freedom to legislate admits of no qualification whatever. Step by step, gradually but surely, the English principle of the absolute legislative sovereignty of Parliament . . . is being qualified.'[28]

It's important to put these comments in context. Other judges on that case, and subsequently, have disagreed with this interpretation, and even judges Steyn, Hope and Hale were only talking about extreme cases. There is no dispute that in the ordinary day-to-day running of things Acts passed by Parliament should not be overturned. But this principle, that there are limits on sovereignty when it is used to infringe on fundamental rights, is becoming more commonplace.

In a more recent 2017 case, brought by trade unions against government attempts to place fees on the use of employment tribunals, Lord Reed said that: 'Even where primary legislation authorises the imposition of an intrusion on the right of access to justice, it is presumed to be subject to an implied limitation . . . the degree of intrusion must not be greater than is justified by the objectives which the measure is intended to serve.'[29]

While these debates about sovereignty have so far been largely theoretical, concerns about executive dominance have undoubtedly contributed to judges' greater willingness to challenge the government via judicial review in creative ways. Thus the large increase in the number of cases lost by government on highly sensitive political issues such as asylum, the rights of prisoners, access to justice, and welfare. Inevitably this has drawn judges more into the arena of both policy-making and political controversy.

For some this has been a largely negative trend that has caused more problems than it has solved. A more conservative-minded judge, Lord Sumption, in a 2011 speech given before he was appointed to the Supreme Court, argued in response to Steyn's comments on executive dominance that: 'I cannot be the only person who feels uncomfortable about the implicit suggestion that it is the function of the judiciary to correct the outcome of general elections.'[30]

He went on to argue that judges like Steyn were wrong to assume that Parliament had declined in power to the point where the courts needed to intervene, because the executive has always been dominant. In doing so he ignored how governments have sought to bypass Parliament in new and creative ways, as set out in the last chapter. To be fair to Sumption this trend has become more pronounced since he gave the speech. Indeed, by 2020, he too was an outspoken critic of Covid lockdown laws, and condemned the government's 'cavalier disregard for the limits of their legal powers' and lack of parliamentary consultation.[31]

Another group of legal academics and practitioners, led by Professor Richard Ekins, under the banner of the 'Judicial Power Project' at the centre-right Policy Exchange think-tank, have become the leading critics of what they see as 'overreach' by the courts. They argue that 'the inflation of judicial power unsettles the balance of our constitution and threatens to compromise parliamentary democracy, the rule of law, and effective government.'[32] In doing so they have become very influential in the right-wing media and on the Conservative Party.

The majority of legal academics and practising lawyers defend the expansion of judicial review as being broadly positive in protecting an expanded array of rights against an overpowerful executive. Indeed some, like Professor Paul Craig, have noted that the constant use of the term 'overreach' is distorting and that, arguably, the courts have been too deferential to government when adjudicating on the Human Rights Act.[33]

It is certainly the case that concerns about judicial overreach need to be balanced by concerns about executive overreach. The Judicial Power Project might argue that the latter is inherently democratic in a way that the former is not, but our model of democracy is based on legislative representation, and if that is undermined it is understandable that a highly flexible constitution would find alternative safeguards, even if that happens in a messy and uncoordinated way.

As Sumption said himself, in the context of Covid: 'Governments hold power in Britain on the sufferance of the elected chamber of the legislature . . . Without that we are no democracy. The present government has a different approach. It seeks to derive its legitimacy directly from the people, bypassing their elected representatives.'[34]

If the executive continues to overpower the legislature then the courts could argue that they are protecting parliamentary sovereignty, in a deeper sense, by overruling government decisions more regularly. The two 'Miller' cases over Brexit are a good example of this given that both saw judges restoring powers to Parliament that the executive had decided it could exercise itself to avoid scrutiny.

Governments take on the judges

Having worked hard to reduce parliamentary scrutiny, government ministers have no desire for that to be replaced by judicial scrutiny. There is here, again, a fundamental failure to understand the value of such scrutiny in improving their own decision-making and helping them achieve the outcomes they want.

As we have seen several of New Labour's home secretaries were fierce critics of the judiciary. Blunkett in particular believed the growth of judicial review to be undemocratic, commenting in his diaries, published after he left office, that it was an 'entirely new arm of our constitution, operated by judges, through judges, and without any redress or accountability to Parliament'.[35]

The Blair and Brown governments did not, though, try to reduce the number of judicial reviews directly. Indeed, by passing the Human Rights Act in 1998 they encouraged its further expansion. But they did pass a law that, while well intentioned, has radically changed the relationship between the executive and judiciary in ways that have proved largely unhelpful.

The Constitutional Reform Act 2005 tried to tidy up a number of apparent anomalies that could, in theory, weaken judicial independence. Chief among these was the role of Lord Chancellor, who was, up until that point, a cabinet minister and Speaker of the House of Lords, as well as the head of the judiciary with overall responsibility for appointing judges. It had long been argued this created the potential for abuse and executive influence on what should be independent appointments. The Act split the role in three. The Lords now elect their own Speaker; the head of the judiciary is the Lord Chief Justice; and the Lord Chancellor is a cabinet minister, usually sitting in the Commons, with their own department, the Ministry of Justice. Critically, they no longer have to be a lawyer.

As critics argued would happen at the time, this has led to a widening gulf between the executive and judiciary. Prior to the changes, the Lord Chancellor acted as their voice in cabinet, arguing for the rule of law and against restrictions in access to justice. In theory it could have been used to compromise their independence, but in practice it did the opposite.

Shortly after the Act passed, one legal academic, Professor Kate Malleson, wrote: 'In the past, the office of Lord Chancellor was the pinnacle of a distinguished legal and political career . . . it had the advantage that the occupant had nothing to gain or lose in terms of promotion by standing up for the judiciary and suffering unpopularity among his ministerial colleagues or even with the Prime Minister. In future the position will be different. The Lord Chancellor may be a mid-career politician inevitably looking for promotion to one of the higher-ranking departments.'[36]

And this is exactly what has happened. Over the past decade the office has been occupied by people like Chris Grayling, Liz Truss and Dominic Raab, all of whom were ambitious, politically minded ministers. They were hardly likely to stand up for the judiciary given how that would have led to criticism in the Tory-friendly press.

Derry Irvine, the last but one of the old-style Lord Chancellors, was a friend of Tony Blair, but he was also a very senior lawyer, who had been a Deputy High Court Judge. He later said that 'on many, many occasions' he had to stand up for judicial independence in cabinet; against, one presumes, the views of people like Blunkett. Now there is no one to perform this role. It is how we ended up with Truss refusing to even condemn the 'enemies of the people' front page for fear it would harm her future career.

The changing role of the Lord Chancellor has had several other detrimental effects that have become clear under the current government. Perhaps the most significant is that they now have their own department, the Ministry of Justice, which has been subject to very significant spending cuts. Successive Lord Chancellors have focused on achieving these savings at the expense of access to justice, whereas previously they could have been expected to stand up for its importance.

Many areas of the state have been drastically cut back since 2010 but legal aid has, perhaps, been hit harder than anything. In 2012 Chris Grayling was made Lord Chancellor. You may remember him as the minister responsible for destroying the probation system in chapter three. That was not the only damage he did. In 2013 he took the LASPO (Legal Aid, Sentencing and Punishment of Offenders) Act through Parliament. This reduced eligibility across the board but completely removed the whole area of civil law from legal aid, including family, employment and welfare law.

The effects have been predictably devastating. The number of people receiving legal aid has fallen more than 80 per cent since 2010.[37] The number of advice and law centres has dropped by 59 per cent since 2012, meaning there are now large parts of the country where no support is available.[38] Stories from family courts are particularly upsetting. Both parties have legal representation in just 20 per cent of family court cases now – which involve the most heartbreaking and serious issues, like child custody, forced adoption and domestic abuse.[39] The Equality and Human Rights Commission (EHRC) has uncovered evidence of domestic abuse victims being questioned by their unrepresented abusers.

One woman explained how she lost her case, having had to represent herself, and her abusive partner was awarded weekly custody visits. She told the authors of the report: 'It's hard when you know he's coming to your door and he's threatening you and your son's in the living room and he's heard it.'[40]

The EHRC also found evidence of children having to represent themselves in court. And more broadly that the cuts had seriously hurt some of the most vulnerable and at-risk children in the country.[41] Meanwhile it has created havoc in a court system that was designed for people to have representation.

One judge told *The Guardian*: '[People representing themselves] are a nightmare. 99.9% do not understand what is going on in court or outside court; they don't know a good point from a bad one; they don't understand the law; they don't understand what they have to prove and they don't know how to ask a question. It is my firmly held view that the courts are full of people who would not be there if they had been able to approach a solicitor.'[42]

The costs associated with this, and the collapse in the numbers seeking mediation, due to lack of advice, has left the family courts with a backlog of over 110,000 cases and higher long-term costs than would be the case if people had been able to access proper legal advice.[43] It is the same story in cases affecting tribunals, and courts, for employment, welfare, housing and so on.[44] The government were well aware that these outcomes were likely, but decided to prioritize saving money in the short term over justice.

As Parliament's Joint Committee on Human Rights put it at the time: 'We are surprised that the Government does not appear to accept that its proposals to reform legal aid engage the fundamental common law right of effective access to justice, including legal advice when necessary. We believe that there is a basic constitutional requirement that legal aid should be available to make access to court possible in relation to important and legally complex disputes.'[45]

When, the following year, Grayling decided to make further cuts to the availability of legal aid for judicial review the same committee noted that the proposals had been launched with a *Daily Mail* article in which he attacked 'left-wing campaigners' for taking cases to court, and that this kind of partisan criticism '[is not] easy to reconcile with the Lord Chancellor's statutory duties in relation to the rule of law'.

They also quoted a former judge's view that 'an independent Lord Chancellor would have stood up against' the proposed restrictions to judicial review and concluded that his failure to do so 'expose[s] the conflict inherent in the combined roles of the Lord Chancellor and Secretary of State for Justice'.[46] Perhaps the government would have made these changes anyway, but it was easier for them to do so with no one to advocate in cabinet on behalf of the judiciary.

Grayling also introduced another Act in 2015 that sought to limit access to judicial review.[47] This was watered down somewhat after the government lost several votes in the Lords, but it was still seen as causing 'unnecessary damage' by lawyers and judges. Lord Dyson, who was then one of the most senior judges in the country, later reflected in his memoirs that 'I was never convinced that [Grayling] believed that access to civil justice was an important social good or that he really appreciated the importance of the rule of law.' And he concluded that the downgrading of the Lord Chancellor role had been an error.[48]

Even if there had still been a judicial advocate in cabinet the current government may have found the opportunity to politicize the issue as too tempting to pass up. There are still three ministerial roles below cabinet level that are held by lawyers. The most important of these is the attorney general, who is the government's principle legal adviser, and oversees the Crown Prosecution Service (CPS). To date governments have maintained the tradition of appointing a barrister, but the role has nevertheless become more politicized.

Theresa May appointed Geoffrey Cox to the role, who did act independently in not giving the legal advice she wanted on her Brexit deal, which eventually led to her downfall. But he was also an opponent of judicial review, which he called the 'judicialisation of politics' in a speech while still in the role, and incorrectly advised the cabinet that Boris Johnson's prorogation of Parliament was constitutional.[49] He was still not pliant enough for Johnson, who didn't consider him enough of a 'team player' – which is the precise opposite of what an attorney general should be.

In February 2020, Cox was reshuffled out of the role to make way for the far more politically ambitious Suella Braverman, who Johnson knew would be prepared to ignore legal qualms that might interfere with the grandstanding he wished to engage in over the Brexit deal he had just signed. Braverman is a lawyer, spending some years at the bar before entering politics, but had more limited experience than most previous occupants of the role. Her 'QC' was granted to her only when she became attorney general.

But more importantly she was a fervent Brexiteer, with strong political ambitions and a desire to build a profile with the right-wing media. As Cox told Johnson's biographers, Anthony Seldon and Raymond Newell: 'The price of survival in Johnson's Cabinet appeared to be subservience. That was short-sighted. In advising on the law, an Attorney General cannot be an acolyte.'[50]

Braverman showed just how damaging an acolyte could be when, in September 2020, she acquiesced in the publication of the UK Internal Market Bill. This would have allowed the government to subvert the Northern Ireland Protocol, a key plank of the Brexit deal, but one that essentially created a border between Northern Ireland and the rest of the United Kingdom. It was during the passage of this bill that the Northern Ireland secretary, Brandon Lewis, famously told the Commons that while it would mean international law would be broken it would only be 'in a specific and limited way'.[51]

This cavalier approach to the law led to a spate of resignations, including the head of the government's legal department, overseen by Braverman. One of the other three ministers in a legal role also quit, saying, 'I have found it increasingly difficult to reconcile what I consider to be my obligations as a law officer with your policy intentions.'[52] Amal Clooney, the highly respected human rights lawyer and wife of Hollywood actor George, resigned as the UK's special envoy on media freedom, writing that 'it is lamentable for the UK to be speaking of its intention to violate an international treaty signed by the prime minister less than a year ago'.[53]

Ultimately the government withdrew the offending clauses before the bill went to a final vote to avoid another defeat in the Lords. But in the meantime enormous damage was done to the relationship between the executive and judiciary. Whether intentionally or through error, Braverman's advice as attorney general was just wrong. As an all-party committee looking into judicial independence noted: 'In providing legal advice on the international law implications of the proposed Internal Market Bill the Attorney General argued that "treaty obligations only become binding to the extent that they are enshrined in domestic legislation". This was a very basic legal error.'[54]

Even worse, the offending clauses of the bill included a provision that would mean they would not be subject to judicial review, a new development in government's attempts to avoid scrutiny. The former President of the Supreme Court Lord Neuberger condemned this approach, saying: 'Once you deprive people of the right to go to court to challenge the government, you are in a dictatorship, you are in a tyranny . . . The right of litigants to go to court to protect their rights and ensure that the government complies with its legal obligation is fundamental to any system . . . You could be going down a very slippery slope.'[55]

The government, through Lord Chancellor Robert Buckland, and the newly compliant attorney general Braverman, were also engaged in yet another attempt to limit judicial review. This followed the 2019 manifesto pledge to 'ensure that it is not abused to conduct politics by other means'. Unfortunately for the government, despite handpicking the review panel, led by a former Conservative minister

Lord Edward Faulks (brother of the novelist Sebastian), it did not come up with the desired conclusion.

Instead it reported that: 'Our view is that the government and parliament can be confident that the courts will respect institutional boundaries in exercising their inherent powers to review the legality of government action. Politicians should, in turn, afford the judiciary the respect which it is undoubtedly due when it exercises these powers.'[56]

This is not what ministers wanted to hear at all. So they decided to pretend they heard something different. A Ministry of Justice press release announced the panel had 'found courts were increasingly considering the merits of government decisions themselves, instead of how those decisions were made – moving beyond the remit of judicial review'.

Lord Faulks promptly headed over to the Radio 4 studios and said that was not a fair summary of his findings.[57] Nonetheless, the government ploughed on, determined to argue that judicial review had been politicized by left-wing activists and liberal judges. This despite, as the Bar Council pointed out, applications for judicial review falling by 44 per cent from 2015 to 2019, after the government's previous rounds of 'reform'.[58] In April 2022 it passed the Judicial Review and Courts Act, which restricted access to judicial review for those who lose a tribunal case; this covers things like asylum applications, welfare claims and access to special-education-needs support for children. There were also proposals to limit judges' discretion in overturning government decisions but these were, again, defeated in the Lords and watered down.[59]

This was not enough for Boris Johnson, who fired Buckland while ratcheting up the rhetoric against 'liberal lawyers' and 'do-gooders' trying to stop his plans to deport immigrants to Rwanda.[60] He replaced him with Dominic Raab, who immediately commissioned advice on how to restrict judicial review even further. Only the government's meltdown in the summer of 2022, followed by Raab's own resignation over bullying civil servants, stopped this from happening.

Initially Rishi Sunak seemed more amenable to the rule of law, negotiating a solution to the Northern Ireland Protocol with the EU in February 2023. But his insistence on appointing Braverman as home secretary rather undermined these hopes. Any attempt to constrain frustrations within the Conservative Party at what they saw as judicial overreach ended when the Supreme Court ruled that the government's Rwanda deportations could not go ahead. The legislation that the government pushed through to override the judges' decision was the most extreme attempt to date to prevent people from accessing justice and the courts from engaging in scrutiny.

The tensions between the executive and judiciary show little sign of improving. A Labour government may take a different attitude – though New Labour were, as we have seen, often hostile to judges too. On the right of British politics, though, it is becoming axiomatic that necessary policies are being blocked by the courts, which could lead to a future government seeking to withdraw from international agreements like the European Convention on Human Rights or, at the very least, using the Rwanda bill precedent to prevent domestic courts from taking it into account. This would make the executive even less accountable and even more overpowered.

All this would lead to is greater conflict with the courts – who have made it increasingly clear that they are prepared to be more assertive in the face of executive dominance – and worse implementation of laws. When the government loses a case it is, nearly always, because they have engaged in bad policy-making, by failing to consult or consider critical evidence. They win the vast majority of cases, including plenty that have tried to overturn welfare or immigration decisions that liberals and progressives disapprove of. Most cases that they do lose could be won by going through a proper process. Few have long-term constitutional significance, and those which do, like Miller 2, only happen when the government has acted with egregious disregard for Parliament or for the most fundamental rights.

It's certainly not ideal for the courts to have to fulfil this role, given that they are unelected, but there has to be scrutiny of the executive somewhere in the system. The expanded role of judicial review in our politics is a function of the weakening of Parliament in a world in which state power has grown and centralized enormously. If politicians want less of it they should strengthen other parts of the state so that the courts do not find themselves as the constitutional guardian of last resort.

As the government's own commissioned review into judicial review put it: '. . . there is a continuing need for respect by judges for Parliament. This is rendered easier where there is evidence of real parliamentary scrutiny,' while noting the increasingly excessive use of secondary legislation and skeleton acts that give huge authority to the executive.[61]

As Kate Malleson wrote back in 2007: 'Where the balance should lie in weighing the disadvantages of unelected judicial power against its capacity to check the "elective dictatorship" is a question of political preference. There are sound democratic reasons for objecting to the expansion of judicial power; but the real answer to concerns about the growing influence of the courts lies in reversing the declining effectiveness of Parliament so that the judges are not called upon to fulfil the role of an unofficial opposition and to provide the sole check on abuse of executive power. Until the question of the revitalisation of Parliament is seriously addressed, the expansion in the role of the judiciary is inevitable.'[62]

She has been proved conclusively right. That is not to say there isn't a good case for increasing Parliament's scrutiny of judicial appointments too. Since the 2005 Constitutional Reform Act it is harder to argue there is democratic oversight. It is not a power that should be given to the executive in any form, given the risk of abuse, but a process of select committee oversight could give judges more authority against attacks. It is certainly the case that the Lord Chancellor role should be split from the responsibility of running the Ministry of Justice. They should have to be a lawyer, and they should have a much stronger duty to defend the rule of law and access to justice from within government. That renewed focus on access should include restoring legal aid funding and support for judicial review.

Appointment abuse

For all the tensions between the executive and judiciary the latter does remain genuinely independent. While the Lord Chancellor can theoretically reject appointments, he or she never has, and the government cannot put its own people forward for roles. Government rhetoric might put pressure on otherwise independent judges to conform, but they are not partisan.

The same cannot be said for appointments to a vast array of other public bodies covering everything from media regulation and food standards to healthcare delivery and compliance with equalities law. Many of these have a quasi-judicial role in regulating public services and private companies. There are now 331 different public bodies that oversee £200 billion of spending, which gives ministers a lot of patronage power. In 2020/21 alone they made almost 1,500 appointments.[63]

This is something that has become vastly more important in recent decades due to what has been termed 'the rise of the regulatory state'. Prior to the 1980s and 1990s there were few of these kinds of bodies, but several trends combined into an explosion of new institutions over the past few decades. Privatization created a need for a swathe of new regulators, especially in monopoly industries like water and gas. There has been a demise of self-regulation in professional sectors like financial services, medicine and higher education, following various scandals, and it has been replaced by state oversight. There is far more intensive oversight of public services through inspectorates like Ofsted. Governments have focused more on risk following intense media focus on market failures (e.g. the creation of the Food Standards Agency in 1999 following the 'mad cow disease' scare). And finally, we have seen the rise of 'social regulation' designed to reduce inequalities and discrimination, for example through the creation of the Equality and Human Rights Commission (EHRC).

This regulatory explosion is an important part of the rapid growth and centralization of the state, explored in section one, that has made it so impossible to manage. As the late Michael Moran – the pre-eminent scholar on the subject – wrote: 'The principle of ministerial responsibility makes responsibility and accountability in the British system intensely personal. But the new regulatory state is so institutionally complex, and so often works independently of ministers, that this personal sense of responsibility makes no sense . . . its growth has been so rapid and so recent that constitutional doctrine has failed to keep up with institutional change.'[64]

This trend has also contributed to the weakening of Parliament, as it has created the need for more open-ended legislation that gives more power to the executive and its agencies, even if they are too overwhelmed to use it effectively. And it has played a role in the expansion of judicial review too, given there are now so many more bodies, and so many more rules, to be reviewed. It emphasizes once again the importance of devolving power in resolving our crisis of governance, not necessarily because people in devolved authorities would be more competent but simply because it would spread the load more.

But in the meantime, we now have a sprawling institutional infrastructure overseen by ministers who often spend a year or less in the job. This means the way they make appointments is critical to state effectiveness. If unqualified or incompetent people are in charge of these bodies it does huge harm. In 1995, the same Nolan principles that led to the professionalization of MPs also put in place rules for the now much bigger array of public appointments. A new post, Commissioner for Public Appointments, was created, and they were given control of choosing the panels that decided if candidates were appointable. Ministers then had the final choice from the appointable list.

This system worked reasonably well but the Conservatives were unhappy that it seemed biased towards Labour, or Labour-adjacent, candidates. For instance, in 2012, the Conservative commentator Fraser Nelson complained, 'Quangos are now stuffed to the gunwales with Labour placemen . . . [David Cameron's] allies say that he has been too much of a gentleman to play Labour's game and start stuffing quangos with Tory placemen . . . Figures out yesterday show that 77 per cent of politically active quango appointees last year were Labour supporters . . . If Cameron feels he is losing too many political battles, this might explain why: he has seemingly forgotten about the need for troops and ammunition.'[65]

And it was true that, of those candidates with political affiliation, far more were Labour (though most did not have an affiliation). But, as the centre-right think-tank Policy Exchange acknowledged, Nelson misdiagnosed the cause. It was not that Labour were being unduly partisan but that far more of their supporters applied, even after they left government. The number of Conservative-supporting appointments was entirely in line with the proportion of applicants who leaned politically to the right.[66]

Labour had no need to fix the process, even if the Nolan system had allowed them to do so. The reality is that most people working with expertise in the fields covered by these bodies – healthcare, the law, charity work, higher education – do have centre-left and liberal politics. This is even more true post-Brexit as both the age and education-level gaps between the two main parties have grown significantly. There are simply not many graduate professionals who vote Conservative. This is undoubtedly frustrating for the party, but rather than wondering why it might be the case, or, alternatively, whether they should be reducing the size of a central state that might oppose their agenda, they instead decided to make it easier to fix appointments.

In 2015, the moment the Conservatives were released from the Coalition, they asked Gerry Grimstone, now a Tory peer, to review the appointments system. Grimstone unsurprisingly recommended ministers should be given more discretion. The commissioner's powers were significantly reduced, with the government given the power to decide who would sit on appointment panels. Ministers became involved at every step of the process and were ultimately given the ability to appoint a person even if a panel considered them unappointable. Indeed, they could now appoint someone without a process at all.[67]

There was no justification for these changes given the previous system was working as well as could be expected given the broader challenges of a vast regulatory state. Anyone paying attention at the time spotted the problem. The Commons committee that oversees public administration said: 'Many distinguished observers of the appointments system have expressed considerable concern about Grimstone's proposals – these must not be dismissed. The system of public appointments must be seen to ensure that appointments are being made on merit. Given the criticisms that have been made, it is clear that, without extensive amendment, the Grimstone proposals will not and cannot sustain public confidence.'[68]

And they were right. Ministers have, inevitably, taken advantage of their new powers over appointments, and have become increasingly cavalier in doing so. This has had two profoundly negative effects. Firstly, more partisan stooges have been appointed to key roles with quasi-judicial powers over whole sectors, thus limiting the ability of people working in those organizations to do their jobs properly. Secondly, people who clearly do not have relevant competence have ended up in key positions. Meanwhile, the one problem Grimstone claimed he was trying to fix, the length of time appointments took, has got much worse, further hindering the ability of agencies to do their job.

Recent appointments to the chair of the Charity Commission are a good example. This is an important agency that regulates the vast majority of charities, which collectively have an income of £88 billion and employ not far off a million people. In 2018, ministers decided to appoint Baroness Stowell, who had been a Conservative cabinet minister three years previously. The Culture, Media and Sport Select Committee unanimously objected to her appointment on the grounds that she had 'little more than six months of negligible charity sector experience, and a complete lack of experience of working for a regulatory body ... Baroness Stowell was unable to demonstrate to the Committee any real insight, knowledge or vision for the charities sector.'[69]

Ministers went ahead with the appointment anyway.

Stowell spent her time pushing culture-war talking points in newspaper interviews rather than improving the quality of Charity Commission services, which are widely seen as poor.[70] While she was there, politically motivated investigations were pursued into the National Trust, for a report noting that several of its properties had been owned by slaveholders, and Barnardo's for publishing a blogpost on racial inequality and white privilege.[71] Both ultimately, and inevitably, found the charities had not done anything legally wrong (whether you agree with their positions or not). But the purpose was newspaper headlines and to pressure other charities into not pursuing causes the government did not like.

When Stowell stood down in 2021, the government failed to appoint anyone for a year, and then chose Martin Thomas, a friend of Boris Johnson, who had to resign four days later after it was revealed multiple complaints had been made against him by women while he was chair of a charity set up to protect women.[72] The (Tory) chair of the select committee expressed his frustration at a subsequent hearing: 'By our viewpoint, what we have seen is a complete shambles in terms of appointments that are in the purview of this committee. They are huge appointments to the good of this country and they have been handled in a way that this committee is actually flabber-gasted to the degree to which there have been such failings.'[73]

Ministers then proceeded to appoint Orlando Fraser, a former Tory parliamentary candidate and founding fellow of a centre-right think-tank. There are similar stories for numerous other bodies. One highlighted by Peter Riddell, who was Commissioner for Public Appointments until 2021, was the process for choosing the new chair of the Office for Students, the body that regulates universi-ties: 'I thought the panel was basically loaded. This is when [Gavin] Williamson was secretary of state for education. And I protested at the time. I expressed my views quite strongly . . . A majority [of the appointments panel] had clear Tory ties.'[74]

They chose another Tory peer, James Wharton, to be chair. Wharton had few obvious qualifications for the role, and quickly got into trouble by appearing at a far-right conference at which a series of racists and anti-Semites also spoke.[75] Perhaps the biggest fiasco was over the chairmanship of Ofcom, which became vacant in 2020. Boris Johnson made it clear that he wanted Paul Dacre, the long-term editor of the *Daily Mail*, supporter of Johnson, and serial critic of the BBC, which Ofcom regulates, for the role. The extent of the briefing meant others did not bother applying. As Riddell says, '[it deterred] good candidates from applying. It's the chilling effect which really concerns me . . . I think only nine candidates applied, that's extraordinarily low.'[76]

Then ministers handpicked a panel that included a Conservative peer. Incredibly, this panel still refused to sign off Dacre as appoint-able following his interview. At this point, ministers rejected any of the appointable candidates and very publicly tried to get Dacre to run again with a new panel, at which point he thew his toys out of the pram, writing to *The Times* that he had withdrawn and complaining that 'if you are possessed of an independent mind and are unassociated with the liberal-left, you will have more chance of winning the lottery than getting the job'.[77] This is something that the many other appointments discussed in this chapter show to be flatly untrue.

Instead, another Conservative peer, Michael Grade, was appointed. Then a few months later the chair of the BBC had to resign after it emerged that during his appointment process he had helped to arrange a large personal loan for Boris Johnson.[78] Meanwhile, another BBC board member, Robbie Gibb, a former director of communications for Theresa May, has been accused of trying to interfere with the Ofcom appointments process.[79] It is a sorry mess.

What this particular set of roles has in common is their importance to the so-called 'culture wars'. The Conservatives were desperate to control these appointments due to a belief that 'liberal-left' beliefs are being spread unchallenged in charities, universities and by broadcasters. Of course, an elected government should be able to challenge institutions, but they need to do so in a transparent way that is open to scrutiny. At any point the government could have legislated to abolish the BBC, ban charities from assessing their links to slavery, or anything else they find unacceptable. But they did not. Instead they tried to get their way by fixing appointments processes, so as to avoid that scrutiny.

In doing so they have left critical parts of the state with weak or absent leadership, unable to perform their functions properly. And though the main focus has been on 'culture war' appointments there has been damage across the state's activities, including in key economic roles. For instance, when John Kingman stood down as chair of UK Research and Innovation – which controls £25 billion of UK investment – he said in his farewell remarks:

The head of Innovate UK – Britain's national innovation agency, with a budget of over £1bn a year . . . [was] left vacant for more than three years as the Government process took us round and round in circles. It is just not sensible that an organization of Innovate's importance can be left without a permanent head for three years. Or take, more recently, the role of head of the ESRC, Britain's social science funder . . . The post has now been vacant for months. But Ministers only in the last few days agreed to even initiate the (inevitably lengthy) process to start to search for a replacement. How is this possible? . . .

[One factor is] the current Government's intense suspicion of appointments proposals that come through the institutional machine, and the deployment of many political advisers around Government, all of whose views are thought to be needed before every stage of every process for every minor appointment can proceed . . . These processes can also lead to strange unexplained decisions – surprisingly often, rejections of people who are clearly world-class. Ministers of course have every right to appoint whoever they want. Nevertheless, there are costs to the UK, and to UK science, in turning superb people down. One does wonder whether this is a luxury the country can really afford.[80]

It is another example of the toxic cycles explored throughout this book. Government becomes overwhelmed, reacts by trying to seize more control and further reduces scrutiny, makes things worse, and gets more overwhelmed. This particular avenue of failure would be easy to close off by ensuring appointments receive more scrutiny. The pre-Grimstone process for appointments should be restored and critical appointments, responsible for big regulatory roles, should require select committee sign-off before going ahead. This already happens with a few roles like the board of the Office of Budget Responsibility and chair of the UK Statistics Authority, and the appointments to both have been non-partisan and high quality.

It is a simple fix but, once more, requires government to acknowledge the damage that excessive executive control does to the state, and be farsighted enough to see the value in improving the implementation of their own policy programme.

6

CIVIL WAR

Why governments always fail to fix the civil service

Jim Hacker: The Opposition aren't the opposition.
Annie Hacker: No, of course not, silly of me. They're just
  called the opposition.
Jim Hacker: They're only the opposition in exile. The Civil Ser-
  vice is the opposition in residence.

YES MINISTER, 'BIG BROTHER' EPISODE,

FIRST AIRED IN 1980

The idea of the civil service as a quasi-constitutional block on ministerial wishes is not a new one. Fictional representations of crafty
bureaucrats twisting the system to their advantage go back centuries.
Mr Tite Barnacle of the Circumlocution Department in Charles
Dickens's *Little Dorrit* is just one of the more memorable examples.
But it was *Yes Minister* that provided the modern cultural archetype
of the senior civil servant in the form of Sir Humphrey Appleby.

While the character was not based on any particular individual,
the writers, Antony Jay and Jonathan Lynn, were inspired by the
experiences of Labour ministers in Harold Wilson's government. The
diaries of cabinet minister Richard Crossman, and his battles with
the first woman permanent secretary, the formidable Dame Evelyn

Sharp, were a key point of reference. Jay and Lynn's main advisers for the show were two of Wilson's most senior appointments: his political secretary, Lady Falkender, previously known as Marcia Williams, and the head of his Policy Unit, Bernard Donoughue.

It is, therefore, a story told from the perspective of political figures who felt they had been frustrated by an out-of-date and stuffy establishment. And there was certainly plenty of truth to that, though Falkender, like Wilson, was unusually paranoid even by Westminster standards. At that time, the senior civil service was nearly all male, mostly Oxbridge with plenty of classicists, like Sir Humphrey, and an attitude that had changed little since the Victorian era. They exerted a strong sense of institutional control and permanency. Between 1947 and 1979 just three people held the role of cabinet secretary, the most senior role in the civil service.

As with so many other topics in this book, it was under Thatcher that things started to change and *Yes Minister* was part of that process. Jay was not just a Thatcherite but one who advised the Conservative Party. The programme, often not very subtly, pushed messages that helped her define the civil service as part of the problem she was trying to solve. Take the first episode of series three, 'Equal Opportunities', in which the minister Jim Hacker battles with Sir Humphrey to fast-track the appointment of a promising woman in his department, Sarah Harrison, only to find that when he eventually succeeds she has decided to quit:

Hacker: *[Stunned]* You were to be my, so to speak, Trojan horse.
Harrison: Well, quite honestly, Minister, I want a job where I
    don't spend endless hours circulating information that isn't
    relevant about subjects that don't matter to people who aren't
    interested. I want a job where there's achievement rather than

196

merely activity. I'm tired of pushing paper. I want to be able to point at something and say 'I did that'.

Sir Humphrey: I don't understand.

Harrison: I know. That's why I'm leaving.[1]

And off she goes to the private sector, with Thatcher no doubt beaming in delight as she watched on the Downing Street sofa. No wonder it was her favourite programme. In 1984, she even participated in a hideously cringeworthy skit with the actors, written by her press secretary Bernard Ingham, and rehearsed twenty-three times with her own civil servants. Appropriately it was performed at an awards ceremony organized by the staunch social conservative critic and prude Mary Whitehouse, where *Yes Minister* was being honoured as an example of 'wholesome entertainment'.[2]

By the time *The Thick of It* (*TTOI*), the second big BBC sitcom focused on Westminster, first aired in 2005 things looked very different. For a start the civil service barely featured. The only official in the main cast was Terri Coverley, Director of Communications for the fictional department DOSAC (Department of Social Affairs and Citizenship), who spends most of her time trying to wearily extricate herself from the madness around her. The permanent secretary never makes an appearance. The stars are the politically appointed special advisers (SPADs), most notably Malcom Tucker, who was very obviously based on Alastair Campbell. The battles are among them, and their ministers.

If *Yes Minister* made civil servants too powerful and too much the cause of national stagnation, even in the early 1980s, then *TTOI* went too far the other way. But it did reflect a genuine, and very significant, shift towards SPADs as the true source of power and influence in Whitehall. It also, in its copious swearing, and sometimes physical violence, accurately reflected a rapid coarsening of the culture that would have distressed poor Mary Whitehouse.

Thatcher, though she found bureaucratic constraints frustrating, usually had good relations with her officials. Indeed, her closest advisers were civil servants who bought into her world view like Ingham and foreign policy adviser Charles Powell, rather than political appointments. But even civil servants who were not politically aligned often eventually developed unexpected feelings of loyalty to her. Caroline Slocock, who worked for her as a private secretary during her final years as prime minister, and whose personal politics were well to the left of Thatcher, wrote in her memoir: 'To her, we were people first, civil servants second. And it was that feeling of being almost part of the family with Margaret Thatcher that prevailed with the private office through thick and thin.'

Thatcher was often closer to her officials than her cabinet or MPs, which contributed to her final demise. As Slocock writes: 'Siding with us rather than her colleagues was a winning formula for her in lots of ways. It helped give her strength to fight what she saw as the good fight against opposition within her own party and beyond . . . But in terms of her support within her own party, it was quite the wrong way round.'[3]

By *TTOI*'s era any sense of family had long gone. Blair's team were his political appointments and that led to big changes in the centre of government. It also changed the culture. There has been a serious breakdown in trust between ministers and officials that has accelerated dramatically during the last few decades, and particularly in the years following Brexit. It is unevenly spread and there are still ministers who work well with, and command the respect of, their civil servants. But the consequences are felt across government through the loss of some of the most talented people in Whitehall, and a growing belief that the best way to get promoted is by telling ministers what they want to hear.

In recent years things have started to come to a head. Dominic Raab's behaviour towards officials was so extreme it forced him into (eventual) resignation as deputy prime minister. It is unusual for civil servants to make formal complaints about bullying and mistreatment, but at least twenty-four did so about Raab, forcing Rishi Sunak to agree to a formal inquiry by the barrister Adam Tolley.[4] In the careful language of a lawyer, Tolley ruled that he had bullied people: 'The combination of unconstructive critical feedback and regular interruption is likely to be experienced as intimidating, in the sense of being unreasonably difficult to deal with, and plainly was so experienced by some individuals.'[5]

While some people who worked for Raab defend his more aggressive approach, most offer similar thoughts to those expressed by Tolley in earthier vocabulary. Stories about his behaviour had been a staple of pub gossip in Westminster for years before the inquiry took place, including how people had to be tempted into working in his private office with extra salary hikes or 'danger money'.

The problem with Raab's behaviour was not just that it made a lot of junior civil servants' lives miserable. It also led to a far worse policy-making process. Because he did not trust anyone around him, he tried to do everything himself, with inevitable consequences.

As one senior official who was at the Ministry of Justice with Raab told me: 'The presumption from Raab was that the civil service were trying to meddle and de-purify his vision. So there would be a constant stream of: "You always do this"; "This is exactly what I knew would happen"; "I want to do something and you'll stop it" . . .

'The way it's supposed to work is ministers give a high-level steer, and then you go [and] work up some options on it. And sometimes what they want to achieve is not directly implementable because it's unlawful, it's expensive, it's whatever, and so you come back and say, "Here are some options" . . . With Raab, he demanded the thing he'd literally written back as the policy. We had to write down literally, word for word, what he said. And then he would say, "What did I say in the last meeting?" If you said, "roughly this", he'd say, "No, literally word for word, what did I say in the last meeting?" '

This refusal to accept advice or criticism meant that it was impossible for officials to divert him off a path that was inexorably going to lead to failure: 'You could never go back and revisit a decision. So if it turned out that subsequently something you were doing was wrong, or something changed that meant what he had decided was wrong, you could never go back and say so.'[6]

Raab's approach meant he ended up writing large parts of his much-cherished new Bill of Rights himself. When published, the draft bill was ripped apart by almost everyone with any legal knowledge from the UN to the Council of Europe to a succession of former senior judges. Critics included the Conservative chair of the Parliamentary Justice Committee as well as Raab's colleague and predecessor in the Lord Chancellor's job, Robert Buckland.[7] Once Raab was out of government it was quickly killed off, never to become law. It was a prime example of how a total lack of trust undermines ministers' own policy goals.

Raab is an extreme case but he is not alone. In February 2020, Philip Rutnam, permanent secretary at the Home Office and a career civil servant for thirty-three years, resigned, issuing a statement that he would be suing for constructive dismissal and strongly criticizing the then home secretary, Priti Patel: 'In the last 10 days I have been the target of a vicious and orchestrated briefing campaign. It has been alleged that I have briefed the media against the home secretary. This, along with many other claims, is completely false . . . One of my duties as permanent secretary was to protect the health, safety and wellbeing of our 35,000 people. This created tension with the home secretary, and I have encouraged her to change her behaviours. I have received allegations that her conduct has included shouting and swearing, belittling people, making unreasonable and repeated demands – behaviour that created fear and that needed some bravery to call out.'[8]

A review by Sir Alex Allan, Boris Johnson's independent adviser on standards, found that allegations of bullying were correct and Patel had broken the ministerial code.[9] Johnson chose not to sack her, leading to Sir Alex resigning. Rutnam's constructive dismissal claim was settled with a £340,000 payout of public money.[10] It was another blow to relations between senior mandarins and politicians. Later in the year, after a fiasco over an algorithm designed to provide exam results in the absence of exams (due to Covid lockdowns), Jonathan Slater, the permanent secretary at the DfE, was fired, with no ministers taking any responsibility.

When Liz Truss took over as prime minister one of her very first acts was to sack Tom Scholar, permanent secretary at the Treasury, which many think contributed to the economic meltdown that followed. Throughout all this chaos the most senior civil servants, the cabinet secretaries Mark Sedwill and then Simon Case, were conspicuously silent – even internally, leaving the rest of the civil service feeling that they'd lost a key layer of protection.

These increasingly strong expressions of executive power have not led ministers, and advisers, to see the civil service as any less of a restriction on their ability to achieve their goals. In recent years the most trenchant critic has been Dominic Cummings, who views the civil service as a major blocker to innovation and a more effective state (though, to be fair, he sees pretty much everyone in the same light).

His core complaint is that personnel management is extremely low quality: 'The most important change [needed] in Whitehall is HR rules: until it is possible to replace people quickly, in the same way that healthy armies fire bad generals fast, and close whole departments and organizations, major improvements are impossible . . . Embedding people with advanced modelling and statistical skills as part-time advisers to ministers would force Ministers and officials to confront the issue of acting on, against, or in the absence of, evidence. Allowing Ministers to hire specific project management people from outside Whitehall, and without Whitehall HR, could greatly improve quality of management.'[11]

That was written in 2013 but his views had hardened even more by the time he was Boris Johnson's chief adviser. A few weeks after the 2019 election victory, he wrote a notorious blogpost asking for people to write to him directly for jobs in No. 10, asking that 'weirdos and misfits' apply. In that post he wrote: 'Over the past five months the No10 political team has been lucky to work with some fantastic officials. But there are also some profound problems at the core of how the British state makes decisions. This was seen by pundit-world as a very eccentric view in 2014. It is no longer seen as eccentric.'[12]

But this has never been an eccentric view, and frustration with the civil service goes back to its creation in the nineteenth century. His complaints are not new. Indeed they are the reason the ranks of special advisers have grown so much in recent decades. Back in 1966, Wilson and his advisers, long before they unloaded their frustrations to the *Yes Minister* writers, set up a review of the civil service under Lord Fulton. When his committee produced a comprehensive report, which appeared two years later, the list of problems they identified were remarkably similar to Cummings's complaints, albeit in somewhat more refined language:

> It is still too much based on the philosophy of the amateur (or 'generalist' or 'all-rounder'). This is most evident in the Administrative Class, which holds the dominant position in the Service . . .
>
> Scientists, engineers and members of other specialist classes are frequently given neither the full responsibilities and opportunities nor the corresponding authority they ought to have.
>
> Too few civil servants are skilled managers.
>
> There is not enough contact between the Service and the community it is there to serve.
>
> Personnel management and career planning are inadequate.[13]

All these issues continue to frustrate civil servants as well as ministers and advisers, which leaves us with the question: Why has no one been able to fix them?

How the weaknesses of the civil service were built in from the start

The problems identified by everyone from Fulton to Cummings are a consequence of the way the modern civil service was formed in the second half of the nineteenth century. Up until then ministers had just appointed whoever they wanted to whatever jobs were within budget, regardless of whether they were necessary or whether the person turned up or not. There was a healthy market in sub-letting lucrative positions.

The Northcote–Trevelyan Report of 1854 is usually seen as the key moment of change as it proposed recruiting civil servants solely on the basis of merit rather than patronage, though in practice it took many years to be implemented and was largely the work of Robert Lowe, Gladstone's chancellor from 1868–73. It took decades to change the culture. In the first stage of reform, departments merely had to put up a selection of candidates for commissioners to choose from. Initially, the Treasury's patronage secretary, William Hayter, paid two people with learning difficulties to 'compete' with ministers' preferred candidates (they were known across Westminster as 'Hayter's Idiots').[14]

Though the eventual shift to merit was clearly a necessary one, the exams developed by the reformers were written to create the very system decried ever since. They were explicitly designed – by the Master of Balliol College, Oxford, Benjamin Jowett – for Oxford graduates, giving most marks to a paper on classical literature. His goal was to ensure a career path for those of his students who did not want to go into either the church or the law, rather than to enable the country to be run more effectively. If that wasn't snobbery enough, those involved in the scheme were snooty about the abilities of those who did not have their educational background.[15]

On top of this the assessments were designed to ensure recruitment would come only from young men, as older recruits with more worldly experience would cost more and be less malleable. They blocked recruits who had joined the civil service in lower-grade clerking roles from the possibility of promotion to what they called 'The First Division' of the senior ranks.[16] The reformers who also believed that training additional skills was unnecessary, actively rejected an existing model established in the Indian civil service, which had set up a training college at Haileybury (later turned into a private school).

As one historian of the civil service puts it: 'The civil service created by Lowe [and Northcote–Trevelyan, and Jowett] deliberately cut itself off from practical men: civil servants were not to be recruited after proving themselves in the real world, nor could they rise from the ranks. Of course, there were practical men who also happened to be brilliant classicists, but the bias veered towards impracticality. Remarkably cultured and learned impracticality, it is true, but this was not really what was needed for the government of the country as it entered the twentieth century. Indeed as Trevelyan's own incompetence in respect of Irish famine relief and the Crimean War demonstrated, it was not what was needed for the government of the country at any time.'[17]

Over time, these restrictions were eased, the classics exam went, and it became possible (though rare) to be promoted from the operational ranks to the senior civil service. But the core structure and culture remained solidly in place. It was not until the immense demands of the Second World War forced Whitehall to temporarily open up recruitment that serious questions started to be asked as to whether this was a desirable way to select the administrators of government.

The growth of the state during the war, and a Labour government eager to approach peacetime with more ambition, caused tensions. An *Observer* editorial from October 1945 noted: 'The Civil Service was built up as a defensive body, safeguarding the old way of life, not as a creative body laying down the pattern of a new way . . . [this had begun] to seem out of place with the growth of social reform. With the coming of socialism it is potentially ruinous. If the socialised industries are to be subject to all the current habits of Whitehall . . . the community will suffer bitterly from the extension to peacetime commerce of the muddles and delays which have often driven us frantic in war time.'[18]

Though Attlee's Labour government was too preoccupied to engage in major civil service reform, the belief that it was a critical barrier to change became increasingly common on the left. The Oxford don and *New Statesman* correspondent, Thomas Balogh, wrote an essay, 'The Apotheosis of the Dilettante', in 1959 that was just as brutal in its assessments as Cummings sixty years later: 'So far as one can make out from a long experience with pupils taking it, [the civil service exams] seem to favour the grasshopper mind and the exhibitionist . . . [Modern] problems far from becoming more universal, are increasingly demanding specialized knowledge yet . . . the dominant branch of the Civil Service has become more and more generalized and, what is worse, more exclusive . . .'

As Balogh went on to emphasize, both the permanent secretary from the civil service and the minister in charge of a department might arrive with no knowledge of the problems they faced. Effective policy 'cannot be formed under these conditions'.[19]

Balogh ended up advising Wilson along with Falkender, and though the prime minister was more conservative, and less convinced the civil service were the problem, they convinced him to establish the Fulton Committee. As we have seen, Fulton largely endorsed Balogh's view, and agreed that 'The Home Civil Service today is still fundamentally the product of the nineteenth-century philosophy of the Northcote–Trevelyan Report.'

But the recommendations they made were fairly limited and did not sustain Wilson's interest for long, as his government wandered into serious economic and political difficulties. The changes that were made ended up being mostly undone over the coming years. The Civil Service Department set up to take control off the Treasury was abolished by Thatcher in 1981 (though survived long enough to be the model for Sir Humphrey's Department for Administrative Affairs). A shift towards more flexibility between 'operational' roles and senior policy ones stuck better, but was partially undermined by the creation of the 'Senior Civil Service' in 1995 that recreated the old idea of a 'First Division'. The Civil Service College, established to improve training, made it to 2012 before being shut down as part of a wave of austerity cuts.

Thatcher's interests lay in reducing the size of the civil service, which she did via privatization and outsourcing (see chapter three). It is the same size now as it was at the end of that Conservative period of government. But she did little to challenge the structures and culture. In turn, senior civil servants themselves were, on the whole, not averse to ridding themselves of cumbersome operational activities, while protecting their policy-making role.

Subsequent governments have done little in the way of serious reform, but have preferred to propose an occasional chunky cut in the number of officials. These redundancy exercises always follow the same pattern. Recruitment is frozen, generous voluntary redundancy packages are offered and often taken by the most talented people who can most easily get employment elsewhere, jobs are lost at random and with no strategy, and then, over time, numbers rise again as government ministers decide they want to take on more responsibilities and announce more initiatives. Those who left are frequently hired back as consultants for multiples of their salary.

The most substantive attempt at reform in recent years came from Francis Maude in 2012 but ultimately it petered out in the face of a lack of interest from David Cameron and other senior colleagues. It ended up being another cuts exercise and had the same result: numbers dropped from 480,000 to 385,000 only to rise to over half a million after Brexit created significant additional work for officials.[20] There have been marginal improvements in increasing external appointments, diversity of staff, and the number of specialists in statistics, economics and management, but the fundamentals have not changed. This is increasingly problematic given the technical demands on modern government, and the vastly bigger array of problems it now has to address.

Maude himself acknowledged the problem when he was asked back to do another review published in 2023: 'There has been a failure over decades . . . Failings identified by the Fulton Committee in 1968, for example the dominance of "generalists", "churn" whereby officials move from post to post in an apparently unplanned and uncontrolled manner, and an excessively closed culture and lack of interchange with external sectors, all constantly recur in reviews of and commentaries on the Civil Service.'[21]

The reason why reform never happens is superficially obvious. It is not in the interests of the senior civil service to upset the status quo too much, and ministers have neither the staying power, nor the ability, to prioritize and see through change when there are usually more pressing political challenges.

As Jonathan Slater, the permanent secretary at the Department for Education fired by Boris Johnson, succinctly put it: 'If you just leave it to ministers, you're never going to really get any change or you're very unlikely to, because it's just typically not their area of competence or interest . . . So that leaves the civil servants. Are they putting ideas, radical changes in front of ministers who are turning them down? No, they're not . . . I guess this is typically because the majority of people at the top of the civil service not having the faintest idea just how poor it is. So why would they?'[22]

But it is not just bureaucratic resistance and ministerial incompetence. Indeed the officials I spoke to tended to be as exasperated with the way things work as Cummings. There is little more dispiriting to a hard-working civil servant than seeing lazy colleagues shuffled between jobs rather than let go. And the need to move constantly around the system in order to get promoted and noticed is frustrating as well.

Rather there is a self-perpetuation problem in that the current system is constantly bogged down in crisis management and the people who are selected for the most senior jobs are, as a result, those that are best at coping with constant chaos, or even thriving on it. Equally, ministers value senior officials who can get them through the day – who are essentially fixers – rather than ones who would focus on running a lengthy change-management process.

As another former permanent secretary, Philip Rycroft, has noted: 'Reform is never, it seems to me, dropped deep enough into the system and I think to me this is exacerbated by the things that are deemed most important, which is essentially chasing after ministers and solving the political problems. And someone like [former cabinet secretary] Jeremy Heywood was brilliant at that . . . but that meant that we were chasing, constantly chasing our tail. So there was no moment of reflection, of stepping back, of saying, no, no, we need a deep, serious reform change programme here.'[23]

The more overwhelmed Whitehall gets, due to the additional responsibilities it is taking on, and the hollowing out of local government, the less time anyone has to step back like this and the more frantic the tail-chasing becomes. This is especially true right at the centre of government, where the role of the cabinet secretary, who nominally is in charge of the civil service, has been diminished and increasingly focused on being a fixer and courtier.

The increasing fixation on communications over policy and the need for a constant stream of announcements to keep the media happy encourages the promotion of those who are good at coming up with quick and journalist-friendly, if superficial, ideas rather than ones who can drive and implement complex reforms. Exceptionally high levels of ministerial churn only exacerbate this trend as the incentive for politicians is to produce headline-catching ideas in order to get noticed in time for the next reshuffle. Why would ministers want, in Cummings's words, to 'confront the issue of acting on, against, or in the absence of, evidence'? Evidence just gets in the way of having something to say that pleases the various interest groups that will decide your future.

There is another reason why reform is harder than ever and the civil service is arguably less effective than it has ever been, despite recruiting large numbers of talented people. The whole principle of the civil service as being independent, and offering impartial advice to government, has been serially undermined in a way that makes all of these other problems worse. This is because reformers who are interested in systems, like Maude and Cummings, are so frustrated by the personnel challenges that are never remedied, that they short-cut the process by increasing executive control.

The SPAD takeover

The biggest shift since the *Yes Minister* age has been in the role of SPADs. The fictional minister, Jim Hacker, brings an adviser with him into government but he is quickly despatched to a distant building, and doesn't even appear in the second and third series. As prime minister, Hacker does have one forceful adviser, Dorothy Wainwright, who was based on Lady Falkender, and this reflected the shift towards political appointments that had begun in earnest under Harold Wilson.

Falkender, or Marcia Williams as she was then, was not the first political appointment. Lloyd George and Churchill had both hired advisers during wartime outside the standard civil service processes. Harold Macmillan had a political secretary, and other ministers had, from time to time, had irregular advisers. But she was the first to see her role in purely political terms and as direct competition to the civil service.

It was in Wilson's second term, starting in 1974, that the current system of SPADs began to take shape. The prime minister expressed his desire to build up a bigger cohort of political advisers explicitly in the context of civil service limitations: '[SPADs offer] a mind more committed and politically aware than would be available to a minister from the political neutrals in the established civil service.'[24]

His ministers were allowed to have their own political hires too. Barbara Castle, for instance, recruited a young Jack Straw, who later went on to be foreign secretary under Blair. By the time Wilson left Downing Street in 1976 there were forty SPADs across government. The numbers fell back under James Callaghan, in the face of Conservative and media attacks on the cost of the new hires. And, initially, Thatcher had only a small cohort, mostly made up of older businessmen like John Hoskyns, who ran her first Policy Unit.

Thatcher personally preferred working with civil servants, as long as they were loyal. She had a tendency to see the need for additional advisers as a sign of weakness in a minister. She did, though, eventually relent and by the end of her time in power it was standard for departments to have two each, one focused on policy and one on politics and communications. She also changed the rules to allow SPADs to ignore those sections of the civil service code which prevented them from doing explicitly political work, like attending party conferences.[25]

It was, though, under the Blair government that SPADs really became a genuine policy-making alternative to the civil service. It is no coincidence that the two prime ministers who did most to introduce SPADs – Wilson and Blair – arrived in No. 10 after lengthy periods of Conservative rule, and with the belief that that civil service would, as a result, be inherently hostile.

Former Wilson (and *Yes Minister*) adviser Bernard Donoughue was brought back into government as a junior Lords minister. He noted the paranoia: '[Blair's ministers and advisors] were young people who had grown up watching the show [*Yes Minister*]. And some of them came in, as a consequence, *excessively* primed, and were out to demonstrate their masculinity by not listening to their civil servants. And I think they went too far. Because they were young, inexperienced Ministers, and they hadn't a clue what to do. So my view was that, in many cases, it would have been better if the civil servants had done it rather than them.'[26]

Increasing the number of SPADs was an alternative to listening to civil servants. The numbers doubled overnight. But more significant than the quantity was the importance given to their positions. Director of communications Alastair Campbell and chief of staff Jonathan Powell had a level of seniority in the No. 10 hierarchy that had never been seen before.

The same was true in other departments, particularly at the Treasury. Ed Balls was essentially deputy chancellor and far fewer officials had direct access to the chancellor than under previous regimes. It was this growing role in direct policy-making that created confusion about the role and purpose of the civil service.

David Omand was a permanent secretary over the transition to New Labour and witnessed the rise of this new culture. For him, and he speaks for plenty of others, it was a turning point in the relations between ministers and officials: 'for almost all of my time at Defence [before 1997] there were no special advisers as we know them today. In my time in the Home Office, the special adviser was an expert on youth justice, Norman (later Lord) Warner. He was a former civil servant, and only a special adviser because he had worked up policy for the Labour Party when in opposition. He was followed by another criminal justice expert, Justin Russell, who became HM Chief Inspector of Probation . . . having them as specialist advisers was really useful. And Jack Straw also helpfully had a PR special adviser, Ed Owen (now a senior communications consultant based in Washington DC), who could go down to the Red Lion [a famous Westminster pub] and do stuff that I would certainly have refused, because it's political.

'But the idea of special advisers who have a crucial role across the board in policy formulation, usually as a stepping stone to a political career, I was very lucky to avoid because, as far as I can see, the effect has been to break the system. That's because nobody's entirely sure about their relation to junior Ministers, who to talk to and how much authority people actually have . . .

'Some senior civil servants now feel they have to run their proposals past the special advisers before they get to the secretary of state. That is a complete collapse of the British system of government . . . I'm not against having special advisers. As long as it's very clear what it is they're doing, and they are doing things which are not the job of civil servants.'[27]

This is a distinction that has long since disappeared. As ever with the British state, because this system has evolved gradually, across multiple governments, without any explicit purpose or goal, the outcome has been a serious confusion of roles and responsibilities. Some SPADs will work in the old way, offering specialist expertise on certain topics, or just doing press management. Others have taken on a quasi-ministerial role, interjecting themselves between ministers and officials, in the style of Ed Balls.

The most extreme example is Cummings himself, when he was Boris Johnson's chief adviser in No. 10. For instance, in their biography of Johnson, Anthony Seldon and Raymond Newell record that during the attempt to prorogue Parliament and avoid scrutiny during the final stages of Brexit there was 'panic among officials as they saw Cummings blocking notes . . . from going to the Prime Minister to keep him in the dark and thus to underplay the emerging risk of prorogation, according to senior civil servants . . . Cummings didn't care if decisions were not taken by the Prime Minister. He tried to take them himself, as if he was the Prime Minister.'[28]

Later on, during the early months of Covid: 'Civil servants began to talk openly about what they termed "Potemkin Government", with the system no longer knowing who was running the country . . . [Cummings] began giving instructions in the name of the PM with no cover from the PM. Says an official, "Don't tell the PM" was a regular Cummings utterance to staff.'[29]

There is an obvious problem here with the lack of accountability. Not only are SPADs not elected but they are very rarely called before parliamentary committees and rarely interviewed in the media on the record. Some, like Cummings and Alastair Campbell, develop a public persona because they are charismatic figures who attract controversy, but the vast majority are completely unknown despite being more powerful than most junior ministers and, in many cases, cabinet ministers.

It has also led to deep confusion over who is responsible for policy-making, often leaving the civil service cut out of the process. This may seem a reasonable response to the historic problems with getting innovative policy advice out of generalist officials, but has only served to make civil servants even less likely to come forward with ideas or to seek them from other outside sources. It is a mentality that has led politicians like Raab to believe the job of their department is merely to implement their exact thoughts.

Yet the quality of SPADs is highly variable and they are too often party hacks with limited knowledge of their ministers' department. Once a minister has found someone they like they will tend to reappoint them whenever they move role. Due to the oddities of the Westminster day and the expectation they will drop everything at any time of day or night to deal with a crisis, SPADs also tend to be young and childless. For many it is a route into either a frontline political career or a highly lucrative gig in one of the public affairs companies that value ministerial connections. People with significant policy knowledge in an area rarely want to associate themselves too closely with a political party, nor would they be trusted to make the political compromises necessary. Increasingly it means no one is really doing serious policy-making. Officials feel frozen out, yet ministers and SPADs do not have the knowledge or, often, the inclination to do it either.

The former deputy prime minister, David Lidington, told me how he'd seen the policy-making capacity of the civil service reduce over time: 'When I worked for Douglas Hurd in the Home Office, in the late 1980s [as a special adviser], the Home Office had a statistics and research department that collated all the stats that were going that looked at foreign countries' experience. They would look what experiments are working well, what the universities were publishing on criminology, and would use that to inform ministers . . . When I went back to Justice [in 2017], I found there was no strategic function at all, nobody in the building was looking at what criminological reports were saying about effectiveness or not, or what the Norwegians were doing about their penal system, or the Californians.'[30]

This is partly due to rapid turnover and the loss of historical memory, exacerbated by regular cuts, followed by waves of new hires. But it is also because it is not what many ministers expect civil servants to do any more, nor something they trust them to do. Unfortunately, this means that no one is really making policy at all. Civil servants no longer feel it is their role, unless specifically asked. But ministers and SPADs often have little knowledge or background in the topics covered by their departments. They may look outside for ideas from politically aligned think-tanks or academics, but have no way of assessing the quality of those ideas. The result is paralysis. Or rather a focus on meaningless media announcements disconnected from real-world issues.

This is a shift that has happened gradually over many years, but relations between ministers and civil servants have certainly got a lot worse in the past decade. Brexit was a major point of fracture. As former deputy cabinet secretary Helen MacNamara told me, officials have traditionally been almost religious in their determination to avoid displaying party-political views: 'It was always completely unthinkable to have any conversation at all ever, about someone's voting intention or personal politics . . . I think politicians, anybody, would be really surprised to understand just how deep that was. I'd have colleagues who I'd be close to and know really personal things about their lives, but it would be totally unthinkable to have a conversation about who they voted for.'

But the Brexit vote was different. As one senior official told me: 'The senior civil service were gutted by it. And it was a real fracture.'[31]

The former permanent secretary at the Foreign Office, Simon McDonald, in a BBC documentary about Brexit, gave a sense of how different this moment was from previous election or referenda results: 'People were in tears. People were in shock. On this occasion, this solitary occasion, I decided to tell my colleagues and therefore let ministers know that I voted to remain in the European Union . . . I was trying to maintain credibility and trying to convey a message to a group of people, most of whom I felt had voted to remain in the EU, that their personal feelings were beside the professional point.'[32]

While McDonald went further than most, this emotional response was repeated across Whitehall. It was a fracture that had profound effects on both sides. Ministers charged with delivering Brexit, particularly those who had campaigned for it, felt even less able to trust civil servants who now seemed affiliated with 'the other side'. They may have felt this was true in the past but now it seemed confirmed; in practice, though, most civil servants asked to work on Brexit did so with full professionalism, and achieved the government's chosen outcome, despite it going against their instincts. But the loss of trust led to the deeply ineffective and aggressive approach taken by Dominic Raab and Priti Patel.

Brexit also led to deep unhappiness within the senior civil service, and many departures, especially after 2019 when it became apparent the government were prepared to risk breaking the law to achieve their aims. John Kingman, former second permanent secretary at the Treasury, left in 2016 to take on private sector roles. He told me: 'Since I left, I've had a constant stream of very good people at all levels – really senior, mid-level, bright young things – coming to me asking, "How do we get out?" . . . I don't think lots of talent left the civil service under Cameron and Osborne even though impos- ing austerity on public services across Britain probably wouldn't have been what they'd ideally have chosen. But I do think that, you know, what we have seen since 2016 has changed that. We've seen government become very casual about breaking the law. We've seen large-scale corruption . . . '[33]

Beyond any specific acts of law-breaking or corruption, there is a broader sense that the space for honest advice has rapidly shrunk. This is partly down to the attitudinal shift from ministers, which has hardened since Brexit, but also rule changes that have made the most senior civil service jobs more precarious and more vulnerable to ministerial displeasure.

During the Coalition years there was a running battle between Cabinet Office minister Francis Maude and the senior civil service due to his determination to give power to ministers in making per- manent secretary appointments. Like Cummings, Maude seems to have channelled his frustration at his inability to properly reform the civil service into a belief that more executive power would provide a short cut. Eventually he forced two concessions. Firstly, permanent secretaries would be appointed on five-year contracts that did not have to be renewed if ministers were unhappy with performance. And secondly, the prime minister would make the final decision on appointments, advised by his or her ministers, from a list of candi- dates considered appointable by the civil service commission.

These changes may seem subtle but they have made a big dif- ference to senior officials' willingness to challenge ministers. It has always been the case that officials are duty bound to follow government instruction unless it involves breaking the law. They are not 'independent' in that sense. But they are supposed to be impartial and give honest advice on policy proposals. Now someone hoping to be a permanent secretary knows that their political masters can veto their appointment, even if they are the best candidate according to their peers, without having to offer justification. And existing permanent secretaries know they will find themselves out of a job within five years if they cause too much trouble.

There have always been ways for ministers to indicate displeasure, and that they would like things to change, but making their power explicit has undoubtedly increased their willingness to use it. Mark Sedwill, who himself was forced out of his post as cabinet secretary, acknowledged to a Lords committee that 'it was not always the objectively best candidate who was selected for a permanent secretary vacancy but the one with whom the secretary of state felt most comfortable'.[34] Nick MacPherson, previously permanent secretary at the Treasury, told the same committee that 'ministers put a lot of pressure on those involved to ensure that their preferred people make it above the line [as appointable candidates]'. The current cabinet secretary Simon Case told them that prime ministers now habitually sign off director-general appointments – the level below permanent secretary – as well.[35]

Perhaps even more concerning is the increasingly aggressive direct dismissals of senior officials. This is not entirely new: if a minister and permanent secretary could not work together the cabinet secretary would always intervene to move things around. But now we have immediate dismissals such as when Truss removed Tom Scholar from the Treasury on her first day in office, and at the same time shifted Stephen Lovegrove out of the critical post of National Security Adviser. Mark Sedwill has argued this move was designed as a 'deliberate signal to Whitehall that political alignment with the new Government's views was the key criterion and that capability . . . and performance were not'.[36]

While Truss went further than anyone else, before or since, Boris Johnson had 'moved on' multiple permanent secretaries, with twelve being replaced in 2020 alone. Cummings was a key figure in determining these changes, even though SPADs are not supposed to have any management role when it comes to the civil service. Between 2019 and 2023 the average amount of time a permanent secretary had been in their current role fell from 6.8 years to 2.4.[37] Ultimately all these things are within the prime minister's power. The Constitutional Reform and Governance Act 2010 introduced into law for the first time the concept that the PM manages the civil service and thus can choose to make appointments or remove people at will.

Most senior civil service appointments do still have an independent appointments process which ensures that the prime minister is choosing director-generals and permanent secretaries from a list of people who meet a quality bar. But for the most important post of all – cabinet secretary there is no set process or rules at all. It is entirely up to the prime minister who they appoint. Historically they were heavily guided in that choice by the outgoing cabinet secretary. But in recent years that process has broken down.

In 2020 Boris Johnson forced Sedwill out of the post and after a convoluted and messy process ended up choosing Case, who had never run a department before, and was widely considered unqualified for the role. As one former permanent secretary put it to me: 'Simon Case would not be cabinet secretary in any normal situation . . . Simon got that job because he was willing to do their bidding. Basically, he was not fit for the job and, nice guy that he may be, that's a politicized appointment if ever there was one.'[38]

This is critically important because, historically, the cabinet secretary has been the guardian of civil service impartiality. Though the constitutional ground was always murky they would have stepped in to try and prevent something like the Scholar and Lovegrove firings, and would have had the authority to do so. Case did not and there has been a serious loss of faith across the civil service in his leadership.

A senior official who has recently worked for a difficult minister explained to me why it has been so damaging: 'I feel there has definitely been a shift. [Until Jeremy Heywood died] there was always a sense that someone had your back. That ultimately when push comes to shove, someone will stand up and say: "No, we're not going to do this." We saw this all the time with a minister who would try and weaponize the civil service code. He would say things like, "You're in breach of the civil service code, if you don't give me that advice." Under Heywood or Gus O'Donnell there was a sense that the Cabinet Office would ride in and talk to the minister and say, "Don't be a dick, you can't weaponize this code. It's not how it works." That has definitely declined. And that means that people are much more afraid of giving impartial advice. Because there is just much more of a sense that you're on your own in departments.'[39]

Sometimes this shift towards a civil service less able to be genuinely impartial in its advice is described as 'politicization'. But this isn't quite right. The people who end up in key jobs – like Case – are not party apparatchiks, or notably enthusiastic about government policy, as they would be in a genuinely politicized senior civil service like America's.

Simon Case's WhatsApp messages released during the Covid Inquiry indicate his deep unhappiness with Boris Johnson and Dominic Cummings. In a lengthy exchange with Sedwill just before the latter quit Case wrote, 'I've never seen a bunch of people less well-equipped to run a country . . . I was quite direct in telling [John-son] that lots of the top-drawer people I had asked [to work in No. 10] had refused to come because of the toxic reputation of the oper-ation.'[40] But he was prepared to take the job and he was prepared to be obsequious to Cummings and Johnson in other exchanges, which meant they felt they could control him better than a more experi-enced appointment. Similarly the people who replaced Tom Scholar at the Treasury or Jonathan Slater at the Department for Education are non-aligned civil servants of high integrity, not Tory party hacks.

What we have seen is the 'personalization' of the senior civil service, in a phrase used by Alex Thomas of the Institute for Gov-ernment. Ministers exercise greater authority over appointments and dismissals so they can have 'their people' in key roles while maximiz-ing loyalty and control. This is the worst of all worlds. An actually politicized civil service would have serious disadvantages, as is clear from Michael Lewis's book, *The Fifth Risk*, about three US govern-ment agencies under the Trump administration.[41] But at least, under good leadership, it means a team of people who support, and will work towards, the government's vision.

What we have is a disempowered civil service, increasingly fearful of genuine impartiality or offering their own policy solutions, but at the same time not signed up to any political vision. It is a recipe for paralysis.

Time for real reform

Should we go all-in on a more politicized approach, and accept that old-school impartiality is never coming back? Perhaps it would break down the barriers that a permanent and untouchable civil service can erect for governments with radical ideas. After all, it is relatively common in other countries. The US is an extreme example, where top officials switch entirely with every change in the Presidency. But there are other options. In Germany, for instance, the top rank of civil servants are explicitly called 'political', and often have party affiliations. Ministers can choose to remove them or recall them as they choose.[42]

The key difference is that those systems have other ways of providing a check on executive power. Both the US and Germany have, for instance, constitutional courts that cannot be overruled by their parliament. And in both countries significant power is held at state or regional level. In the UK, the executive is enormously powerful already, with high levels of centralization, and increasingly dismissive of Parliament when they have a majority. That makes genuinely impartial, and high-quality, advice from the civil service acutely important. Without it, ministers are much more likely to scupper their own intentions through bad policy design and a lack of focus on implementation.

The frustrations of reformers like Maude and Cummings are understandable and, indeed, shared by many civil servants. Over fifty years since the Fulton report it is still the case that there is too little specialist knowledge; far too little effective performance management; and too little focus on practical questions of delivery.

But their desire, as a result, to increase executive control even more is entirely wrongheaded. In a 2023 report for government, Maude proposed giving ministers more control over appointments and dismissals, and putting all senior civil servants on four-year contracts.[43] As one response put it: 'This would fundamentally change the incentives for senior officials to give confident, honest advice . . .

incentivizing pliant or conditioned behaviour.'[44] This is exactly what has happened already by doing the same for permanent secretaries.

Misuse of executive power has clearly made things worse. The rise of SPADs has created confusion because of the lack of clear rules about their remit, or mechanisms to apply the rules that do exist. Sometimes these two alternative systems for policy-making can work harmoniously together, but often it has meant pushing civil servants further away from giving honest advice. Repeated botched attempts to 'reform' the civil service by simply cutting jobs in an arbitrary way have led to a loss of talent and a huge amount of wasted time. Incredibly tight rules, imposed by ministers on senior officials, requiring approval to make basic operational decisions about their departments have hamstrung the system even more. Every attempt to exert control leads to greater dissatisfaction and a less effective system. It is yet another vicious spiral.

The alternative is the – admittedly harder – route of proper reform. But that requires understanding why every previous effort has failed. There has, no doubt, been some Sir Humphrey-like protection of the status quo over the years. However, the main fault lies with successive governments. Partly because, like many issues covered in this book, they have not prioritized it, despite its obvious importance in delivering their agenda successfully. And partly because it does not suit them to do so because their personal incentives are also entirely misaligned with good governance.

It is far easier to launch endless attacks on lazy, feckless, 'fat cat', 'woke' civil servants, and blame them for your failings. Announcing another set of arbitrary cuts or salary freezes or new 'tough' rules to stop people working from home will always get you a few friendly headlines. But doing it properly would require really thinking through the incentives created for officials. At the moment, as Blair's chief of staff Jonathan Powell put it, 'there is very little gain for an individual official who succeeds in resolving a problem and huge downside risk for permitting something to go wrong'.[45] Increasing executive control has only made this worse by exacerbating the 'blame culture'.

Before attempting any big-bang reform, the authority of the civil service needs bolstering to encourage many of those who have left to come back. Permanent secretaries need to have the authority, within their budget, to pay the salaries needed to recruit the right people and to reallocate funds from one project to another without being second-guessed at every stage by the Treasury.

They also need to be confident they will not be fired simply because a prime minister or secretary of state takes against them. That does not mean taking away all ministerial oversight over the process but increasing transparency. If the prime minister wants to remove someone, he or she should need to explain their reasons in full, with right to reply, and parliamentary scrutiny. It should be a power used only very occasionally and not as a tool to force ideological compliance. Likewise, while the prime minister should have the final say on the person running the civil service, the appointments (and dismissal) process should be open and transparent.

Once confidence has been restored, more substantive changes would be possible, as long as the prime minister made it a priority and appointed a cabinet secretary whose primary job was to drive through those reforms. Jonathan Powell proposed that: 'A prudent leader would introduce a new bargain whereby the government reduced the number of civil servants substantially, kept the best ones, ensured they had the right skills and paid them properly. Such a policy would come under fierce attack from the *Daily Mail*, which used to weigh in every time we appointed a highly paid expert to run a failing part of the bureaucracy, complaining about the waste of taxpayers' money. Actually employing an outsider to sort out the Immigration and Nationality Division in the Home Office, would save the taxpayer massively more than even a £1 million annual salary.'[46]

Almost everyone I spoke to agreed this was the right approach. It is obviously absurd, for instance, to think the government can have a world-class approach to digitizing public services while paying multiples less of the going rate for programmers. It would need to be accompanied by performance management based on achieving success rather than avoiding failure. It would need intensive well-designed subject-specific training programmes, as opposed to the extremely tokenistic and poor-quality courses currently available.

None of this is conceptually complicated or new. It is just that doing it is counter to all the incentives currently in the political system. Which is why governance needs to be tackled across the board rather than just seen as a civil service problem. Unless we improve the incentives for ministers, we will never get them right for anyone else. In the next part of the book, we turn to how changes to media coverage of politics have made these incentives so much worse.

PART 3

OVERDRIVE

7

THE RANDOM ANNOUNCEMENT GENERATOR

How PR became more important than policy

'We're beyond not believing the bullshit; mostly we don't even hear it now, dismissing it at the same deep level, below attention, where we also block out billboards and Muzak.'

DAVID FOSTER WALLACE, 'UP, SIMBA'[1]

'The purpose of a system is what it does.'

STAFFORD BEER

It was the first week of September 2010, and students were returning to school after the summer holidays. That meant it was 'schools week' on the Downing Street Grid. The Grid was first introduced by Alastair Campbell in 1997, as a day-to-day plan for coordinating government communications across different departments. But it quickly evolved into a way of controlling policy from the centre. A process designed as a way to sequence announcements to provide a steady diet of news quickly became a permanently hungry beast, demanding more and more policy from ministers and their advisers.

As an adviser in the Department for Education I had to feed the beast. Every September a 'Back to School' week appeared in the Grid, which meant three or four big policy announcements were required. In 2010 we hadn't yet finished developing our policy plans so had to scrabble around for ideas. Over the past several months we had been considering an idea to reward pupils who did a particular mix of more traditional subjects at GCSE. But no proper work had been done by the department and we had not talked to any headteachers about it yet. However, the minister, Michael Gove, was due to go on the BBC's Andrew Marr programme that Sunday and he needed something to say, so we decided it was the best idea we had.

At the time the department was leaking a lot so the announcement was worked up by a tiny team of ministers, advisers and one or two trusted officials. There was no consultation and it was done in two days. That Sunday Gove announced a new 'English Baccalaureate' to Marr.[2] (He called it that because it sounded European and *The Guardian* would like it.)

In the years since the announcement, that policy has had an enormous impact on schools. Some of it has been positive, in that it has delayed the total demise of foreign language teaching at GCSE. Some of it was negative, as there has been a big drop-off in many of the subjects, like music, that were not included. The core objective of the policy arguably makes sense. But there were better ways to do it and certainly better ways to gain the support of school leaders and teachers, who were understandably alienated by the absence of any consultation. The need for a rapid, and exclusive, announcement meant we ended up with a worse policy than necessary.

Over time I figured out how to appease No. 10 with announcements that sounded 'tough' and 'new' but were in fact both meaningless and harmless. We announced that we were giving headteachers the power to issue 'same-day detentions' to unruly pupils, a power they already had, several times. A favourite repeat announcement of Dominic Cummings was giving Ofsted the ability to launch 'dawn raids' to catch out schools that were gaming inspections. This was despite the fact that schools were not open at dawn for much of the year.

To give Dominic credit he thought, like me, that this process was mad – tactics in the absence of strategy. It was him who came up with the term 'random announcement generator' as a way of describing the Grid in the Cameron era. When he became Boris Johnson's senior adviser in Downing Street he largely ignored the Grid. But it was still there, sucking the life out of departments, and spewing out a constant stream of nonsense into the papers and TV news.

Our frustrations are widely shared. Nothing came up more regularly in the interviews for this book than the impossibility of making good policy in a world where media management is the overriding priority of government.

David Cameron's former head of policy Camilla Cavendish spoke for many when she told me: 'I hated the Grid, because the Grid creates another pressure: the amount of time that No. 10 spends worrying about the cycle of announcements, controlling the announcements made by other departments and the timetable. It's insane. It makes no sense at all. And then you're obsessed by the six and the ten o'clock news. And now 24-hour rolling news . . . '[3]

At the time of writing, there are twenty-five special advisers in No. 10 working on the political and media side and just twelve on policy. There is one adviser whose sole job is to manage the Grid. Liz Truss had fifteen advisers working in her press team (along with dozens of civil servants) and one adviser responsible for all public services including health, education and welfare.[4]

Despite the fact that almost everyone across government agrees this is a serious problem, no one can see a way out of the trap. Most expect it to get worse. As one former senior adviser to the Conservatives put it to me: 'I'm generally very bearish on politics . . . [because of the] long-term impact of social media and the media world we have on our ability to take long-term, consistent decisions. I can't see an answer to it because it's clearly deteriorating all around the world.'[5]

How and why has media management achieved such domination over policy?

The comms takeover

The symbiotic relationship between press and politics is not, of course, new. The modern political system emerged in the eighteenth century, alongside a proliferation of aggressive pamphleteering, so partisan (and often scatological) as to make even today's tabloids look positively sedate.

As the electorate grew so did newspaper circulation and thus its importance to anyone hoping for a successful political career. Most of the papers still around today emerged in the nineteenth century, with the *Daily Mail*, in 1896, the first to cater to the newly literate lower-middle classes, moving away from stuffy columns of society news and offering prizes, puzzles, gossip and sensation.

By the early twentieth century, politicians had learned the value of close relationships with newspaper proprietors. In 1901, Winston Churchill, who had made his name as a journalist reporting from the Boer War, arranged for his maiden parliamentary speech to appear on the front page of *The Times*. After defecting to the Liberals, he found a colleague, in David Lloyd George, even more attuned to using the press to his advantage. Lloyd George's relationships with editors were critical in helping him replace Herbert Asquith as prime minister in an unfriendly takeover during the First World War. The historian A.J.P. Taylor wrote of him that 'the editor of *The Times* has often thought himself more important than the prime minister. Lloyd George was the only prime minister who apparently shared this belief.'[6]

Once in No. 10, Lloyd George used profits from illegally selling honours to buy his own newspaper, *The Daily Chronicle*, which he then used to praise himself and place positive news stories. He also made a substantial profit on selling it eight years later.[7] The press was particularly important to Lloyd George because, having split from Asquith's Liberals and going into a precarious alliance with the Tories, he often needed to appeal over the heads of parliamentary colleagues. Likewise, Churchill was never fully comfortable in any party and ultimately became prime minister only because of the extreme circumstances of 1940. It is no coincidence that the two premiers who, as we saw in chapter one, did the most to build up the role of the prime minister as the centre of government, prior to Thatcher, were the two who also spent the most time buttering up newspaper proprietors.

Some of the more conventional prime ministers of that era found the growing importance of the media less appetizing. During a particularly vicious by-election in 1931, Stanley Baldwin attacked the owners of the *Mail* and *Express* in a way no modern politician would dare: 'The papers conducted by Lord Rothermere and Lord Beaverbrook are not newspapers in the ordinary acceptance of the term. They are engines of propaganda for the constantly changing policies, desires, personal wishes, personal likes and dislikes of two men.'

He went on, in his most famous line, written for him by Rudyard Kipling: 'What the proprietorship of these papers is aiming at is power, and power without responsibility – the prerogative of the harlot throughout the ages.'

Yet it was under Baldwin that the future relationship between politics and media in the UK was established, during the general strike of 1926. With government struggling for control, as the trade unions shut down Britain's infrastructure, ministers initiated the first Lobby briefings. The Lobby had existed as an accreditation system for a handful of selected political journalists since the late nineteenth century. It gave them access to the Members' Lobby in Parliament, where they could talk to MPs. But it was only during the strike that the government started to invite them in collectively, and separately from other journalists, for off-the-record briefings. It would be another five years before these briefings were regularized by the first Downing Street press secretary George F. Steward, after which the Lobby became a key component of the political system.[8]

The second innovation of the strike was government manipulation of the BBC, founded four years earlier to make use of new radio technology. With no newspapers available during the critical days of the strike, as print workers joined in, radio, for the first time, became essential to getting the government message out. Not only did the government insist that their line be broadcast, they also strongly discouraged BBC management from allowing the Labour leader Ramsay MacDonald or the Archbishop of Canterbury to respond with an alternative point of view. The BBC were facing a review of their funding and backed down. It would not be the last time the national broadcaster found itself in a compromised position.[9]

During the Second World War the press was subject to censorship and control on a level not seen before or since. But from 1945 relations normalized. There was, from this point on, always a press secretary in No. 10. Lobby briefings continued and broadcast news

234

became increasingly important as more households bought TVs. Suddenly how a politician looked, and how well they could handle the new medium, mattered.

Of all the prime ministers in the twenty years after the war, Anthony Eden was the most obsessed with the press, not that it did him much good. He was notoriously thin-skinned and bad-tempered, and would ring up editors, and BBC managers, to yell at them about unfavourable coverage. But it was Harold Wilson, another obsessive, who first understood the potential of modern media. He hired the first press secretary who was a political adviser rather than a civil servant, Joe Haines, and carefully crafted a genial pipe-smoking persona for TV appearances. Wilson's attention to detail was such that he called the BBC director-general to ask, successfully, that an episode of the enormously popular sitcom *Steptoe and Son* be delayed on the evening of the 1964 election until after the polls closed, worried that working-class Labour voters would stay home.[10]

Even under Wilson, though, the press was nowhere near as important to the day-to-day running of government as it was to become. Politicians of all stripes wanted to be popular, and influence public opinion, but the infrastructure of government was built around policy not communications. Most announcements were made in Parliament, and were not particularly coordinated. The small number of special advisers were mostly subject experts with little interest in communications. There was also far less media to manage, with only the papers and the (typically deferential) BBC and ITV, to worry about.

As Robin Butler, who was a senior civil servant in No. 10 under every prime minister, bar Callaghan, from Heath to Blair, told me: 'The media really, in my early years in No. 10, were not a very important factor. I mean, it wasn't a factor that dominated our lives. The press office did its thing. Donald Maitland [Heath's press secretary], you know, dealt with the press.'

But over his time in government: 'Politics changed. The age of deference ended, there was more challenge from the media, more penetration by the media, I think, of government. So the power of a No. 10 press office became more important.'[11]

Back in the Heath era, *The Times* still employed twelve journalists just to report proceedings of Parliament – three times as many as they had in the Lobby.[12] But as power centralized in favour of the prime minister and chancellor, Parliament lost importance. The focus shifted much more onto the Lobby and the soap opera of personalities and relationships. As Butler says, the soft-serve obsequious style of TV interviewing gradually changed thanks, initially, to presenters like Robin Day and Brian Walden, and then a new generation with a much more aggressive approach, led by Jeremy Paxman, who joined the BBC's *Newsnight* in 1989.

On the government side, it was Thatcher's press secretary Bernard Ingham who first properly understood how to harness this new interest in the prime minister to her advantage. He was technically a civil servant, but regularly went well beyond the civil service code into political territory and adored Thatcher. It was Ingham who introduced the first version of what later became the Grid, insisting all planned announcements and media appearances by ministers were cleared by his team.[13]

Thatcher was unusually (for a politician) uninterested in newspaper coverage – and was quite happy to skim Ingham's daily digest – but she fully understood the importance of image, especially as the first woman prime minister. She took editors into her confidence and was close to interviewers like Walden and commentators like Woodrow Wyatt, both of whom were disillusioned former Labour MPs. Walden, rather unethically, given he was then heading ITV's main politics show, wrote one of her election broadcasts. Neither was she above helping out proprietors, holding an infamous meeting with Rupert Murdoch as he was trying to buy *The Times* and *Sunday Times*, a purchase which the government ended up not referring to the Monopolies and Mergers Commission.[14]

Ingham figured out how to maximize the value of the Lobby, at this point still secretive and entirely off the record, to help burnish Thatcher's image. He handed out stories to journalists, using access to reward compliance, and rubbished any potential rival to her crown. Some journalists found him overbearing but most appreciated that he was making their job easier.

In contrast, John Major, despite being another media obsessive, had a series of very proper civil servants perform the press secretary role for him, like future cabinet secretary Gus O'Donnell. This meant everything was very above board but not helpful for his image, nor the government's ability to control the media agenda. Even papers traditionally friendly to the Conservatives like *The Sun* and *Telegraph* were mostly hostile as he stumbled from one hapless crisis to the next. The arrival of Sky News in 1989, the same year Parliament was televised for the first time, increased the intensity of the news cycle. The BBC later launched their own 24-hour channel, and their first online news service, in 1997.

Tony Blair was determined to avoid Major's fate. He centralized power into No. 10, reduced the role of cabinet, and gave his new press secretary, later upgraded to director of communications, Alastair Campbell, far more power than any of his predecessors.

Campbell explained the thinking to me: 'from talking to ministers in John Major's government and from civil servants, I knew that there was something not quite functional about it. The relations between media and politics had changed very, very quickly and they hadn't adapted to what was becoming a very different media landscape. My big thing in opposition had been strategic communication, the idea that you devise, execute and narrate strategy, and all three have to work together. I just felt the government didn't do that. And that was one of the reasons why John Major found it so frustrating. It was not necessarily anyone's fault. It was just that the systems didn't lend themselves to it. We exploited that, and we knew we had to change the systems when we got in, to avoid that being done to us.'[15]

With this in mind, Campbell introduced the modern Grid where weeks were allocated to particular topics, which departments were expected to support. Ministers who were not on message were kept away from interviews and every policy had to be considered with communications in mind, rather than it being an afterthought. The shift was obvious.

In October 1997 the journalist Matthew d'Ancona wrote: 'What distinguishes this government from its predecessors is the belief that presentation is not a secondary activity to be delegated to officials, but the first and most pressing task of every minister. New Labour does not regard news management as an ancillary function of government, but as its very essence.'[16]

For officials across government working on communications it was a shock. Jill Rutter was in charge of communications at the Treasury when New Labour arrived: 'They certainly thought that we were hopelessly amateurish and naïve. That was the Alastair Campbell and Charlie Whelan [Gordon Brown's media adviser] critique. And frankly, Ken Clarke [the outgoing Conservative chancellor] didn't particularly care about the press and the only newspaper that the Treasury cared about was the *FT*.

'Equally it's true to say that we applied much higher standards in dealing with the press. We didn't "manage" the press, feeding stories to favourites, or harangue journalists who put out stories we did not like. We didn't put out or confirm confected stories. And that was what made being the official press secretary to Gordon Brown completely impossible because you never knew what rubbish Charlie was spinning to the press.'

Rutter left after a few months, though she later returned to the civil service in policy roles. Her experience was not unique. Those who stayed either had political sympathies with the goals of the new government or were happy with a more aggressive approach to press management. Only a few months into the government there was a parliamentary inquiry into the politicization of government communications and Robin Butler was asked why so many civil service leads had quit, something he agreed was a 'disturbing and unsettling matter'.[17]

A narrative quickly developed around 'the dark arts' and 'spin', helped by the growing tensions between the Blair and Brown camps, which led to vicious briefing and a higher than desirable public profile for Campbell and Whelan. Campbell put Lobby briefings on the record, though journalists had to call him and his successors 'the prime minister's spokesman'. But that just meant the really juicy stuff was handed out to a smaller group of friendly journalists.

By the early 2000s, Campbell was arguably the best-known figure in the government after the prime minister and chancellor. This was especially so after he became embroiled in a bitter and very public row with the BBC over the death of Iraq War whistleblower David Kelly. He left government in 2003 after the row was resolved, largely in his favour, in an inquiry by former Lord Chief Justice of Northern Ireland, Lord Hutton.

But the model Campbell and his colleagues developed became embedded and, despite the initial controversies, it soon normalized. The modern era of government communications had begun. Increasingly ministers were promoted due to their ability to stay on-message and avoid making unwanted news in as unobtrusive a way as possible. Those who understood the value of providing a steady diet of announcements for the press were even more valued. Real policy knowledge, being increasingly centralized, was less relevant.

After the 2005 election the new Conservative leadership criticized the culture of spin in public while wholeheartedly adopting the New Labour model of media management. Cameron and Osborne were advisers during the Major era and sympathized with Campbell's diagnosis of out-of-date amateurism. One of Osborne's first jobs in politics was to prepare John Major's press digest in the months running up to the election, so he was well aware of the risks of poor media management. They professionalized the press and political operation, bringing in former *News of the World* editor Andy Coulson in 2007 to sharpen up their communications. Conservative Party headquarters had, by the time I was working there in 2009, become a factory for producing stories for friendly media outlets.

Papers like the *Mail* and *Telegraph* had always been helpful to the party (Major excepted) but by this point they would often print whatever they were given. The client journalism first used consistently by Ingham, and which had been institutionalized under Campbell, was now standard. And it was easier for the Tories because the written press was structurally biased towards them, due to the views of their proprietors.

By the 2010 election, there was not even the slightest pretence of independence. After Nick Clegg performed strongly in the first televised debate among prime ministerial candidates, Tory HQ went into a panic and everyone was ordered to dig up any dirt they could find on the Liberal Democrat leader. Story after story was handed over to *Mail* journalists, including one suggesting Clegg had made a 'Nazi slur' against the British people.[18]

This Campbell-esque approach to communications has drifted into becoming a habit rather than having any purpose. New Labour prioritized communications to win elections and manage media pressure but it was still in the service of a wider strategy and meaningful policy.

Increasingly the tactics have remained but the strategy has gone. It is a self-reinforcing problem. The more effort governments put into generating tactical announcements, and finding on-message ministers, the less scope there is for policy-making and long-term thinking. This panics central government into wanting more tactical announcements. If these ever had much effect on the public they don't any more.

It is like snacking on sweets and crisps when hungry rather than eating a proper meal – the empty calories may induce a brief feeling of satisfaction but often do harm in the long term. For instance, a favourite announcement over the years has been increasing prison sentences for whatever crime is in the news a lot at the time. This is one reason prisons are now completely full, and some criminals are being let out on early release, leading to bad press, and a real-world problem. How have the government responded? With more announcements about prison sentences.

As Theresa May's chief of staff Nick Timothy told me: 'whether you view the Grid as a proper strategic function or a short-term, tactical thing makes a huge difference. That's another way in which the modern No. 10 could work better.'[19]

The desperation for announcements has also meant smaller and smaller policies getting sucked into the Grid vortex. The less the government has anything genuinely significant to say, the more they have to squeeze news out of tiny non-events to fill the void.

Someone who used to work as a senior official at the Department for Education offered a good example of the kind of problems this causes: 'The annoying thing about the Grid is it's in too much detail. Right? Everything has to go through it. A lot of the time it was just operational stuff that you need to get out. Like you need to tell schools what they're supposed to do next week. And you can't . . .

'The coronation teaching materials [for King Charles' coronation] went out late because of the Grid. It's just a bloody lesson plan for primary teachers, and they need it in advance so that they can use it. But they got it two days before. It just didn't need to be in the Grid. The lesson plan for Key Stage Two, to be able to teach about the coronation, is not Grid-worthy.'[20]

Budget briefings and balls-ups

The traditional set pieces of the British political year have also been distorted by the all-encompassing needs of the Grid and the hunger for content. Budgets are a great example. Since Gladstone Budgets have been an annual opportunity for the chancellor of the day to set out the state of the economy and make changes they deem necessary. There have always been chancellors who used the opportunity to showboat, and a long history of overly aggressive corrections and counter-corrections, creating economic instability.

But under Gordon Brown Budgets morphed into a grander political event, an opportunity to take centre stage and set out a wide policy agenda that went well beyond the chancellor's normal remit. His spin doctors, like Whelan, and later Damian McBride, also used the opportunity to build up their boss's profile and keep journalists onside by feeding them titbits in advance. McBride was commendably honest about this process in his memoirs:

> In the fortnight before the speech, you want as little speculation about the Budget as possible, to keep your powder dry . . . So I'd tend to leak a few stories or planned announcements from other departments that could be guaranteed to cause a bit of distraction and keep the journalists busy for a day or two . . . If all that activity worked successfully, it meant we would get to the weekend before the Budget without a single good story from the package having leaked . . .
>
> That's where it became fun. From the forty to fifty readymade stories in the Budget, we would generally decide two or three that had to be held back until the day at all costs, and a few dozen that were too complicated, boring or unpopular to do in advance. That left us with about fifteen that could be released before the day, equating to one each for the main Sunday and daily papers.[21]

The two or three stories that were to be held back were the 'rabbits' (from a hat) – the surprise announcements that were supposed to grab attention, guarantee positive coverage for the chancellor and distract from bad economic news or changes that the Treasury did not want coverage for.

This whole process was so useful to Brown that his team built up the autumn statement – which had been introduced in 1975 as a fairly run-of-the-mill statutory requirement for a second economic forecast to be published each year – as almost a second Budget. This allowed for another stream of stories and announcements.

What was useful for profile building was terrible from a policy point of view. The need for pre-announcements and 'rabbits' has led to constantly changing and highly unstable tax policy. It is a key reason why the amount of tax law has proliferated so much in recent years and why the system, taken as a whole, makes so little sense, with random cliff edges and high marginal tax rates all over the place. Between 2004 and 2015 the number of annual tax measures grew from thirty to eighty a year.[22]

There have also been all sorts of reversals and embarrassments as tax plans made in secret with no consultation have unravelled when made public. Brown introduced the 10p income tax threshold in 1999 but then removed it in 2007 to pay for a reduction in the standard rate. This led to a major party revolt, much unfavourable media coverage, and a costly attempt to reverse the damage the following year.

George Osborne's 2012 Budget ended up unravelling so badly that it will forever be known as the 'omnishambles Budget'. A variety of apparently minor tax changes to VAT on things including hot food sold by bakeries and supermarkets, and static caravans, led to a bizarrely intense backlash and lots of U-turns. The problem was that Osborne's Lib Dem coalition partners had leaked all the 'rabbits' that the tax increases were paying for, leaving the papers with nothing positive to run on the day. It was a failure of media management but also an indictment of a process.

Phillip Hammond, as chancellor, tried to readjust, committing to only one annual set of tax changes. But in the chaos that followed his departure in 2019 things reverted back to multiple, and highly dysfunctional, sets of announcements each year. Most notably Kwasi Kwarteng's 'mini-budget' unravelled so badly that it brought down both him and his boss.

A former senior adviser to the Conservatives acknowledges that: 'The tax policy process is totally fucked because chancellors want to own this twice-a-year Budget process. Budget secrecy is necessary but it's massively abused to spring these half-baked ideas. We came in with good intentions [in 2010] but by year three, four or five, with an election looming, Budgets become these political opportunities. And that's what dominates everything. It's no mystery why we some-times make bad policies. It's very, very obvious.'[23]

It is not just tax policy. In 2011, when I was at the DfE, we got a call the night before the Budget to tell us the chancellor would be announcing tens of millions of pounds for another round of 'Uni-versity Technical Colleges' (UTCs), a pet project of Thatcher-era education minister Kenneth Baker. Michael Gove and the DfE offi-cials had not wanted to pursue this project further, and had not given any consideration to how it might be implemented. Unsurprisingly, many of the UTCs have ended up as expensive failures.

These 'night before' phone calls from the Treasury are dreaded across Whitehall. Vince Cable's former adviser Giles Wilkes told me about a similar experience from when his boss was business secretary: 'The 2011 Budget isn't much discussed because of the shambles of the year after. It had all sorts of sudden changes to North Sea tax, to environmental taxation, the introduction of carbon pricing. I had the CBI [Confederation of British Industry] on the phone to me saying what the actual has just happened. And I have no ability to be prepared for this, because the Treasury put these things up on its own. We've learned when the Budget came out, or maybe got a call twelve hours before.'[24]

The ability to leave things so late is one reason so much bad policy emerges from Budgets and autumn statements. Last-minute tweaks and fiddles can have unintended consequences. As a former senior official in the Cabinet Office told me: 'A chancellor like Ken Clarke had to finalize the Budget weeks in advance, so it could go to the printer. And then he'd go to the cricket. Whereas now, the day before, the night before, Budgets, they're still being tweaked and finalized. The scorecard still isn't really nailed down. And that's just an appalling way of doing business. And they do it because they can.'[25]

Pointless conferences and performative legislation

The same problem applies to party conferences. These used to be genuinely important events for parties to come together in the pre-internet era. There were meaningful debates about policy and dramatic moments of conflict like Neil Kinnock taking on the hard-left militants in his party in 1985, as they shouted back in outrage. But their purpose has become much less clear now that parties have shifted from being genuine mass movements to their modern hollowed-out state.

This is most true of the Conservatives, who had 2.8 million members in the early 1950s and now have around 150,000. But Labour have also dropped from a peak of over a million to around 400,000.[26] Conferences have become more stage managed, with fewer, shorter speeches, and those by ministers and shadow ministers are vetted closely in advance. They have become more expensive to attend, as their main role today is a fundraising opportunity, as hordes of lobbyists pay large sums for access to politicians. It is quite standard to attend events at conferences that have more lobbyists, think-tankers, and sector specialists than party members themselves.

A big part of the stage management is ensuring enough announcements to keep journalists occupied and out of trouble. If they have nothing to write about, they might go and find some crank at a fringe event being racist or spouting a mad idea and turn that into a story. Or they will try and manufacture a row between different party factions. The media management process is similar to the one McBride described for Budgets except it is coordinated by No. 10 not the Treasury.

As with Budgets, it leads to bad policy being designed on the hoof, and in secret, so as to have something to say. But unlike Budgets, where at least the media is very focused on the policy, at conferences, there is always a risk of more spicy, personality-based stories getting the attention. So, all the work on announcements does not even guarantee any positive coverage. In 2006 Gordon Brown's detailed speech was entirely ignored after it was claimed that Cherie Blair was overheard saying 'well, that's a lie' when the chancellor claimed he considered it a privilege to work with her husband. The allegation was denied but the damage was done.

It can be expensive though. In 2012, Nick Clegg was desperate for an education announcement for the Liberal Democrat conference. He used up a bargaining chip with David Cameron to get permission to announce a new £50 million a year 'catch-up premium' for eleven-year-olds who were behind at the start of secondary school. I, along with civil servants who did the bulk of the work, had to invent this thing in a few days. It was announced, got barely any mention anywhere at all, lasted a couple of years, and was binned by the Conservatives after the 2015 election. It was never evaluated and almost no one knows it ever happened.[27]

The following year Clegg and Cameron struck a bigger deal. The prime minister got permission to announce a marriage tax allowance worth £600 million a year at his conference, and in return his deputy got the go-ahead to spend £600 million on free school meals for all four-to-seven-year-olds.[28] The former was a complete waste of money. Even if you think the tax system should incentivize marriage, an allowance worth £200 a year maximum is not going to do that. Even the most abstemious wedding would cost several multiples of that.

There was some evidence base for expanding free school meals, but unfortunately no one told the Department for Education, because it had to be secret until the last minute. This meant no one had pointed out to Clegg that lots of primary schools did not have big enough kitchens. So, there was a mad scramble to implement the policy, with lots of other priorities dropped to make way. It is a hopeless way to run a country. And the public barely noticed either announcement anyway.

Rishi Sunak's shambolic announcement, at the 2023 conference, that he was going to replace the Manchester leg of HS2 with a variety of other transport projects, some of which turned out to already exist, was down to a similar lack of time and consultation.[29]

As if Budgets and conferences were not enough opportunity for badly thought through announcements, there is also a (usually) annual King's Speech. This is when the government set out their legislative programme for the next session of Parliament. Governments have, of course, always sought, when possible, to pursue legislation that voters would support. Until the New Labour comms revolution, though, those bills were actually meant to do something that would have a real effect in the real world.

As we saw in chapter four, the introduction of bill timetabling as standard has made it easier to jam legislation through Parliament quickly, with fewer opportunities to cause delays if a party's own backbenchers are onside. This has led to 'performative' legislation that has no purpose other than to show the government 'cares' about a public concern. The King's Speech is an opportunity to fill the news agenda for a few days with this type of legislation, though individual bills can be introduced at any time while Parliament is sitting.

It is hard to assess the growth in this phenomenon given no bill is formally designated as being performative. There are plenty of examples though. One is the rise of legislated targets where a government 'enshrines in law' their commitment to do something. This can have some value if there is a clear sanction on government for failing to meet the target, or if it creates a lever for campaigners to start a judicial review if the target is missed. On the whole, though, it is used, as 'a low-cost way for the government to give the appearance of vigorous action without actually having to commit to take measures in the short term', as one report wryly put it, 'so that Governments . . . [can] take political credit for their boldness without having to engage in proper policy discussion of the measures needed to achieve it.'[30]

In practice almost none of the legislated targets have stuck or made any difference. Ones introduced by Labour on fuel poverty (2000) and child poverty (2010) did not come close to being achieved. The Conservatives repealed the latter Act in 2016 with barely a murmur of criticism, despite supporting the initial legislation. The former is still in place, which, given almost no one knows about it, rather testifies to its lack of effectiveness. Cameron passed legislation to force the government to spend 0.7 per cent of GDP on overseas aid but when Boris Johnson chose to drop that commitment in 2021, he just used a large loophole in the initial Act to do so. In 2010 the chancellor Alistair Darling passed an Act enshrining a commitment to halve the deficit by 2014, which was a lot easier than actually cutting spending (the Tories repealed the Act in 2011).[31]

Other types of performative legislation are more subjective, as most bills claim to be doing something meaningful even if they are not. Did Tony Blair really need quite so many counter-terrorism Acts? Have we really needed a new criminal justice or policing Act in more or less every parliamentary session since 2000? A lot of unnecessary work has gone into making sure governments can point to legislation as evidence of action.

We have had two Acts relating to asylum seekers, one in 2022 and one in 2023, where almost the sole purpose was to indicate the government cared about the issue. The 2023 Illegal Migration Act acknowledged in the introduction to the bill that it was likely not to be legal, but it was passed anyway. Why? Because Rishi Sunak had, as one of his five big pledges on becoming prime minister, promised to pass an Act to stop small boats crossing the channel. He hadn't pledged to actually stop them, but to pass an Act.

An even more unsubtle example was the Strikes (Minimum Service Levels) Act introduced in January 2023. This was rushed out in order to create a 'dividing line' with Labour after various public sector and transport unions announced industrial action at the end of 2022. The Conservatives wanted to put forward legislation that Labour could not support so they could get lots of headlines about their opponents being in the pockets of the unions. This they achieved, but the Act itself was a complete mess and entirely unnecessary. The bipartisan Regulatory Policy Committee gave it a red rating and called it 'not fit for purpose', saying, bluntly, that 'the Department makes use of assumptions in the analysis which are not supported by evidence'.[32] The Joint Committee on Human Rights, another bipartisan group of MPs and lords, said it failed to meet human rights obligations.[33] It passed anyway.

This drift towards legislation designed for the news cycle rather than the real world is, perhaps, even more damaging than the misuse of Budgets and party conferences. It represents a phenomenal waste of time for departments, ministers, MPs, and all the organizations that have to engage with the legislation. There is also an opportunity cost. This is taking place while all the real problems that need attention are languishing in the 'too difficult' box.

The dozens of announcements required for the Budget and conferences, plus eye-catching legislation needed for the King's Speech, plus manifestos, plus the day-to-day need to fill the Grid and keep journalists busy, creates an enormous burden to keep cranking out policy. It is not unusual for the same announcement to be made half a dozen times in different ways, rather than governments actually fixing problems. It is one reason the civil servants that get promoted quickest are not necessarily the ones best suited to working on delivery and long-term reforms but are the best at coming up with gimmicks for the Grid.

It is also a major cause of the centralization into No. 10 and the Treasury, described in section one, because the need to have control over every announcement inevitably reduces autonomy in departments and at local level. Giving away power means having fewer things to put in press releases. And it is connected to the increasing attempts to evade scrutiny discussed in section two. Announcements and bills designed mainly for media consumption are not something governments want to be scrutinized, plus rushed announcements and poorly thought through laws lead to more judicial reviews. Overall, this focus on perception rather than substance produces such frantic activity that proper government becomes impossible. It is no wonder the public have tuned out.

Reasserting the primacy of policy

A world in which communications tactics and message discipline have become the driving force behind politics is the only one in which Liz Truss could have ended up as prime minister. She was a minister for a full decade before getting the top job, yet did not have a single significant achievement to her name, nor even any substantive policy ambition associated with her.

As Rory Stewart, who was a junior minister to Truss at DEFRA (Department for Environment, Food, and Rural Affairs), notes in his memoir: 'I was told she had been promoted faster than anyone because she was a "strong media performer". Intrigued by this, I had watched a number of her interviews. In none of them had she reflected, apologised, explained, emphasised, or attempted to persuade. Nor did she ever, except in the rarest cases, answer a question. Instead, she approached interviews as broadcasts, opportunities to repeat the party attack line, never giving ground, or varying her tone. I wondered how Cameron had developed any views on her skills as a minister.'[34]

Her approach to policy-making was to see it as an opportunity for coverage rather than to make any real-world difference. At one point she asked Stewart for a plan for National Parks, and when he asked for a month to do it properly, he was told, 'You have three days . . .

We need to get it into the *Telegraph* on Friday.' He writes: 'The details, it seemed, hardly mattered at all, nor did their implementation, for this was only a press release, masquerading as a plan . . . she used provocative policy statements to create an impression of forcefulness.'[35]

Not only did this approach ensure Truss got repeated promotions, but it also helped her build her profile with the Tory membership who read the papers that uncritically print these press releases and policy statements. That meant she was well placed to win the leadership, and her campaign, even more than usual, was all about using image to define herself to this audience.

Ultimately, whatever the stated purpose of an organization is, ambitious people within it will follow the incentives that exist in reality. If that incentive is to focus on media and image in order to get more rapid promotions and build profile, then that is the route politicians will follow, even if they find it somewhat undignified (not something that ever seemed to bother Truss). They will privilege relationships with the most important political journalists over the success of the government as a whole. Truss was known as one of the most inveterate leakers in cabinet.

There are still ministers who work away quietly on genuine policy change. Rory Stewart cites David Gauke, his former boss at the Ministry of Justice, as an example. The easy route for justice ministers is just to try and sound as tough as possible on sentencing, given criminals are not the most popular group with the public, and the papers love crackdowns. But Gauke was well aware that the evidence of the benefits of short sentences for low-level crimes is weak. They are expensive, take up precious prison space, and do not lead to lower levels of reoffending than community sentences. So he developed a policy to scrap sentences of less than six months.

But even when you get ministers prepared to try and govern, at the cost of personal profile (Gauke was widely attacked in the Tory press), they are rarely in post long enough to see any reform through. Gauke left government when Boris Johnson became prime minister, and his successors scrapped the reform, reverting back to endless press releases and legislation about being tough on sentencing, despite an unsustainable and unaffordable rise in the prison population. What's the point in thinking long-term when there is a negative impact on your career from doing so and there is nothing you can do about it anyway?

The only way this will change is when party leaders, and their top teams, prioritize policy over communications again. At the moment they are trapped in a game they cannot win, believing that a certain way of doing politics is the only choice available. Naturally many of those in senior communications roles have no interest in dispelling this belief. But it very obviously isn't working, even on its own terms. The public have switched off because they can see the chaos behind the headlines.

Politicians cannot 'manage' the media cycle as they did in Alastair Campbell's day and attempting to do so is proving counterproductive. The more effort put into trying to control the narrative, the less attention voters are paying to what the parties are saying. Despite a huge increase in time and resources put towards communications, politicians of all parties are less trusted than ever before.[36] The deprioritizing of policy in favour of tactical announcements may get you through the day, but it gives you nothing to talk about after years in office.

The idea that politicians could choose to reorient the system might sound Panglossian. It is easy to understand why so many interviewees feel trapped by a system they cannot control. But there are reasons for hope. For one thing, there is a better strategy already available and already used by the more effective ministers.

As Gabriel Milland, who ran communications for several government departments, told me: 'I have a mantra that good policy is good comms. In the end if you have the right policy, the newspaper columns will be good. As long as you don't fuck it up . . . I mean, leave the comms people to obsess with the comms. But if policy officials and ministers have decided to focus on the comms, then you've probably got a bad policy.'[37]

This echoes Alastair Campbell's stated principle that comms should be in the service of wider government strategy, even if it's not one New Labour always stuck to. The issue is that it takes a lot of confidence to go with this approach. It also requires an actual interest in policy and the ability to develop and implement it. In this sense solving this problem is downstream of solving the problems set out in the first two sections. A better-functioning government, that is making better use of the wider British state, will rely less on tactical comms to survive.

Politicians could, though, make their lives easier by scrapping the big set-piece moments that drive so much of the announcement fever. Many think-tanks and commentators have argued that the government should move from two fiscal events a year – a Budget and an autumn statement – to one, so as to reduce complexity in the tax system due to a constant stream of new measures.

But why does there even need to be a Budget, in the way we currently hold them, at all? Why not treat finance legislation as the same way we treat any other, with draft proposals as and when they are needed, that can then be subject to proper debate and scrutiny? There is no intrinsic need to change the tax system every year, or have a single document packed with random policy announcements from across government to keep the media happy.

Why, you might wonder, would ministers be willing to give up the opportunity to seize the agenda and boost their poll ratings? The answer is that is never does. The average poll change from Budgets since 2010 has been 0.1 per cent. All that work, all that rushed policy, for no benefit.[38] The opportunity cost is vast.

The same is true of party conferences. They also require a huge amount of work. There are lots of announcements that create even more work. And what is the benefit? At best parties get through the week unscathed and avoid falling out publicly. Conferences raise a bit of money for the party coffers but it is not remotely worth the cost and could easily be replaced with more low-key regional events.

The Grid needs to stay in some form – there needs to be some coordination of big policy announcements to avoid clashes. Departments should, though, be given far more freedom to release information, that is of limited general interest, to their sector. Communications do matter. Persuading people of your plans and explaining them clearly are important functions of government. But it must be subservient to policy.

8

HIGH SPEED CRASH

How the internet turned politics into a frantic mess

'Social media is basically a plague on politics.'

TONY BLAIR[1]

'What's the news? Just tell me what the fucking news is and I'll put it on the front page. It's not like we're the Independent. *We can't just stick a headline saying CRUELTY then stick a picture of a dolphin or a whale underneath it.'*

ADAM KENYON, FICTIONAL *DAILY MAIL*
NIGHT EDITOR IN *THE THICK OF IT*

To many readers it will, no doubt, seem ridiculous, that something as ephemeral as Twitter could make a big difference to the way government works (I refuse to call it 'X', whatever Elon Musk says). Fewer than half of British adults have ever used Twitter and most that do check it only occasionally and rarely, if ever, post. But in Westminster, everyone is on it and most check it obsessively. It has changed the way politicians and officials consume information, and completely changed the job of a political journalist.

For politicians who experienced the transition from the pre-social-media age the effect has been profound, as Ed Balls explained

257

to me: 'The intensity of the news cycle just changes things so much. When Margaret Thatcher was prime minister she didn't experience anything like the news cycle intensity that politics has now . . . When we were in opposition, the only reporting was John Sergeant and Robin Oakley on the BBC six and nine o'clock news. And there was time to stand back. See what had happened, work out what you were going to say, and then go do it.

'By the time you get to later Blair and Brown, then you could have a story which is started at any time and that is iterating with its own life on broadcasts and social media. And so the pressure builds and it's much harder to not say something immediately. And I think that is a real material difference.'[2]

In the 2000s, pioneering political bloggers like Iain Dale and Paul Staines (aka 'Guido Fawkes') became required reading across Whitehall. There was a watershed moment in April 2009. Staines acquired emails sent by Brown's adviser Damian McBride that encouraged a friend, running a Labour-supporting website, to publish a bunch of unsubstantiated rumours about senior Conservatives. For the first time a major political story, that led news bulletins, had been broken by a blogger. This was the changing media landscape that Balls was referring to.

Twitter launched in 2006 but was, at first, barely used. It was seen as a bit of a joke where boring people told you what they'd had for lunch. But then a few celebrities, most notably Stephen Fry, started signing up and gaining thousands of followers. By 2009, political journalists were seeing the potential benefits.

Paul Waugh, who joined the Lobby in the late 1990s, was one of the first: 'I thought it was amazing. But at first the rest of my colleagues were all really anti. I just could tell straight away that this was perfect for hacks, because it just replicates the way we work. Yes, the gossipy stuff, the slightly nerdy stuff, you know, the good and the bad. And so, that I think was a big moment, particularly as more and more politicians and more and more journos saw the value . . . Then hacks could see you could get stories from this medium, because the politicians had joined it . . . So they might say something there that they wouldn't say somewhere else.'[3]

The shift, once it started, happened fast. In a July 2009 interview, David Cameron may have said that 'too many tweets make a twat', but within a few years of his government taking power, most of his MPs were happily tweeting, and it was changing the whole way the media worked.

Gabriel Milland has worked on both sides of the divide, as a Lobby journalist for the *Express* newspaper from 2006–10 and then, from 2011–17, running press and communications at several government departments as a civil servant. He explained to me how the rise of social media, and online news, changed the relationship between media and government: 'We no longer have a cycle that begins every morning afresh, with news editors going into newsrooms having conversations with political editors and saying: "What's the news today? What are we going to follow up from yesterday? What's going to happen today?" Those conversations do happen, but they're not as important as they used to be. We now have a news stream, which can be switched on or switched off. It can last for five minutes, or it can last for five weeks. Something will be incredibly important for five minutes. Or it will be incredibly important for five weeks. Social media will drive a lot of that.'

The speed and suddenness with which stories emerge puts pressure on ministers and departments to spend even more of their time monitoring, responding and managing this constant stream of news. As Milland told me: 'It basically means that you just have to be quicker. Much quicker. Government communications, civil service communication, is not particularly well set up for this at all, although the best government spinners are without doubt the best spinners anywhere in the business. I think there's two approaches you can take. And there's a tension between the two approaches. The first one, which has ebbed and flowed inside Whitehall many times, is that news no longer matters nearly as much as it did. That fewer and fewer people are reading newspapers. Which is true. And their content matters less, which is sort of true, but not entirely. This is what the civil service communications, bureaucracy, and some ministers think, although not all of them. And what most ministers think is, "Oh, my God, the *Daily Mail* has said this about me, stop them saying this about me," or, "I want the *Daily Mail* to say this about me and my policy . . . we need it in the *Daily Mail*." '4

All the incentives, in terms of promotion and future leadership prospects, are to take the second path and obsess about the news stream. Ignoring it will significantly improve your chances of developing good policy but probably harm your career. This is even more true during periods of extreme political instability, of the kind the UK has experienced since Brexit, when no one has any sense of security in their current role.

For Milland there is a way through the tension. When he was at the Ministry of Justice he was working for Michael Gove, a rare minister who was genuinely interested in policy change, and who wanted to take a fairly similar approach to the one David Gauke later tried: 'We were trying to run a very liberal prisons policy. We were going to make prisons places that were not warehouses of awfulness, but were actually functional. And we wanted to send fewer people there. My job there was to communicate this to the Tory press and to keep them as onside as possible. We needed to have the political cover to do it . . . We did it by centering the victim at all times . . . saying "we're doing this because we want fewer people to be bashed on the back of their heads", creating some messaging that we knew would work with the Tory press, with reactionaries. While the previous regime at MoJ had effectively banned journalists from prisons, we opened them up. We needed people to know just what a disgusting state most were in – although they have probably got worse since then. If reform was going to happen, we needed a burning platform. In other words, we needed people to believe it was an urgent and acute problem, not a chronic one which could be effectively forgotten about. The media was vital for that. So we did things like let the BBC broadcast live from inside a prison for the first time ever. That's one way you can use the media to achieve political and policy objectives in government, though it's high risk and I had a few sleepless nights.'[5]

But, as he acknowledges, this is a hard trick to pull off and required existing good relations with the Tory press, which Gove had from his time attacking the left-wing 'Blob' as education secretary, and because of his support for Brexit. Most ministers prefer to appease the press without trying to win them over to a noble cause they will not naturally support. Especially as all that policy work again turned out to be pointless. Like Gauke after him, Gove was fired before he could drive through any real change.

The Lobby takeover

The growing intensity of the 'news stream', hasn't just changed the behaviour of politicians but the whole structure of the political news industry. In turn, this has degraded the quality of coverage and made it easier for politicians to pursue bad policy and avoid scrutiny.

For a start, the increasing dominance of online news has changed the economics of the media business. The sale of physical newspapers has collapsed over the past fifteen years. As of September 2023 the *Daily Mail* had a circulation of 729,000, a 66 per cent drop from 2,144,000 in September 2010. It is continuing to fall at 1–2 per cent a month. According to industry insiders, it nevertheless outsells *The Sun*, which no longer publishes circulation figures, but was selling almost 3 million copies a day in September 2010.[6]

Most of the larger newspapers have found a way to achieve profitability in the face of such headwinds, but it has required a major reduction in the number of specialist journalists. When I started working in education policy, every major newspaper had at least one education specialist. There are still a few but it is a much diminished group. This is true in every sector.

The centralization of policy development and communication within Westminster has been mirrored by a centralization of policy coverage within newspapers. These days, the Lobby write the big policy stories, as well as covering political news about who's up and down, and which politicians have fallen out with each other. This has several consequences. Firstly, the number of general Lobby correspondents has stayed the same size, or grown at some papers, even as overall staff numbers have plummeted. Secondly, they have to write far more stories about far more things they cannot possibly have expertise in. Which means government can get away with far more.

The demands of the news cycle create just as much frantic, and often pointless, activity for journalists as they do for politicians and their advisers. As Francis Elliott, who has spent most of his career in the Lobby, and was political editor at *The Times* from 2013 to 2021, told me: 'What's changed most is that political journalism now feels much more like ball-by-ball commentary, and much less like a match report. Which means essentially you're doing two jobs. You are getting out there, on social media, everything that you think won't hold. It incentivizes immediate disclosure of information. But if you're a good, or aiming to be a good, journalist you're simultaneously trying to keep back your bangers as exclusives. It's exhausting.'[7]

Paul Waugh compared the job today to what it was when he started: 'When I arrived you'd start at half nine, you'd read all the papers, you'd chat to your news desk, you'd come up with a rough list of stories based on the order paper [Parliament's agenda for the day], then you go to a Lobby briefing at Downing Street at 11 a.m. You'd discuss it with your colleagues, then you go to lunch. Normally a long liquid lunch, and then before you know it, it was the 4 p.m. afternoon briefing. And then after all that process, you'd write a story, maybe two. The pace of things was different . . . And there was time to step back and make a decision . . . And to build a relationship.

'Obviously, people still have lunches and cups of tea, which is crucial. That's the lifeblood of this place . . . But now in that middle stretch of the day you'll be tweeting, you'll be contributing to a podcast, you'll be on various bits of media that are not your own media . . . You'll be helping the broadcasters fill out time. And again, that's good for promoting yourself and your paper, you know, it's good for the brand. And so your employers like you to do it, but it shortens the amount of time you've got to do other things.'[8]

The lack of time to think would be bad enough if the Lobby were just writing the types of story they have always written. But more and more they also have to cover policy stories. As Milland explains: 'The *Express*, when I worked for it, was selling well over a million copies a day and making a lot of money. There were over a hundred journalists. There are now maybe thirty, some ludicrously small number.

But there is still a Lobby team of three at the *Express*. It's an extreme example but it's happened to some degree everywhere. So the economics of newsroom budgets dictate some stories that would not have been Lobby stories, that would have gone to specialists before, now get done by the Lobby. The Lobby do stories in a different way to other journalists . . . The instinct of every single Lobby hack is to cover every single policy story as a row or a scandal . . . Even very good ones do this. I can think of one upmarket national daily which seems to have decided this is the main way it's going to cover Westminster – as a succession of scandals.'[9]

The broadcasters – BBC, ITV and Sky – have now followed the papers into making nearly every story a Lobby story, partly because they have made cuts of their own, but also because they follow the pack. Policy is increasingly covered in terms of what it means for the political fortunes of those involved, which is what the Lobby knows, and not whether it is actually achievable or not, whether it might have positive effects, or what the historical precedents might be, which would require specialist knowledge.

The more technical the policy area, the more this is the case. Talk to an expert on online safety, AI regulation or international trade deals about the coverage of their area, and they will quickly have their head in their hands. Many viewers were frustrated during the pandemic to see press conferences, with medics and scientists, dominated by political correspondents trying to pick apart internal disagreements within government rather than ask about the health implications of various policy decisions. Arguably more scrutiny from specialist health correspondents could have forced the government into better decisions.

Economics is another area to suffer. In 2022 the BBC commissioned a review of their economics coverage, which highlighted the instinct to turn every story into a political one as a major issue: 'We agree with the many interviewees who said an elephant in the room is politics. Close attention to politics feels as though it ought to nurture impartiality. We find that without similarly close attention to the economics, it can be a threat to impartiality. Politically led news is vulnerable to groupthink, just as politics itself can become a bandwagon, while other perspectives, perhaps from other specialists, speaking to the interests of other groups, are overlooked or crowded out.'[10]

As one of their interviewees put it: 'Political editors are being asked to be experts in the economy, macro-economics, the Constitution, trade, law, political negotiations and who's up and who's down in four different administrations and nobody can do that. The only possible result of asking a political editor to front all of those things is they look foolish.'[11]

This fixation on the political, at the expense of the important details, not only means the public are less well-informed but also makes it easier for politicians to avoid scrutiny. Lobby journalists don't know the really difficult questions to ask.

Moreover, they prize novelty above all else and measure themselves against their competition on the basis of exclusives. As Francis Elliott says, it is 'how they keep score' and build their personal brand. Even being the first to announce something on Twitter by thirty seconds can build your following versus others. Ultimately every political correspondent is a sole trader for whom access to information is their main commodity, precisely because they are not experts or specialists.

This curiosity, this obsession with uncovering the new, has real value. It is what made journalists like Pippa Crerar, now at *The Guardian*, and ITV's Paul Brand, spend months uncovering the

Partygate scandal, with a succession of revelations that built into the storm that eventually finished off Boris Johnson.

As Waugh says, this hunting for exclusives 'is the lifeblood of what we do in the sense that you want to be not just first, but first with the good stuff. And that does get you up in the morning because you want to find out something new and you want to share it. That's the *raison d'etre* and why I'm so excited by doing this damn job . . . But the exclusivity bit, yeah, I can see if you're not in the business it seems almost like a waste of energy. But I think it's useful because it does drive the competition.'[12]

As a mentality, this is important, if what you are doing is covering political stories like the Blair/Brown disagreements or a Boris Johnson scandal. These things really matter. But when political correspondents are asked to cover complex and long-running policy stories it is much less helpful. For a start, the obsession with novelty drives the need for the endless stream of new government announcements that can be given out, like sweeties, as exclusives to different papers.

It also means the government can be relatively confident that the outcome of a policy will get far less coverage than the initial announcement. A minister primarily motivated by press coverage will focus on the attractiveness of the announcement – particularly its ability to create controversy that suits their political positioning – rather than the workability of the policy. In the long run, failure might become visible to voters but by that point the minister will likely have moved on to a different job.

Immigration policy is the perfect example. On any measure the Conservative government have failed to tackle the basics of managing the asylum system. This is regardless of whether one has a broadly liberal or conservative view of what the system should look like. The speed with which the Home Office process asylum seekers has fallen dramatically, leading to a large and expensive backlog of immigrants unable to work and stuck in hotels. Removals of those whose asylum applications have failed has also completely dropped away in recent years.

Yet these serious failures have been largely ignored in favour of, at times almost daily, stories briefed by the Home Office about some new way to be 'tough' on immigrants, who already have utterly miserable lives, stuck in limbo with barely any money. Many of these announcements never happen in reality, or are distractions that make things worse by sucking up officials' time. There were, in 2023, far more articles about the *Bibby Stockholm* – the barge used to house a small number of migrants – than any of the real reasons why the backlog of asylum seekers has grown so large in the first place. Proposals to deport people to Rwanda have been front-page news since they were first announced in spring 2022 but, as of writing, not a single person has been removed via this route.

One reason these tactics work, at least in the short term, is that these policies are seen, by friendly papers, as ones that will help the Conservatives politically (with little evidence – in September 2023 83 per cent of the population thought the government was handling immigration policy badly).[13] But it is also because the novelty of these contentious policies suits political correspondents of all stripes. The BBC have also covered Rwanda, and the use of barges, far more than any of the real issues with the asylum system. And despite the poor polling, it has worked politically for the now former home secretary Suella Braverman, who has become the darling of the right of the Conservative Party, and is regularly touted as a future party leader, despite having achieved less than nothing while doing the role.

The shift in the business model of the biggest newspapers has had another, more subtle, detrimental effect, precisely because the physical paper is no longer as important to the bottom line. Their money is now made primarily online either from advertising, like the *Mail* or *Sun*, or from subscriptions, like *The Times*.

Somewhat paradoxically, the less financially important the physical paper is, the more it can become a plaything of proprietors and editors. The difference between the *Mail Online* and the daily paper is instructive. The former is ecumenical when it comes to what it covers and the tone it uses. If there are clicks to be gained by criticizing a government policy that the daily paper has fully supported, they will happily write and promote that story. But the core purpose is to maximize traffic, page views, and time spent on each page, leading to more advertising revenue.

The daily paper meanwhile has become, more than ever, a mechanism for government propaganda, pushing the agenda of a faction within the Tory party. The target audience are Conservative Party backbenchers and broadcasters, who might feel they have to follow up a story, not the public. Likewise, the government often use these newspapers to communicate with, and manage, their own back-benchers rather than the wider public, for whom there are better avenues. Increasingly the whole thing is becoming a closed loop that is less and less connected to any real-world audience.

Covid was a good example. The remaining readerships of the *Mail* and *Telegraph* were strongly in favour of lockdowns, given they are mostly retired and, thus, were both at higher risk from the virus, and not overly worried about pursuing an exciting social life. Yet the papers pursued a strongly anti-lockdown line. The intended audience was not their subscribers but Tory MPs and Downing Street.

As Milland, who was brought back into government to help with

268

communications during the pandemic, explains: 'What *The Daily Telegraph* said was extremely uninfluential with the public during the pandemic. It was ludicrously unpopular and out of touch . . . But it was highly influential on policy development, because the prime minister had a kind of oedipal relationship with *The Daily Telegraph*.'[14]

Boris Johnson made his name as a *Telegraph* journalist, reporting, with wild inaccuracy, on the EU. More recently he had been a highly paid columnist for the paper. Their view mattered to him a lot. Dominic Cummings confirmed that their anti-lockdown stance played heavily on Johnson's mind, and that he even referred to the paper as 'my real boss', when one would have hoped he'd have considered that the British public held that role.[15]

Johnson was unusually personally susceptible to press influence. But even prime ministers who try to be a bit less media driven, like Theresa May or Rishi Sunak, cannot ignore the impact that these newspapers have on their own party, even as their circulation dwindles. For instance, in 2023, the Department for Education had to spend an enormous amount of time reviewing sex education, and looking at how to give parents access to information about what was being taught to their children, following an extensive press campaign by backbencher Miriam Cates, which appealed to many of her colleagues. There was no real problem here, no widespread public concern or outrage. But it became a focus for policy nevertheless.

Until recently, broadcast news had been fairly well protected from these trends. The BBC, in particular, comes in for huge criticism from all sides, and can sometimes take an overly defensive posture when it knows this criticism is coming. But, like Sky and ITN, they do at least aim to produce non-partisan news, even if they sometimes miss the target. As such they are more trusted than the papers by the public, and BBC online news is by far and away the most widely used source of information in the UK. In 2021 though, an overtly partisan cable news channel, GB News, was launched, followed by Talk TV (which subsequently went online-only) the following year. The regulation of broadcasters by Ofcom is in theory supposed to be stronger than for written media, but it has been shown up to be largely toothless. In any case, the rise of social sites like YouTube and TikTok as a way of accessing news makes Ofcom's remit appear increasingly redundant.

The partisan TV channels have small audiences, but again a large part of their purpose is political influence rather than profitability. As of late 2023, GB News employed four Conservative MPs as presenters, including the then deputy chairman of the party Lee Anderson, and provided a platform for a growing faction within the party. Which means they can't be ignored by the Tory leadership, despite having a vastly smaller audience than the BBC or ITV. There is also cross-fertilization of ownership. Talk TV is owned by the Murdochs. One of the main shareholders in GB News is hedge fund billionaire Paul Marshall, who is also heading a bid to buy the *Telegraph*.

As Tim Montgomerie, who founded a political website called Unherd, funded by Marshall, acknowledges: 'Paul really believes in freedom of speech and liberty and he fears the British economy is going the wrong way. He wants to shape the wider culture, so he is investing because of a political agenda.'[16]

Stanley Baldwin was bemoaning the niche interests of proprietors back in the 1930s, but what has changed is the business model. Marshall, if he buys the *Telegraph*, can make money on online advertising and subscriptions, while using the physical paper and his loss-making TV channel to strongly influence the Conservative Party. John McTernan, who was, among other roles, Tony Blair's director of political operations, had an interesting analogy for this phenomenon: 'For me, the current relationship between the government – the Tories – and the media is a similar relationship we [Labour] used to have with the trade union movement, which was to attach ourselves to a drowning man. Don't go near a drowning man, they'll drown you to stabilize themselves.'[17]

The difference, though, is that the trade unions were permanently weakened by legal changes under the Thatcher government, and more broadly by deindustrialization, which made it possible for Labour to, at least partially, detach themselves under Tony Blair. The media industry has been destabilized, and it has caused serious problems for the Conservatives, who are increasingly attached to a group of newspapers and TV stations that have limited public appeal. But these companies are not drowning; they are mostly profitable because of their online operations. This is going to make it hard for the Conservatives to manage their way out of this new equilibrium, given it could continue for some time.

While this is a bigger problem on the right of politics it also causes headaches for Labour. They cannot simply ignore the fringe right-wing media complex, because it still has an oversized influence on the less-partisan media that most voters do consume. The BBC, who spend much fruitless time trying to convince the right they aren't a bunch of 'latte-sipping liberals', often make a point to reflect the news agenda elsewhere. For instance, Labour advisers were deeply frustrated in early spring 2023 when Keir Starmer made a speech about cracking down on criminal anti-social behaviour, only to see a very similar speech by Sunak get far more extensive BBC coverage the following week. This was, in part, because it had received much more coverage in the right-wing press.

New Labour made significant efforts to keep the right-wing press as onside as possible, while knowing they would never get outright support (except from *The Sun*, which is a rare paper that does occasionally shift its support). As Lance Price, who worked for Alastair Campbell in the early years of the Blair government, wrote, 'the number of hours I spent with ministers planning new "crackdowns" on drugs, asylum seekers and benefits cheats' testifies to the obsession with coming up with announcements for these papers. Even if one considers this a good use of time and energy, or even a necessary evil to create space for policy ideas, it may no longer be an option for a Labour government.

As McTernan says: 'I think we [New Labour] put a lot of effort into managing the media, and it was probably necessary. And they could be managed in a way they can't be managed now. No. 10 would give anything to fly off to an island in Oceania and have a meeting with Rupert Murdoch, and settle all the issues as Tony did [referring to a meeting in 1995 that is considered the critical moment in winning the support of *The Sun* for the 1997 election].'[18]

As things stand the relationship between media and politics is more damaging to the creation of good policy than it has ever been. No party has yet figured out an approach to the new equilibrium. The rise of social media may be playing a part here too.

Nostalgia politics and the death of new ideas

Back in 2011, the writer Simon Reynolds published a book called *Retromania* about the decline of innovation in pop music. His thesis was that the permanent availability of every song, whenever it had been released, was making it impossible to look forward: 'In the 2000s the pop present became ever more crowded out by the past, whether in the form of archived memories of yesteryear or retro-rock leeching off ancient styles. Instead of being about itself, the 2000s has been about every other previous decade happening again all at once: a simultaneity of pop time that abolishes history while nibbling away at the present's own sense of itself as an era with a distinct identity and feel.'[19]

You only need to look at the line-up of aging rockers headlining Glastonbury to see the validity of Reynolds's point. A list of the top ten most followed rock bands on Spotify includes Queen, Guns N' Roses and AC/DC. Coldplay, who top the list, are comparative youngsters; lead singer Chris Martin is only in his late forties. It is not that there is no new music at all: all sorts of new micro-genres appeal to niche audiences but there are very few new acts able to fill a stadium.

The same is true in other areas of culture. Every one of the top ten grossing films from 2013–23 is either a sequel (*Avatar: The Way of Water*); a remake (*Lion King*); a homage to a decades-old film (*Top Gun: Maverick*; *Jurassic World*) or part of a long-running franchise (Marvel and Star Wars).[20] Of the top fifteen most streamed TV series in 2022 several were filmed years ago (*Seinfeld, Gilmore Girls*); others have been running for decades (*NCIS, The Simpsons, Grey's Anatomy*) or are based on old series (*Cobra Kai, Wednesday*). The most streamed of all – *Stranger Things* – is a pure nostalgia trip through 1980s pop culture.[21]

This flattening out of time, the ability to access culture from any period at the click of a button, has made it much harder to break through into the mainstream with something genuinely new or different. The same thing has happened with political culture. The reference points for modern politicians have drifted ever further back into the mythology of the past, crowding out progress.

Our discourse is packed with historical clichés. Every trade union dispute is 'a return to the winter of discontent' which happened forty-five years ago. Conservatives determined to stand firm in the face of strike action refer to the miners' strike (forty years ago). Centrists demand Labour have a 'clause four moment' (twenty-eight years ago). Every perceived gaffe is referenced back to ancient examples from political lore. A politician is messily dressed? Michael Foot's 'donkey jacket' at the cenotaph will be mentioned (forty-two years ago; and it wasn't a donkey jacket). A party leader seems too triumphalist? Neil Kinnock's 'Sheffield Rally' just before the 1992 election (thirty-one years ago) will come up. A politician tries, and fails, to look cool: William Hague's baseball cap (twenty-six years ago) and so on.

As another music writer, Fergal Kinney, puts it: 'British politics' retromania is what happens when politics is drawn heavily from those who have studied politics – the line is blurred between practitioners and, well, fans. It creates a language that's off limits to younger voters who might look for inspiration to figures in tech or in activism instead of cultivating a working knowledge of Labour's grand old men.'[22]

But, as in music, film and TV, it is the internet that allows 'fandom' to dominate political culture by creating an immediately and easily accessible archive. As Reynolds said, 'there has never been a society in human history so obsessed with the cultural artifacts of its own immediate past'.[23]

Naturally, the key reference points for political parties and their partisans are their periods of greatest electoral, and ideological, success. For the Conservatives, this means Thatcher, who, a third of a century after leaving office, and long dead, continues to dominate the party's psychodramas. All Tory politicians who want to succeed have to pay tribute, but Liz Truss went further than anyone by literally cosplaying Thatcher, dressing in the same clothes and doing photoshoots in the same locations during her campaign for the party leadership.[24]

Dressing up as Thatcher was not an option for Rishi Sunak but he did get her chancellor, Nigel Lawson, to write an endorsement in *The Daily Telegraph* headlined 'Rishi Sunak is the only candidate who understands Thatcherite economics'.[25] He has continued to try and connect his decisions to her legacy in government. A number of commentators noted that when he told the Conservative conference in 2023 that 'we've had thirty years of a political system which incentivizes the easy decision, not the right one – thirty years of vested interests standing in the way of change', he picked a cut-off date just after Thatcher's defenestration as Tory leader.

For Labour, Tony Blair is starting to play the same role, albeit in a more complex way due to the more factional nature of politics on the left. In the summer of 2023, Keir Starmer made a symbolic appearance at a conference held by Blair's foundation and was interviewed by the man himself. It was a clear signal to the media that the new leader had the blessing of the old.

Starmer has also taken to using historical references to emphasize the type of leader he will be. At a speech shortly before his Blair interview, he highlighted his commitment to changing the party by saying: 'This project goes further and deeper than New Labour's rewriting of clause four . . . This is about rolling our sleeves up, changing our entire culture, our DNA. This is clause four on steroids.'[26]

This is a perfect example of using a reference that, to most voters, would be obscure as a placeholder. Actual activity is replaced by referring back to past success. As Kinney noted, in another section of the same speech Starmer was delivering 'the deluxe Greatest Hits box set': 'If you think our job in 1997 was to rebuild a crumbling public realm, that in 1964 it was to modernise an economy overly dependent on the kindness of strangers, in 1945 to build a new Britain, in a volatile world, out of the trauma of collective sacrifice – in 2024, it will have to be all three.'[27]

This turn towards nostalgia in politics is fully supported by media outlets whose audience is getting older. Just as music and film magazines are filled with endless retrospectives of long-dead bands and fifty-year-old movies, so the political pages of newspapers look to offer the comfort of the past. Here's just a few example headlines from the *Daily Mail* and *Daily Telegraph* from the past few years:

'A return to Margaret Thatcher's Right to Buy home scheme will always be loathed by the Left – and loved by voters'

'I saw how Margaret Thatcher flashed her steel against the unions. Now Boris Johnson must show his mettle, writes former Tory minister'

'Why there was only one Iron Lady, by Henry Kissinger'

'Rishi Sunak should follow Margaret Thatcher and defend using private health'

'We've blown Mrs Thatcher's legacy. Now Rishi must confront the truth'

'Britain needs bold tax cuts to make Mrs Thatcher's shareholder democracy dream a reality'

'Rishi Sunak hasn't yet grasped the secret of how Mrs Thatcher inspired Britain to strive'[28]

It is hardly a surprise that Conservative candidates who wish to appeal to their membership, who read these papers, feel the need to constantly refer back.

This obsession with the past has baleful consequences for the present. The mythologies created around previous eras distort the past and mean the wrong lessons are learned. We have seen during the course of this book that, while Thatcher and Blair, in different ways, were hugely important figures, they also made many mistakes. The commitment to Thatcher's memory has prevented the Conservative Party from considering whether certain totemic policies – whether utilities privatization, outsourcing, or Right to Buy – have had long-term negative effects. Centrist Labour's focus on Blair's successes have also blinded them to the excessive centralization of his era or his adoption of less successful Thatcher-era economic policies.

Even where Thatcher or Blair made the right calls, a superficial adherence to their memory can hide an approach that is very different in reality. Truss managed to secure the 'heir to Thatcher' label almost entirely through vibes: clothing, aggressive speech, photoshoots and so forth. But as more astute right-wing commentators noted, her policy approach was nothing like Thacher's.

As Simon Heffer wrote a few months after her downfall: 'The "Thatcherite" Truss promised dramatic tax cuts to stimulate economic growth, but gave little indication in her campaign of where the money to do this would come from. For all her desire to emulate – or rather, to imitate – Thatcher, her grasp of the history of the Thatcher years was manifestly poor. Thatcher never made unfunded tax cuts, and certainly never borrowed money in order to cut them. Indeed, early on in her premiership she raised taxes to create a sound economic base from which borrowing and spending could be cut, and growth could then proceed, to ensure the markets were not alarmed by her stewardship of the economy.'[29]

Perhaps even more problematically, the past-focus of British politics is preventing the identification of new solutions to our current crisis. The policy problems of our age – from climate change to the fracturing of institutions – are not the same as the past. Yet manifestos and speeches are packed with sequels and reruns. Judging new ideas against whether they would have appealed to Thatcher, Blair, or any other historical figure, acts as a block on innovation. Ironically, the most significant prime ministers are those – like Thatcher, Blair, or further back Lloyd-George and Attlee – who have broken with past consensus, or at least modified it, to create something new.

Even the language of politics seems stuck. We see it in the tired repetition of words or phrases that have historical resonance to politics fans but are never normally used, like 'frit' – a dialect version of frightened that Thatcher used at a 1983 Prime Ministers' Questions – or 'Crisis? What crisis?' a phrase falsely attributed to James Callaghan by *The Sun* forty-five years ago – or 'events, dear boy, events', a phrase supposedly uttered by Harold Macmillan but for which no one can identify an original source.

Politicians themselves use a set stock of jargon that doesn't seem to have changed in decades and is never used in any other context:

'I will take no lectures from . . .'

'I won't comment on hypotheticals . . .'

'Hard-working families up and down the country . . .'

'On the doorstep . . .'

The use of these phrases is partly just a mechanism to fill time when politicians are trying to avoid saying anything. None of them speak like that in private. But there is also a ritualistic quality to all this, an exclusive language which sets a fanbase apart from those with a passing interest. It is, of course, at its most extreme in the House of Commons where the refusal to change archaic jargon is undoubtedly linked to this desire to enjoy politics as a historical artefact rather than something that could be used to change our future. It is, as yet, unclear how our culture can break free of the past in an age where everything that has happened is available all at once. But finding a way to do so is important in the battle to put policy rather than communications, at the heart of politics again.

Misery and confusion: the challenges of 'always on' politics

As we have seen, social media, and the rise of internet culture, has had an enormous impact on politics by speeding up decision-making, increasing the dominance of communication over policy, and boosting nostalgia above the present and future. It has also made working in politics a much more unpleasant, stressful and sometimes downright scary experience. Former MP Charlotte Leslie, who was in Parliament from 2010 to 2017, joined Twitter in 2014.

She did so reluctantly, as she told me: 'I thought, "What is the reality of Twitter conversations? Folks will chat and it's not really real. So if people say terrible things about me on Twitter it doesn't really matter." Something around early 2014 tipped and I thought "it is real". By 2017 social media was toxic, you had all sorts of crazy troll people saying diabolical things that would never have been said before. And it changed the way people talked to you in real life too – on the doorstep.'[30]

During the 2015 election Leslie's father was followed home, after putting up posters for her, and her parents' house was vandalized, with the garden and several cars destroyed. The family also received harassment calls.[31] It got to the point where the police were camped out near the house after any contentious vote in the House of Commons. It is this kind of real-world toxicity that Leslie attributes to the rise of social media.

A number of the interviewees for this book were either prospective candidates to become MPs or have given the idea serious consideration. For all of them, the prospect of a constant stream of social media hatred – and the real-world effects of that hatred – weighed heavily on their minds. The risk to family was forefront in their minds and they are right to be concerned. In 2020 Rakeem Malik was jailed for threatening to murder and rape the Labour MPs Rosie Cooper and Jess Phillips.[32] Cooper has since stood down as an MP, partly because of the mental toll of dealing with these threats. We have also seen two MPs – Jo Cox and David Amess – brutally murdered since 2016.

Isabel Hardman's 2019 book *Why We Get the Wrong Politicians* – which is a fair bit more sympathetic to MPs than it sounds – examined this increased sense of personal risk in depth, and considers it a major reason why good potential candidates are deciding against running. She quotes Ellie Cooper, the daughter of Labour MP and now shadow home secretary Yvette Cooper: 'I am scared when I scroll through the replies to her tweets calling her a liar and a traitor. I am scared when our house gets fitted with panic buttons, industrial-locking doors and explosive bags to catch the mail.'[33]

It's not just the fear of physical violence that makes social media so toxic for MPs. As Hardman says: 'One MP told me that after a year of being in Parliament and on Twitter, she was starting to believe what the trolls told her every day about how stupid and useless she was. It is a similar tactic to the one that domestic abusers deploy, wearing down their victims with a constant stream of comments about what they are getting wrong each day, to the extent that the victim agrees with them and believes they deserve the abuse.'[34]

Advisers and officials tend not to have public accounts on social media but are still affected by scrolling through hatred towards their bosses or invective about policies they have spent months working on. It reinforces the sense of being in a permanent defensive posture and can lead to destructive behaviours.

The corrosive effects of social media on people's ability to think clearly and calmly has been exacerbated further in recent years by the increasingly widespread use of WhatsApp. The messaging app has been around since 2009 and became the most popular in the world in 2015. It is used by almost everyone in Westminster, as it is by most Britons. (Though not by Ken Clarke, who kept getting missed out of key meetings with MPs during the Brexit saga. 'I wasn't on WhatsApp, so everybody forgot to tell me.'[35])

When used for informal messaging between colleagues or friends it is unproblematic. The problem is that, increasingly, the platform is used by a mix of ministers, advisers and officials, not just to communicate, but to make decisions.

Analysis by the Institute for Government in 2022 found that, in key departments, the use of WhatsApp on work phones was widespread. In the Treasury it was being used by 629 officials alongside special advisers and ministers, and in the Cabinet Office 1,704 people.

As the authors of the report say: 'Instant messaging may be quick, but it is a superficial way to make decisions. Unlike formal written submissions, presentations, discussions and even emails, WhatsApp encourages short messages that do not allow for much detail or nuance, which risks key information, perspectives or challenge being missed. It can help support other decision-making or resolve a specific block, but not when it is to the detriment of detailed policy decisions. Lack of control also risks different overlapping group chats and parallel conversations duplicating each other and causing chaotic decision-making.'[36]

We saw this in abundance during Covid when, alongside the normal pressures of government, there were also many officials working from home, while senior politicians and advisers were from time to time forced into isolation.

We know that there were multiple WhatsApp groups used to discuss priority policy issues. One Whitehall official involved in the pandemic response told the Politico website: 'These groups all had slightly different members and remits, with names including "Covid No 10 Coordination", "CSA-CMO-Matt-PM-Dom" and "Numberten action" . . . People were having parallel conversations and one half of a team was behind the other half because they had already had this conversation over WhatsApp and it was really confusing. You didn't know what time people had taken decisions and made different steers.'[37]

The official Covid Inquiry set up by the government, with the legal power to compel evidence, struggled to force leading players to hand over their WhatsApp archives but ultimately managed to collect 'approximately 250 separate WhatsApp groups from over 24 custodians, in addition to thousands of pages of one-to-one WhatsApp threads'.[38] This gives a sense of the scale of the conversations happening via instant messaging.

To date few of these messages have been released to the public. However, the ones that have indicate how it added to the general confusion. One shows Health Secretary Matt Hancock in a confused discussion with multiple senior No. 10 advisers, and Chief Scientific

Adviser Patrick Vallance, about what he should say about the use of masks at an imminent press conference.[39]

Not only were these overlapping groups with semi-arbitrary memberships a bad way of communicating decisions, but they also contributed to more traditional decision-making processes being undermined. They gave participants a false sense of security that action was happening when it was not. I spoke to several civil servants who were in No. 10 during that period. They all confirmed that it was an absolute shambles, with no proper systems put in place to manage the crisis. For example, a relatively junior official told me that they sent an email to senior staff asking whether there was a plan on care homes, pointing out how they were suffering in France and Italy.

As they said: 'I just got no response. Just got no response for about two weeks, I think. And then when I did, because I sent a chaser, the response was "yeah, okay, good point, you should cover it".'[40]

The failure to act on this point, or to have any forum in which it could be raised, led to care homes not being properly protected. Between mid-March and mid-June 2020 almost 20,000 care home residents had Covid when they died, and the true number will have been considerably higher due to the lack of testing early on.[41]

Another official who was in the Cabinet Office at the time confirmed this sense of drift and confusion: 'I was sending emails in mid-March saying we were going to run out of PPE [Personal Protective Equipment] . . . I raised the alarm to everyone. And people were like, "Surely it can't be that bad. Surely they've [the Department for Health and Social Care] got it under control." And I was telling them "they really don't". We suggested some quite rational things like using the government procurement service, or Crown Commercial Services, these huge organizations that buy and sell things all the time . . . But it was just so hard to get a rational decision to happen.'[42]

Ultimately the Department for Health and Social Care (DHSC) ended up panic-buying large amounts of PPE at inflated costs and dropped all procurement controls, leading to the process being declared unlawful in the courts.[43] The department wrote off almost £10 billion of taxpayer money spent on overpriced, unusable or undelivered PPE.[44]

Clearly these problems were not caused purely by instant messaging but it was part of the confusion. Others involved with the process say that traditional formal processes were followed alongside the WhatsApp groups but the insane sense of pace meant that many important issues were missed. What's worse, the bad habits developed during the pandemic have stuck.

Amy Gandon, who used to be a civil servant, has interviewed fifty of her former colleagues as part of a project to understand ongoing challenges with morale and high turnover. Excessive pace, leading to confusion and short-termism, has been a major theme: 'I do think that the stuff about pace is a digital thing, an online thing. But It's also been massively accelerated by Covid and everyone being able to contact everyone all the time. One of the director-level participants spoke about ministers getting an addiction to Cobra [the name of the briefing room where meetings are held about emergencies]. They got used to being able to pull the government together to do something like a lockdown within three hours and that's become the expectation.'[45]

As one very senior former civil servant put it to me: 'The Brexit and Covid pace and drama was addictive to many, many people in the Cabinet Office. And they've recreated other stuff in that image to try and get that buzz. They miss that adrenaline. But the systemic creation of adrenaline is terrible.'[46]

In many ways, this is an accurate description of the challenge of policy-making in the social media age. The whole political system has become addicted to adrenaline, and it is killing us.

Shaping the new world

Politicians' ability to influence the state of the media industry is limited. Freedom of the press is a critical component of democracy. We should all be wary of governments proposing to, for instance, reduce misinformation in the media. Ministers' views of what is and isn't true should not be a factor in what newspapers and broadcasters can say.

But that does not mean there is nothing governments can do. There is a real lack of pluralism in media ownership. Just three companies (DMG Media, News UK and Reach) account for over 90 per cent of national newspaper circulation and the vast majority of traffic to commercial news websites. Two companies (Bauer and Global) own 65 per cent of analogue commercial radio stations. Perhaps most significantly, Meta and Google now take around 80 per cent of all online advertising spend, giving them huge control over the industry.[47] Existing law allows the government to block media mergers if it would concentrate too much power but not to make an assessment of plurality as it changes over time. Giving the Competition and Markets Authority that power, and the ability to propose changes, would help.

More urgently, government could step in to save local media, which has suffered immensely as the result of the shift online.

Revenue from classified adverts, on which the business model of local papers rested, collapsed by 96 per cent in the twenty years from 2004. Circulation has also disappeared – even the biggest and best known rarely sell more than 5,000 copies.[48] We have been left with a host of cluttered and unreadable websites full of clickbait about daytime TV and lottery numbers put there in the desperate hope of producing an income stream. The number of local journalists has collapsed by two thirds in just over a decade. As the former Conservative leader William Hague has written: 'In most of Britain, local news is hollowed out and on the verge of extinction.'[49]

Yet local media is critical to providing real coverage of the policy changes and failures that affect people's lives, rather than Westminster rows. It will be even more important if governments do decide to devolve power and build more state capacity at local and regional level. There are still some excellent local journalists, fighting against the dying of the light, including a new online initiative called *The Mill* providing subscription-based and substantive coverage in several northern cities.[50] But they need help.

There are a number of things government can do, including diverting more of their own large advertising budget to high-quality local media. More radically, they could ask Google and Meta to divert some of their advertising revenue to local news initiatives in return for not making it a legal requirement to do so. While it may not seem in governments' short-term interest to help those trying to make their lives more difficult it would, in the long run, help reorient politics towards policy, which is in everyone's interest.

While all these changes would help, the world is not going back to the way it used to be. The news stream is not going anywhere, even if it fragments across a wider range of platforms. As recently as 2018 more than half of people still used newspapers – either in print or online – as an important source of news. By 2023 it had fallen to 39 per cent and just over 30 per cent among people aged under thirty-five.[51]

Papers can still have oversized influence by setting the agenda for the broadcasters but they are now on the wane too. Older people still rely heavily on TV news for information but social media has already overtaken it in importance among under-35s according to Ofcom surveys. For 12–15-year-olds TikTok is now the single-most important source of news, followed by YouTube and Instagram.[52] These trends are all only going in one direction. The traditional media world will continue to lose influence, while the disaggregated, and harder to regulate, news stream, will grow in importance.

The vast majority of people working in political communications are more familiar with traditional media. It is why the Campbell formula – shorn of its strategic purpose – remains the dominant approach twenty-five years on. Occasional attempts by politicians to use Instagram or TikTok are usually painful to watch. But that will change over time as younger people who grew up with social media explore more novel ways to reach new audiences.

It will certainly create the opportunity to circumvent traditional media gatekeepers. The personal preferences of the *Mail* and *Telegraph*'s proprietors will matter less. But it also means that organizations like the BBC, that have at least tried to offer a bipartisan lens, will decrease in influence too. The dangers are clear from watching the behaviour of politicians who have harnessed social media, in countries that do not have a history of non-partisan media, from Donald Trump in the US, to Jair Bolsonaro in Brazil and Rodrigo Duterte in the Philippines. In addition, the algorithmic designs of platforms like Twitter and Facebook can exert the kind of influence

Lord Rothermere could only dream of, but are much harder to detect, let alone do anything about.

Governments will need to look at how to broaden Ofcom's existing powers to manage an era of more aggressively partisan broadcast media, as well as the increased dominance of social media platforms as a source of news. But it will be far harder to regulate than a landscape of five TV channels and a handful of talk-radio stations. This all heightens the importance of the recommendations in sections one and two about devolving power and strengthening scrutiny.

As with media, the changes the internet has wrought to working patterns and behaviours is irreversible. We also cannot expect advisers and civil servants to go back to the formalities of paper records and making every decision at an in-person meeting. Nor should we want to.

Technology has brought benefits as well as challenges. Sometimes speed matters and being able to get a cabinet minister's attention when they are on a constituency trip, or on a plane over the Atlantic, is useful. Social media can be distorting, maddening, and occasionally deeply scary and upsetting, but it can also provide rapid expert responses to questions, and provide valuable new sources of information. We cannot and should not put these tools back in a locked box. But we need to figure out how to maximize the benefits and limit the costs.

The answers to the negative trends around centralization and executive power, described in sections one and two, involve changing the structures of our political system. But there are more limited options for structural change when it comes to dealing with the speeding up of politics. The Institute for Government have, sensibly, called for new rules to be put in place regarding the use of WhatsApp and other forms of instant messaging.

These include amending the ministerial and civil service codes to be clear that all government business must be done on government devices, and that groups need to have a planned membership. Critically there is a need to ensure all messages are archived, both for transparency and scrutiny but also so that those who need to implement decisions have a paper trail.[53] Increasingly politicians and advisers are setting their WhatsApp messages to delete automatically after seven days, to avoid embarrassments of the kind being revealed by the Covid Inquiry. Needless to say, if important decisions are being made, this cannot continue to happen.

To date Westminster has not adapted well to the internet age. It has exacerbated the existing obsession with media coverage over substance by considerably weakening serious news coverage; destroyed local news; contributed to a nostalgia explosion which has shut down new ideas; increased the stress and pressure on MPs; and contributed to rushed and confused decision-making processes. If government doesn't get better at offsetting the downsides, while banking the benefits, it will keep making all the other problems outlined in this book harder to resolve.

CONCLUSION

Ending Our Crisis

Watching the news can be a bleak experience these days. As I write this, in the first week of January 2024, hospital trust after hospital trust is declaring a critical incident as accident and emergency departments are overwhelmed. There has been another dip in economic growth. This will be the first Parliament in modern history where families' disposable income will be lower at the end than the start. One million children are living in destitution – without adequate food or shelter; 300,000 households are homeless, 100,000 of them with children, the highest on record. Several local authorities have effectively gone bankrupt, including Birmingham, which is the largest. The trains don't even run on time; more than 30 per cent were delayed last year.[1]

There isn't a single cause of a set of problems on this scale. It is partly down to an unusually bad run of global crises: the 2008 financial meltdown and the 2020 pandemic followed by an inflationary surge set off when Russia invaded Ukraine. In the middle of that Britain chose to exit the European Union, which made it harder for businesses to trade abroad and gummed up government. Partially due to the chaos unleashed by that EU referendum,

Britain was afflicted with the worst run of prime ministers we have ever had.

But underpinning all of it has been our crisis of governance. The global picture meant the past fifteen years would always have been difficult, even without Brexit or Boris. The weakness of our institutions has, though, made it so much harder. Worse, it has made it easier for bad politicians to wreak havoc. Ultimately, even if things do recover somewhat from this particular nadir, we will remain hopelessly vulnerable to the next external shock that hits us until we fix the core foundations of the state. Nothing will work properly until we have institutions fit for the modern world.

Take the NHS. As we saw in chapter two, the NHS has been highly centralized from the start, unlike other taxpayer-funded health systems in countries like Denmark and Spain. As that system has become bigger and more complex, with improved treatments and an older population, managing it centrally has become harder. New Labour poured a huge amount of money into healthcare, and with the intensive use of targets they got waiting lists right down. But even at this point, when public satisfaction with the NHS was at its highest, problems were building up.

While the targets drove real improvements, they were also narrow. There was little focus on long-term trends in public health around obesity and mental illness. The now-dominant Treasury were giving more money to the NHS but only, at best, on a three-year cycle, making it harder to plan. Even in these years of relative munificence, spending on longer-term infrastructure projects and equipment was well below the average for developed countries. Meanwhile repeated centrally driven reorganizations sucked up attention and money for little obvious benefit. The NHS National IT programme, which was announced in 2002 and involved an immensely complex web of outsourced contracts, was a disaster, wasted billions and set back the health system by years.

The Public Accounts Committee, in one of their many similar critiques of public sector procurement, said: 'This saga is one of the worst and most expensive contracting fiascos in the history of the public sector . . . It should be plain to anyone that we are witnessing systemic failure in the government's ability to contract.'[2]

Then the financial crisis hit. The Coalition and then the Conservatives kept the NHS budget steady but, without the big Labour funding increases, targets started to be missed, and were thus downgraded. Public health funding, for things like programmes to help people exercise more or eat better, was handed to local government so it could be cut while 'protecting' the NHS. 'Treasury brain' short-termism meant that money was repeatedly diverted from infrastructure to acute crises in hospital care. There were more deeply misconceived reorganizations that Parliament failed to scrutinize properly, with inexperienced civil servants failing to spot some big problems. A succession of health secretaries and prime ministers promised, on repeat, to 'slash fat-cat management', which garnered cheap headlines but was hardly an effective answer to what a weakly managed system needed.

When the pandemic hit, the health system was running far too hot, with nowhere near enough capacity, which meant it fell over faster than in other countries. Chaotic procurement and a lack of local government capacity meant billions were wasted on unusable protective equipment and an infection tracing system that did not work properly, leading to more pressure on hospitals. After the pandemic, doctors went on strike over pay cuts. Rather than negotiate, the government decided to pass a meaningless law to create a 'dividing line' with Labour, designed with friendly newspapers in mind; well over a year later, the strikes were still not settled.

And so we were left with record waiting lists, thousands of people stuck in A&E for more than twelve hours every day, and tens of thousands of 'excess deaths' a year. In addition, there were more than 1.5 million people aged from 50–69 not working, primarily due to ill health, which constrained economic growth. Centralization, lack of local capacity, outsourcing disasters, minimal scrutiny, judicial reviews, a weakened civil service, and a desire to keep the media beast fed – the full set of governance failures – all contributed to this sorry picture.[3]

The same process can be applied to almost any policy problem we have. Housing supply? As we saw in chapter two, local authorities used to build a lot of social housing, but were effectively stopped from doing so by Thatcher during her war on local government. Subsequent governments have done nothing to change this, which has pushed more and more people into renting privately. That, in turn, has pushed up the housing benefit bill, which is harder for the government to control than social housing subsidies because land-lords can raise rents when benefits rise.[4] Rather than admitting the problem, chancellors (exhibiting 'Treasury brain' again) have just cut housing benefit, forcing many more people into homelessness and creating higher long-term costs as overwhelmed councils struggle to cope with the trail of human misery.

Private housing developments are regularly blocked by local authorities who have no financial incentive to want a bigger popula-tion, as their income is largely unrelated to even the small proportion of tax paid locally. It is far easier to heed the call of local NIMBYs who do not want their view spoilt. Instead council executives spend their time bidding for central government handouts rather than seeing local growth as their route to success. Repeated changes within central government – we have had twenty-four housing ministers in the last twenty-three years – have led to repeated initiatives, media announcements and U-turns that have left developers wary of starting projects.

Worried about high levels of low-wage immigration and the inability to remove failed asylum seekers? The former has been driven by the short-term boost it gives public finances, helping the Treasury meet their arbitrary fiscal rules, and the latter by instability in the Home Office, compounded by a lack of parliamentary scrutiny and chaos caused by repeatedly losing judicial reviews. In addition, successive governments have repeatedly attempted to keep the media happy with an endless string of announcements showing how 'tough' they are on asylum, but these suck up time and resources that could have been better used for something useful.

The criminal justice system? It is on the brink of collapse, with prisons full and an unmanageable courts backlog. That's again due to short-termist approaches to investment combined with severe policy instability (twenty-one prisons ministers in twenty-three years) and the lack of anyone standing up for the judiciary or access to justice in the cabinet. Meanwhile ministers have been strongly incentivized to announce ever tougher sentences to fill up the Grid while making a complete mess of the probation system through yet another disastrous outsourcing exercise.

Pick any policy mess you like and the problems go back to the fundamental flaws in institutions outlined in this book. This doesn't mean that individuals don't matter too. Having sharper, more thoughtful, emotionally intelligent people, with integrity, in high office will always makes things better. Conversely having Boris

Johnson and Liz Truss in charge will always make things worse. But individuals are highly constrained and incentivized by the system they are working within.

Even the most brilliant prime minister could not take the volume of decisions they are now personally responsible for and properly understand all the issues involved. The most effective cabinet minister, equipped with an experienced and knowledgeable team of advisers, would still be hamstrung by crushing Treasury oversight of the smallest spending decisions, a cowed and weakened civil service, the lack of state capacity to deliver policy at a local level, the endless procurement failures, and the pressures created by the all-encompassing news stream. The best local authority chief executive imaginable could only do so much given the need to stitch together hundreds of different and arbitrarily changing pots of money, while remaining tied down by reams of Whitehall-imposed rules.

All these constraints make government jobs far less attractive to high-quality candidates. We should be grateful that many good people persist with public service despite the frustrations. But how many great potential MPs do we lose when being a backbencher comes with so little authority or opportunity? How many good civil servants are lost because their bosses will no longer stand up to ministers for fear of losing their jobs, or because they are fed up with having to switch jobs every five minutes to get promoted? How many local government leaders give up because they have so little ability to get things done?

People matter, but systems matter more and we will get nowhere until we fix our systems. Good government is just not possible while we have a handful of politicians making every decision about a central state that is far too large, with far too little scrutiny, and operating under a terrible set of media-driven incentives. Government is overwhelmed, overpowered and in permanent overdrive.

All over the world, developed democracies are facing challenges. Politicians will always be incentivized to make the decision that will cause them less short-term pain with the electorate, and to pretend difficult trade-offs don't exist. This is even more true in a world with fewer media gatekeepers and a far more dispersed flow of information and misinformation. But democracy is vastly preferable to any alternative, even if it will always be messy.

It just makes it even more important to design your systems of government as effectively as possible, and shows why such a centralized state, with so much executive power in the hands of a government always elected by a minority of voters, is so dangerous. Some readers might be surprised there has been no mention of proportional representation in this book. A variant of PR would be preferable to our first-past-the-post system simply because it would be more democratic: a better reflection of voters' interests. But I am not convinced it would resolve any of these governance problems. It is certainly nowhere near as important as building state capacity, sharing power more widely and ensuring better democratic scrutiny by elected MPs.

The best way to fix everything sounds simple but it is painfully hard: we need to disperse power.

What does that mean in practice? Most importantly it requires building up meaningful local and regional sources of power that can make many of the decisions currently sat with ministers, and deliver much more of what the state now does. Mayoral combined authorities are a promising route to achieving this, with real voter buy-in, but are still new, and largely untested. Nor is there any particular rationale why they have certain powers and not others. Creating a proper national network of these bodies, with clear criteria for what gets devolved, needs to be a priority.

Critically, they need powers over taxation. Without this they will have neither the necessary levers to succeed, nor proper account-ability, nor the right incentives to grow and build houses and infrastructure. We also need to accept that some of these bodies will fail, or get involved in scandals. That is inevitable but it is still preferable to concentrating power in Westminster where there is a single point of failure. In any case, mayors trying a range of differ-ent approaches will give us a better sense of what works and what does not.

If we get it right there are major benefits. Firstly, growing our larger cities outside of London is critical to improving our econ-omy in the long term, and doing so would have a halo effect on other nearby towns that have been the focus of doomed centrally driven regeneration efforts. Secondly, it would build local delivery capacity that would reduce our dependency on outsourcing to large unaccountable profit-seeking contractors and private-equity-run ser-vices. Finally, it would free up Whitehall to focus on the big strategic challenges that can only be handled nationally: major infrastructure projects, climate change, AI, energy security and so on.

They will only deal with those enormous challenges if there is adequate scrutiny of their plans too. Which means dispersing more power, this time to Parliament. This is not about recreating some golden era that never existed, but designing a new institution fit for far greater complexity and professional MPs. The focus needs to be on strengthening the power and status of MPs that are not in govern-ment. Being a backbench MP needs to be as attractive, or even more attractive, than being a minister. That means much more powerful select committees with statutory rights to pre-scrutinize legislation and set the timetable for bills, call witnesses under oath, demand government documents, and sign off appointments to public bodies. Committee members and chairs should be paid the equivalent of ministerial salaries to signal equivalent prestige.

This would fundamentally change the balance of power. The executive would still set the agenda but Parliament would have much more ability to interrogate its actions and behaviour, forcing compliance to higher ethical standards, and making it harder to pass bad laws that gum up the state. There would, of course, be poorly led committees, and grandstanding chairs. Again, the question is not, would it preferable to some utopian ideal, but is it preferable to what we have now: extreme executive power in a highly centralized state leading to high levels of instability.

A properly functioning House of Commons would take the burden off those other parts of the state that have stepped in to offer alternative forms of scrutiny. The House of Lords would be under less pressure to rewrite or reject laws despite not being elected, and itself could be strengthened by a cap on numbers and proper scrutiny of appointments. The Johnson and Truss resignation honours lists should mark the end of the current system. Likewise, the increased involvement by the courts in political battles would likely recede if Parliament was in a position to intervene earlier in irrational or unreasonable policy decisions.

A less frantic government that was subject to proper scrutiny would be in a position to reform the civil service in the way that has been needed since it was first set up. The role of the cabinet secretary should be to see this reform through, rather than be a courtier and fixer. It would require a quid pro quo: real control over their departments for senior civil servants, and the opportunity to pay the going rate for the talent they need, in return for greater willingness to manage out poor performers and keep experts in the jobs that suit them for longer.

As for the incentives on politicians, a combination of much less operational control, and reduced ability to endlessly fiddle, combined with proper scrutiny, should make it harder to succeed just by feeding the media beast. Local media should be supported as a counterweight to the preoccupations of the Westminster Lobby. Social media is here to stay, and has some benefits, but makes the dispersal of power even more imperative.

There is a beguiling alternative to the suggestions I have put forward, which is to centralize power even more. The leading proponent of that approach is Dominic Cummings, who would agree that our state is broken but thinks that a small team of brilliant individuals (who he has yet to identify but presumably include him) is the only way to break through the impasse. We saw what that approach looked like when he was in government, where he tried to cut the actual prime minister out of decision-making and was prepared to use executive power in a way that our constitution, such as it is, appears to allow but no one ever intended.

His advice to Rishi Sunak, when they met clandestinely in 2023, was, in his own words: 'That he should, unlike his predecessors, actually *use his full constitutional power to control the government*, rather than only use a fraction of power and *pretend* to "run the government" like Cameron et al.'[5]

This is pretty much the opposite conclusion I have drawn. You can see the attraction: a benignly intentioned super-genius seizing total power and sweeping through all the decaying remnants of our state and replacing them with efficient and competent ones. But, of course, anyone grounded in reality can also see the problem. Such a person does not exist, and even if they did, that level of unchallenged authority would distort their intentions. There is a reason why 'power corrupts and absolute power corrupts absolutely' is one of the most commonly used quotes in political history.

What's more, attempting to use the openness of our constitution to maximize executive power, beyond even its current levels, would be challenged. We have seen how the Lords and the courts have adapted their own constitutional position in the face of executive dominance. The Cummings approach has already led to one big constitutional clash in the courts and it would keep doing so until eventually full-blown crisis ensued. What has happened in Israel over the past few years, with a prime minister intent on maximizing his power in a country with no codified constitution, is a good case study. It has led to constitutional paralysis and a major breakdown in society, not more effective government.

Ultimately you cannot strengthen your institutions by weakening them. Power dispersal is the only way to end the crisis of government and put ourselves in a better position to cope with our current policy challenges and those of the future.

The problem, of course, is how you get politicians to do so when it rarely suits their short-term interests. All the trends of the past forty years of politics have encouraged centralization. In isolation, many decisions to centralize further look rational. Ministers have often taken more power because they want to get a grip on an issue of national importance. But the net effect has been to destroy local government, and seriously constrain state capacity. Paradoxically, the state has been left more powerless.

It is also not hard to see why ministers have wanted to bypass a more rebellious and professional Parliament, or why they have tried to limit judicial review of their decisions and give themselves more power to appoint whoever they want to critical jobs. These constraints can seem like a nuisance standing in the way of their agenda. Even more so when they face so much pressure to come up with endless announcements to fill the news stream and build their profile.

Within Whitehall, the trends have also been towards more central control – it is a long time since anyone believed the fiction that the prime minister is merely the chair of the cabinet. The role is now presidential, albeit with far fewer resources and more actual power than most presidents. The prime minister is likewise expected to behave like one by the press and public. The Treasury has ensured it has iron control over other departments, without any accountability of its own. Communications teams have become more powerful than policy ones, meaning even the smallest decisions need to be turned into a centrally controlled announcement. The only two things that matter now in Westminster are the Treasury scorecard and the No. 10 Grid.

Two things give me hope things can change. The first is that we have seen glimmers of recognition. The creation of mayoral authorities, and cross-party support for them, does suggest the problems of centralization are starting to be realized, even if the shift so far has been messy and limited. Likewise, the rise of select committees over the past few decades has shown a desire among MPs to play a greater scrutiny role, and indicated that governments will occasionally acknowledge that.

The second reason is more stark. We cannot go on as we are. Public trust in politicians and politics – never high – has crashed through the floor. Politicians themselves are overwhelmed by a system so big and complex they can barely understand it. Advisers spend all their time coming up with nonsense announcements. It just very obviously does not work. The history of UK politics is a cycle of crises and each crisis comes to an end when there is no alternative left but to do things differently.

What this resolution looks like, though, is in the hands of the government. They can accept the diagnosis and move to disperse power in an ordered and coherent way; building stronger and better institutions. They can give themselves the time and space to focus on the most important issues and prioritize policy over communications. There is the opportunity for someone to be one of those rare prime ministers who really makes a difference to the long-term future of the country. The ideas are there and there are hundreds of thousands of people across the public sector who desperately want to be able to make a difference, waiting to be given the chance. We just need to find someone willing to call time on this crisis cycle.

Alternatively, they can keep using the machinery we have, making promises they can't keep, pulling levers that aren't there, filling newspapers with announcements of actions that never happen, until politics breaks altogether. If future governments fail in the way that recent ones have, we will hit a point where the public's patience snaps altogether and they try more radical alternatives on offer from extremists and charlatans. We have seen this happen already in countries with a more flexible voting system. But it will happen here too if nothing changes. And when it does, politicians will find themselves asking: why didn't we do things differently when we had the chance?

ACKNOWLEDGEMENTS

I first conceived of this project three years ago while lying in hospital following a near-death experience, so my first thanks are to the doctors and nurses at Northwick Park who saved my life and looked after me. Without them there would be no book.

Once recovered I started a new career as a writer with the generous support of my boss Lucy Heller. As I didn't have a clue how to find a publisher I am very grateful to my agent James Pullen at The Wylie Agency for helping me write and sell a proposal.

The publisher who bought it, Pan Macmillan, have been exceptionally helpful in guiding me through the process as a first-time author. Mike Harpley, my editor, has made the book far easier to read, and Ian Allen, the copy-editor, saved me from a number of embarrassing errors. The whole team have been incredibly supportive.

I have spoken, over the years, to an enormous number of people who have helped me develop the ideas discussed. I'd like to offer particular thanks to Tom Shinner, who read the whole manuscript, as well as Hannah White, Robert Saunders, Meg Russell, Michelle Clements, Anthony Breach, Tim Bale, Tim Leunig, JP Spencer, Amy Gandon and Rachel Wolf, for helpful conversations about various sections. Jesse Norman invited me to give a talk setting out the nascent themes to a high-powered group at All Souls College, which was valuable. I made wide-ranging use of dozens of reports done by my brilliant colleagues at the Institute for Government. Of course, all opinions and any remaining errors are mine alone.

I did nearly a hundred interviews for the book, as well as using material from interviews done for other projects. I'd like to thank the following interviewees for their time and insights: Ed Balls, Gavin Barwell, Robin Butler, Alastair Campbell, Camilla Cavendish, Francis Elliott, David Gauke, Ian Fletcher, Helen Ghosh, Donna Hall, Rupert Harrison, Gavin Jones, Samanatha Jones, Kate Josephs, John Kingman, Paul Kissack, David Laws, Charlotte Leslie, David Lidington, Polly Mackenzie, Helen MacNamara, Nick Macpherson, Ciaran Martin, John McTernan, David Miliband, Sally Morgan, Gus O'Donnell, David Omand, Jonathan Portes, Joanne Roney, Jill Rutter, Nick Timothy, Robin Tuddenham, William Waldegrave, Paul Waugh, Giles Wilkes and David Willetts. I'd also like to thank the dozens of current and former advisers, officials and ministers who spoke to me off the record. And Rosie Inwald for transcribing many of the interviews.

Doing a project like this is far easier with a strong support network around you. Special thanks go to my closest friend of thirty years, Ben Morgan, for all his advice (and teaching me to write when we were at school). My wife Linda has been brilliant, as she always is. I still have no idea how I managed to end up married to someone so clever, kind and generally wonderful, but I am grateful every day that I did.

My children Ava, Oscar and Grace, have been supportive too, in a somewhat more sarcastic, but ultimately loving, way. The elder two, who are twins, became teenagers while I was working on this book and offered to contribute. But their main idea – that 'Rishi

ACKNOWLEDGEMENTS

Sunak is a knobhead' – didn't really fit with my systems rather than people focus.

Finally, I want to thank my parents. My dad, author of many successful books, read the manuscript, and gave lots of useful feedback. My mum, the first woman to be Professor of Tax Law at Oxford University, contributed plenty of insights from decades of frustrating attempts to make our tax system less mad. But beyond their help with this book I am so deeply grateful for everything they have done for me. I was ill for most of my childhood and they spent endless hours shepherding me through hospitals, while also feeding my burgeoning curiosity about history and politics. This book is dedicated to them.

NOTES

INTRODUCTION: THE CRISIS CYCLE

1   This account is pieced together from Bernard Donoughue, *Downing Street Diarchapter*: Volume Two (Pimlico, 2009), p. 153; plus author interviews with Sir Robin Butler, a private secretary to Heath at the time, and Lord William Waldegrave, who was Heath's political secretary.

2   Russell Jones, *The Tyranny of Nostalgia* (London Publishing Partnership, 2023), p. 72.

3   Interview with Robin Butler.

4   See e.g. Mastroianni, A.M., Gilbert, D.T., 'The illusion of moral decline', *Nature* 618, pp. 782–9 (2023) https://www.nature.com/articles/s41586-023-06137-x

5   Phil Tinline, *The Death of Consensus* (C. Hurst and Co., 2022), p. 333.

6   Or at least it seemed that way. It later turned out that Treasury estimates of the financial position were overly pessimistic.

7   Quoted in Peter Hennessy, *The Hidden Wiring* (1996, Indigo), p. 22.

8   Interview with Rupert Harrison.

9   Interview with Camilla Cavendish.

10   John Burn-Murdoch, 'Britain and the US are poor societies with some very rich people', *Financial Times*, 16 September 2022, https://www.ft.com/content/ef265420-45e8-497b-b308-c951baa68945

11   Interview with Helen MacNamara.

12   Action for Children, 'All worked out? The limits of work as a route out of poverty and hardship', February 2023, https://www.actionforchildren.org.uk/our-work-and-impact/policy-work-campaigns-and-research/policy-reports/

all-worked-out-the-limits-of-work-as-a-route-out-of-poverty-and-hardship; Department for Levelling Up, Housing and Communities, 'Statutory homelessness in England: April to June 2023', 30 November 2023, https://www.gov.uk/government/statistics/statutory-homelessness-in-england-april-to-june-2023.

13 https://www.spectator.co.uk/article/full-text-rishi-sunaks-tory-conference-speech/

14 https://www.ipsos.com/en-uk/ipsos-trust-in-professions-veracity-index-2023

CHAPTER 1: NO NINJAS

1 Patrick Wintour, 'Cabinet secretary has David Cameron "by the balls", says former Tory adviser', *The Guardian*, 19 November 2014, https://www.theguardian.com/politics/2014/nov/19/cabinet-secretary-david-cameron-balls-dominic-cummings-jeremy-heywood

2 Quoted in Peter Hennessy, *The Prime Ministers* (Penguin, 2001), p. 64.

3 Quoted in Jack Brown, *No. 10: The Geography of Power at Downing Street* (Haus, 2020), p. 16.

4 Brown, p. 272.

5 Interview with Polly MacKenzie.

6 Brown, p. 19.

7 Interview with Nick Timothy.

8 Brown, p. 48.

9 Hennessy, p. 206.

10 Hennessy, p. 96.

11 Brown, p. 218.

12 Interview with Sally Morgan.

13 Interview with Alastair Campbell.

14 Suzanne Heywood, *What Does Jeremy Think?* (William Collins, 2021), p. 114.

15 Heywood, p. 117.

16 Interview with senior civil servant.

17 Michael Barber, *Instruction to Deliver: Fighting to Transform Britain's Public Services* (Methuen, 2008).

18 Nehal Panchamia and Peter Thomas, 'Public Service Agreements and the Prime Minister's Delivery Unit', Institute for Government, 2014, https://

www.instituteforgovernment.org.uk/sites/default/files/case%20study%20
psas.pdf

19 Michelle Clement, 'The Art of Delivery: The Prime Minister's Delivery
    Unit 2001–2005', blogpost, 26 August 2022, https://history.blog.gov.
    uk/2022/08/26/the-art-of-delivery-the-prime-ministers-delivery-
    unit-2001-2005/

20 Heywood, p. 315.

21 Nicholas Watt and John Vidal, 'Forests sell-off abandoned as Cameron
    orders U-turn', *The Guardian*, 16 February 2011, https://www.
    theguardian.com/environment/2011/feb/16/forests-sell-off-cameron-
    uturn; Toby Helm, Jamie Doward and Nicholas Watt, 'Writers furious
    at plan to axe free books scheme for children', *The Observer*, 25
    December 2010, https://www.theguardian.com/books/2010/dec/26/
    booktrust-funding-cut-pullman-motion

22 Heywood, p. 358.

23 *The Economist*, 'Why Boris Johnson is recreating Tony Blair's "delivery
    unit"', 13 May 2021, https://www.economist.com/britain/2021/05/13/
    why-boris-johnson-is-recreating-tony-blairs-delivery-unit

24 Interview with a senior official.

25 Public Administration Select Committee, 'On Target? Government By
    Measurement', 10 July 2003, https://publications.parliament.uk/pa/
    cm200203/cmselect/cmpubadm/62/62.pdf

26 Panchamia and Thomas, p. 6.

27 Conservative Party Manifesto 2010, p. 37, https://general-election-2010.
    co.uk/2010-general-election-manifestos/Conservative-Party-Manifesto-
    2010.pdf

28 Interview with Gus O'Donnell.

29 For more on the history of Gladstonian spending control see: Nicholas
    Macpherson, 'The origins of Treasury control', transcript of speech
    delivered 16 January 2013, https://www.gov.uk/government/speeches/
    speech-by-the-permanent-secretary-to-the-treasury-sir-nicholas-
    macpherson-the-origins-of-treasury-control

30 Quoted in Brown, p. 134.

31 See Robert Skidelsky, 'Keynes and the Treasury View: The Case for and
    against an Active Unemployment Policy 1920–1939', in *The Emergence
    of the Welfare State in England and Germany*, edited by W.J. Mommsen
    (Routledge, 1981).

32 https://www.gov.uk/government/speeches/speech-by-the-permanent-secretary-to-the-treasury-the-treasury-view-a-testament-of-experience

33 Quoted in MacPherson, 'The origins of Treasury control'.

34 Aeron Davis, *Bankruptcy, Bubbles and Bailouts: The Inside History of the Treasury Since 1976* (Manchester University Press, 2022), p. 37.

35 Interview with Nick MacPherson.

36 Ibid.

37 Clarke's predecessors, Nigel Lawson and Norman Lamont, had both argued for giving the Bank of England independence in setting interest rates but were overruled by prime ministers nervous about giving away such an important political lever. Gordon Brown took the leap a few days after the 1997 election.

38 Interview with Ed Balls.

39 Interview with Dame Helen Ghosh.

40 Interview with Nick MacPherson.

41 Interview with Ed Balls.

42 Thomas Pope and Peter Hourston, 'Fiscal rules in the UK since 1997', Institute for Government, 16 March 2022, https://www.instituteforgovernment.org.uk/explainer/fiscal-rules-history

43 Phillip Inman and Larry Elliott, 'Head of OBR says lack of budget details led to "work of fiction" forecasts last year', *The Guardian*, 23 January 2024, https://www.theguardian.com/politics/2024/jan/23/head-of-obr-says-lack-of-budget-details-led-to-work-of-fiction-forecasts-last-year

44 Thomas Pope and Peter Hourston, 'Current UK fiscal rules', Institute for Government, last updated 27 November 2023, https://www.instituteforgovernment.org.uk/explainer/current-fiscal-rules

45 Interview with Giles Wilkes.

46 Interview with Paul Kissack.

47 Interview with John Kingman.

48 Tom Belger, 'Risk of school buildings collapsing now "very likely", DfE says', *Schools Week*, 19 December 2022, https://schoolsweek.co.uk/school-building-safety-funding-repairs-fears-collapse/

49 Richard Adams, 'Repair bill for schools in England doubles to over £11bn, finds survey', *The Guardian*, 27 May 2021, https://www.theguardian.com/education/2021/may/27/repair-bill-for-schools-in-england-doubles-to-over-11bn-finds-survey

50 Jennifer Williams, Peter Foster and George Parker, 'Treasury
bans capital spending by Michael Gove's Whitehall department',
Financial Times, 7 February 2023, https://www.ft.com/content/
ee18f02c-7fa5-4ddb-aa41-4dd67743548b

51 Heywood, p. 178.

52 Interview with Nick Timothy.

53 Commission on the Centre of Government, 'Power with Purpose',
Institute for Government, 2024; Giles Wilkes and Stian Westlake,
'End of the Treasury?', NESTA, 2014; 'What's Gone Wrong with
Whitehall?'/'Designing Government for a Better Britain', Commission
for a Smarter Government, November 2020/June 2021.

54 Commission for a Smarter Government, 'What's Gone Wrong with
Whitehall?', p. 16.

55 Helen MacNamara, witness statement to UK Covid-19 Inquiry,
9 October 2023, p. 63, https://covid19.public-inquiry.uk/wp-
content/uploads/2023/11/03103311/INQ000273841.pdf

CHAPTER 2: ENEMIES WITHIN

1 Quoted in *Failure in British Government: The Politics of the Poll
Tax*, David Butler et al (OUP, 1994), p. 265.

2 Ministry of Housing, Communities and Local Government,
'New government guidance on weekly bin collections',
4 January 2014, https://www.gov.uk/government/news/
new-government-guidance-on-weekly-bin-collections

3 Carrington Walker, 'Councillors slam "ridiculous" criteria for
wildlife road signs', *Weston Mercury*, 5 February 2021, https://www.
thewestonmercury.co.uk/news/local-council/20505975.councillors-
slam-ridiculous-criteria-wildlife-road-signs/; Planning Inspectorate,
'Common land guidance sheet 10: highways and cattle grids', last
updated 27 September 2023, https://www.gov.uk/government/
publications/common-land-guidance-sheet-10-highways-and-cattle-
grids; Charles Thomson, 'Haringey Council faces government probe
into "rule-breaking" magazine', *Ham & High*, 21 February 2021,
https://www.hamhigh.co.uk/news/21325471.haringey-council-faces-
government-probe-rule-breaking-magazine/; Mark Sandford, 'Will online

council meetings be extended beyond 6 May?', House of Commons Library, 19 April 2021, https://commonslibrary.parliament.uk/will-online-council-meetings-be-extended-beyond-6-may/

4   Paul Swinney and Anthony Breach, 'The role of place in the UK's productivity problem', Centre for Cities, 16 November 2017, https://www.centreforcities.org/publication/role-place-uks-productivity-puzzle/

5   Interview with John Kingman.

6   Hugo Bessis, 'Competing with the continent: How do UK cities match up to the rest of Europe?', Centre for Cities, 22 September 2016, https://www.centreforcities.org/publication/competing-with-the-continent/

7   Swinney and Breach.

8   https://parlipapers.proquest.com/parlipapers/result/pqpdocumentview?accountid=14511&groupid=1418965&pgId=86b744cc-ada0-4914-a549-218956e873d7#0 p. 335; Sir Michael Lyons, 'Place-shaping: a shared ambition for the future of local government', March 2007, p. 6, https://assets.publishing.service.gov.uk/government/uploads/system/uploads/attachment_data/file/243601/9780119898545.pdf

9   Interview with Paul Kissack.

10 Tony Travers and Lorena Esposito, 'The Decline and Fall of Local Democracy: A History of Local Government Finance', Policy Exchange, 2003, p. 31, https://www.localis.org.uk/wp-content/uploads/2003/08/Travers-T-Esposito-L.-The-Decline-and-Fall-of-Local-Democracy.-A-History-of-Local-Government-Finance.pdf

11 Nicholas Timmins, *The Five Giants: A Biography of the Welfare State*, Third Edition (William Collins, 2017), chapter 6.

12 Butler et al, p. 269.

13 Ibid., p. 274.

14 Margaret Thatcher, 'Speech to 1922 committee', transcript of speech on 19 July 1984, https://www.margaretthatcher.org/document/105563

15 David Parker, 'The 1988 Local Government Act and Compulsory Competitive Tendering', *Urban Studies*, October 1990, 27(5):653–67, https://www.researchgate.net/publication/237291559_The_1988_Local_Government_Act_and_Compulsory_Competitive_Tendering

16 Stuart Adam et al, 'Social Housing in England: A Survey', Institute for Fiscal Studies, November 2015, https://ifs.org.uk/sites/default/files/output_url_files/BN178.pdf

17 Frank Eardley, 'Right to buy: Past, present and future', House of Lords Library, 17 June 2022, https://lordslibrary.parliament.uk/right-to-buy-past-present-and-future/

18 Richard Disney, 'The right to buy public housing in Britain: a welfare analysis', Institute for Fiscal Studies, February 2015, p. 2, https://ifs.org.uk/sites/default/files/output_url_files/BN162.pdf

19 Cassie Barton, 'Local authority data: housing supply', House of Commons Library, 1 December 2023, https://commonslibrary.parliament.uk/local-authority-data-housing-supply/

20 Transcript of James Callaghan's 'Ruskin College' speech, 18 October 1976, https://education-uk.org/documents/speeches/1976ruskin.html

21 Education Act 1980.

22 Butler et al, p. 271.

23 Stuart Wilks-Heeg, 'New Labour and the Reform of English Local Government, 1997–2007: Privatizing the Parts that Conservative Governments Could Not Reach?', *Planning Practice & Research*, 24:1, 23–39 p. 30, https://www.tandfonline.com/doi/full/10.1080/02697450902742130.

24 Ibid., p. 32.

25 Eric Pickles, 'The Localism Bill reverses a century of centralization', Conservative Home, 18 November 2011, https://conservativehome.com/2011/11/18/in-pursuit-of-localism-restoring-a-100-year-democratic-deficit/

26 Local Government Association, 'The General Power of Competence', July 2013, https://www.local.gov.uk/sites/default/files/documents/general-power-competence--0ac.pdf

27 Jennifer Williams and William Wallis, 'English councils "forced to the pawnshop" in fire sale of assets', *Financial Times*, 28 February 2024, https://www.ft.com/content/9d79cd59-bbfb-4a8c-b62a-b616aed63ffc?shareType=nongift

28 Graham Atkins and Stuart Hoddinott, 'Local government funding in England', Institute for Government, last updated 21 July 2023, https://www.instituteforgovernment.org.uk/explainer/local-government-funding-england

29 Mark Sandford, 'Council tax: local referendums', House of Commons Library, 4 January 2023, p. 10, https://researchbriefings.files.parliament.uk/documents/SN05682/SN05682.pdf

30 Interview with Robin Tuddenham, CEO of Calderdale Council.

31 TRL Insight, 'Fragmented Funding', Local Government Association, 22 September 2020, https://www.local.gov.uk/publications/fragmented-funding-report

32 Interview with Joanne Roney, CEO of Manchester City Council.

33 'Fragmented Funding', p. 30.

34 Malcolm Tait et al, 'Fair Funding for Devolution?', The University of Sheffield, September 2022, https://www.sheffield.ac.uk/city-region/news/researchers-university-sheffield-reveal-costs-regeneration-funding-england

35 Interview with Joanne Roney.

36 Husna Anjum, 'Levelling up "rule" that saw Birmingham snubbed revealed by Culture Secretary Michelle Donelan', *BirminghamLive*, 19 January 2023, https://www.birminghammail.co.uk/news/midlands-news/levelling-up-rule-saw-birmingham-26023200

37 Levelling Up, Housing and Communities Committee, 'Funding for Levelling Up', 22 May 2023, https://publications.parliament.uk/pa/cm5803/cmselect/cmcomloc/744/report.html

38 Ibid., p. 17.

39 Public Accounts Committee, 'Selecting towns for the Towns Fund', 2 November 2020, https://committees.parliament.uk/publications/3373/documents/32489/default/

40 Eleanor Shearer and Paul Shepley, 'Towns Fund', Institute for Government, 22 September 2021, https://www.instituteforgovernment.org.uk/article/explainer/towns-fund

41 Graeme Atherton and Marc Le Chevalier, 'Funding levelling up: who really benefits?', Centre for Inequality and Levelling Up, 2023, p. 5, https://www.uwl.ac.uk/sites/uwl/files/2023-04/SBT2517%20University%20of%20West%20London%20Funding%20levelling%20up%20Report%20v4%20WEB_0.pdf

42 Department for Environment, Food and Rural Affairs, 'More than £1.2m funding for councils to clean up chewing gum from our streets', 6 July 2023, https://www.gov.uk/government/news/more-than-12m-funding-for-councils-to-clean-up-chewing-gum-from-our-streets

43 Department for Levelling Up, Housing and Communities, 'Installing chess tables in parks and public spaces: prospectus', 1 September 2023, https://www.gov.uk/government/publications/

installing-chess-tables-in-parks-and-public-spaces-prospectus/
installing-chess-tables-in-parks-and-public-spaces-prospectus

44 Department for Levelling Up, Housing and Communities, 'Changing
Places toilet fund', 6 February 2023, https://www.gov.uk/government/
collections/changing-places-toilets-fund

45 Interview with Gavin Jones, CEO of Essex Council.

46 Mark Sandford, 'The abolition of regional government', House of
Commons Library, 27 March 2013, https://researchbriefings.files.
parliament.uk/documents/SN05842/SN05842.pdf

47 Local Democracy, Economic Development and Construction Act 2009.

48 Michael Heseltine, 'No Stone Unturned', October 2012, p. 9, https://
assets.publishing.service.gov.uk/government/uploads/system/uploads/
attachment_data/file/34648/12-1213-no-stone-unturned-in-pursuit-of-
growth.pdf

49 Interview with Rupert Harrison.

50 Interview with John Kingman.

51 Ibid.

52 Interview with Martin Reeves.

53 Ibid.

54 Philip Britteon et al, 'The effect of devolution on health: a generalised
synthetic control analysis of Greater Manchester, England', *The Lancet*,
volume 7, issue 10, E844-E852, October 2022, https://www.thelancet.
com/journals/lanpub/article/PIIS2468-2667(22)00198-0/fulltext

55 Anthony Breach, Stuart Bridgett and Olivia Vera, 'In Place of
Centralisation', Resolution Foundation, 8 November 2023, https://www.
resolutionfoundation.org/events/in-place-of-centralisation/

56 Interview with Rupert Harrison.

CHAPTER 3: CONTRACT KILLINGS

1 Interview with former government adviser.

2 Business, Energy and Industrial Strategy and Work and Pensions
Committees, 'Report on Carillion', 16 May 2018, https://publications.
parliament.uk/pa/cm201719/cmselect/cmworpen/769/769.pdf

3 Tom Latchem and Dan Evans, 'Celebrity-Run Children's Care Home
Shuttered by Ofsted Again after Child Taken to Hospital', *Byline Times*,

12 March 2024, https://bylinetimes.com/2024/03/12/celebrity-run-childrens-care-home-shuttered-by-ofsted-again-after-child-hospitalised/

4 Report on Ofsted Monitoring Visit to AP Care Homes Limited, 3 January 2024, https://reports.ofsted.gov.uk/provider/2/2724911

5 Report on Ofsted Monitoring Visit to AP Care Homes Limited, 30 January 2024, https://reports.ofsted.gov.uk/provider/2/2724911

6 Caitlin Webb, 'Revealed: Spiralling cost of children's homes', *Local Government Chronicle*, 19 March 2024, https://www.lgcplus.com/services/children/revealed-spiralling-cost-of-childrens-homes-19-03-2024/

7 Competition and Markets Authority, 'Children's social care market study', 10 March 2022, p. 9, https://assets.publishing.service.gov.uk/government/uploads/system/uploads/attachment_data/file/1059575/Final_report.pdf

8 Ibid., p. 5.

9 Tom Wall, 'Revealed: hundreds of vulnerable children sent to illegal and unregulated care homes in England', *The Observer*, 13 April 2024, https://www.theguardian.com/society/2024/apr/13/vulnerable-children-illegal-unregulated-care-homes-england

10 Tom Sasse et al, 'Government outsourcing: What has worked and what needs reform?', Institute for Government, September 2019, pp. 26–7, https://www.instituteforgovernment.org.uk/sites/default/files/publications/government-outsourcing-reform-WEB_0.pdf

11 Serco website, accessed 6 January 2024.

12 Matt Ford, 'The ongoing electronic tagging scandal', Centre for Crime and Justice Studies, 25 June 2015, https://www.crimeandjustice.org.uk/resources/ongoing-electronic-tagging-scandal

13 Alan White, *Shadow State: Inside the Secret Companies that Run Britain* (Oneworld Publications, 2016), pp. 6–19.

14 Ibid., pp. 122–31.

15 David Laws, *Coalition Diaries 2012–2015* (Biteback Publishing, 2017), pp. 202–3.

16 Richard Adams, 'Ofsted to end third-party contracts and employ school inspectors directly', *The Guardian*, 29 May 2014, https://www.theguardian.com/education/2014/may/29/ofsted-end-third-party-contracts-employ-school-inspectors-directly

17 Jamie Grierson, 'Why HMP Birmingham has been brought back under state control', *The Guardian*, 20 August 2018, https://www.theguardian.

com/society/2018/aug/20/why-hmp-birmingham-has-been-brought-back-under-state-control

18   Denis Campbell, ' "Inadequate" Hinchingbrooke hospital to be put in special measures', *The Guardian*, 9 January 2015, https://www.theguardian.com/society/2015/jan/09/hinchingbrooke-hospital-special-measures-cqc-report

19   Lawrence Dunhill, 'Revealed: Trusts' estimated savings potential', *Health Service Journal*, 5 January 2016, https://www.hsj.co.uk/finance-and-efficiency/revealed-trusts-estimated-savings-potential/7001364.article

20   Crispin Dowler, 'Exclusive: Hinchingbrooke backtracks on controversial £50 referrals offer', *Health Service Journal*, 24 July 2014, https://www.hsj.co.uk/north-west-anglia-nhs-foundation-trust/exclusive-hinchingbrooke-backtracks-on-controversial-50-referrals-offer/5073309.article

21   Public Accounts Committee, 'Circle's withdrawal from Hinchingbrooke Hospital update report published', 18 March 2015, https://committees.parliament.uk/work/4345/an-update-on-hinchingbrooke-health-care-nhs-trust/news/185264/circles-withdrawal-from-hinchingbrooke-hospital-update-report-published/

22   Ian Dunt, *How Westminster Works . . . And Why It Doesn't* (Weidenfeld & Nicolson, 2023), p. 3.

23   Alan Travis, 'Two companies to run more than half of privatised probation services', *The Guardian*, 29 October 2014, https://www.theguardian.com/uk-news/2014/oct/29/justice-probation-contracts-private-companies

24   Beckie Smith, 'Working Links, outsourcer with £1bn of public contracts, collapses', *Civil Service World*, 19 February 2019, https://www.civilserviceworld.com/professions/article/working-links-outsourcer-with-1bn-of-public-contracts-collapses

25   Dunt, p. 21.

26   HM Inspectorate of Probation, 'Chief Inspector welcomes government action over Working Links and publishes damning report on Dorset, Devon and Cornwall CRC', February 2019, https://www.justice inspectorates.gov.uk/hmiprobation/media/press-releases/2019/02/ddcrc/

27   HM Inspectorate of Probation, 'Probation in the news for all the wrong reasons', 2 February 2023, https://www.justiceinspectorates.gov.uk/hmiprobation/2023/02/02-february-2023-probation-in-the-news-for-all-the-wrong-reasons/

28 HM Inspectorate of Probation, 'Independent Serious Further Offence review of Jordan McSweeney', January 2023, https://www.justiceinspectorates.gov.uk/hmiprobation/media/press-releases/2023/01/jmsfor/

29 National Audit Office, 'Transforming Rehabilitation: Progress review', 1 March 2019, https://www.nao.org.uk/wp-content/uploads/2019/02/Transforming-Rehabilitation-Progress-review.pdf

30 Mark Wallace, 'Serco and G4S ripped us off – the public sector must start to play hardball', *The Guardian*, 13 March 2014, https://www.theguardian.com/commentisfree/2014/mar/13/serco-g4s-public-sector-hardball-government-taxpayers

31 Sam Gruet, 'Avanti sorry after leaked presentation cheers "free money"', BBC News Online, 16 January 2024, https://www.bbc.co.uk/news/business-67997916

32 Tony Stott, 'Market Testing and Beyond: Privatisation and Contracting Out in British Central Government', *Teaching Public Administration*, Spring 1994, vol. XIV, no. 1, pp. 36–48, https://journals.sagepub.com/doi/epdf/10.1177/014473949401400104

33 Polly Curtis, 'PFI projects not best value for money, says watchdog', *The Guardian*, 28 April 2011, https://www.theguardian.com/politics/2011/apr/28/pfi-not-best-value-money

34 Treasury Select Committee, 'Private Finance Initiative', 18 July 2011, https://publications.parliament.uk/pa/cm201012/cmselect/cmtreasy/1146/114605.htm

35 National Audit Office, 'PFI and PF2', 18 January 2018, pp. 44–5, https://www.nao.org.uk/wp-content/uploads/2018/01/PFI-and-PF2.pdf

36 Ibid., p. 4.

37 Nicky Phillips, 'Revealed: The true scale of school PFI debts', *Schools Week*, 4 March 2016, https://schoolsweek.co.uk/the-true-scale-of-school-pfi-debts/

38 Public Accounts Committee, 'Strategic Suppliers', 24 July 2018, https://publications.parliament.uk/pa/cm201719/cmselect/cmpubacc/1031/103106.htm

39 White, pp. 78–80.

40 Ibid., p. 85.

41 Work and Pensions Committee, 'Employment and Support Allowance and Work Capability Assessments', 16 July 2014, p. 28, https://

publications.parliament.uk/pa/cm201415/cmselect/cmworpen/302/302.pdf

42 White, p. 88.

43 Rajeev Syal, 'Maximus miss fitness-to-work test targets despite spiralling costs', *The Guardian*, 8 January 2016, https://www.theguardian.com/society/2016/jan/08/maximus-miss-fitness-to-work-test-targets-despite-spiralling-costs

44 Mark Say, 'DWP signs Atos for PIP IT service', *UK Authority*, 14 June 2022, https://www.ukauthority.com/articles/dwp-signs-atos-for-pip-it-service/

45 John Pring, 'Disabled mum took her own life after actions of DWP and Capita "magnified" anxiety', *Disability News Service*, 25 May 2023, https://www.disabilitynewsservice.com/disabled-mum-took-her-own-life-after-actions-of-dwp-and-capita-magnified-anxiety/

46 John Pring, 'DWP tried to prevent Atos winning £338m assessment contract, court documents suggest', *Disability New Service*, 10 August 2023, https://www.disabilitynewsservice.com/dwp-tried-to-prevent-atos-winning-338m-assessment-contract-court-documents-suggest/#:~:text=court%20documents%20suggest-,DWP%20tried%20to%20prevent%20Atos%20winning,assessment%20contract%2C%20court%20documents%20suggest&text=The%20Department%20for%20Work%20and,benefit%20assessments%2C%20court%20documents%20suggest

47 Adam Leaver, 'Out of time: the fragile temporality of Carillion's accumulation model', Open Democracy, 17 January 2018, https://neweconomics.opendemocracy.net/index.html%3Fp=2214.html

48 Ibid.

49 National Audit Office, 'Investigation into the government's handling of the collapse of Carillion', 7 June 2018, https://www.nao.org.uk/wp-content/uploads/2018/06/Investigation-into-the-governments-handling-of-the-collapse-of-Carillion.pdf

50 Business, Energy and Industrial Strategy and Work and Pensions Committees report on Carillion, p. 67.

51 National Audit Office, 'Investigation into the government's handling of the collapse of Carillion'.

52 Business, Energy and Industrial Strategy and Work and Pensions Committees report on Carillion, p. 3.

53 Kalyeena Makortoff, 'KPMG to be fined £14m for forging documents over Carillion audit', *The Guardian*, 12 May 2022, https://www.theguardian.com/business/2022/may/12/kpmg-fined-frc-audit-carillion

54 Mark Wembridge and Michael O'Dwyer, 'Former Carillion executives fined over "misleadingly positive" statements', *Financial Times*, 28 July 2022, https://www.ft.com/content/7eb26473-96a2-4b07-af02-0c0b7e8b8eda

55 Cristina Lago, 'Another Carillion director banned for over a decade', *Construction Management*, 17 July 2023, https://constructionmanagement.co.uk/second-carillion-director-banned/#:~:text=Earlier%20in%20July%2C%20another%20of,from%20January%20to%20September%202017.

56 Jennifer Rankin, 'Serco shares crash after latest profits warning', *The Guardian*, 10 November 2014, https://www.theguardian.com/business/2014/nov/10/serco-profits-warning-shares-crash

57 Andrew Bowman et al, *What a Waste: Outsourcing and how it goes wrong* (Manchester University Press, 2015), chapter 4.

58 David Foster and Rachael Harker, 'Adult Social Care Funding (England)', House of Commons Library, 17 January 2023, https://commonslibrary.parliament.uk/research-briefings/cbp-7903/

59 Omar Idriss et al, 'Social care funding gap', The Health Foundation, 11 February 2021, https://www.health.org.uk/news-and-comment/charts-and-infographics/REAL-social-care-funding-gap

60 Bob Hudson, 'The failure of privatised adult social care in England: what is to be done?', Centre for Health and the Public Interest, November 2016, https://chpi.org.uk/wp-content/uploads/2016/11/CHPI-SocialCare-Oct16-Proof01a.pdf

61 Grace Blakeley and Harry Quilter-Pinner, 'Who Cares? The Financialization of Adult Social Care', Institute for Public Policy Research, September 2019, https://www.ippr.org/articles/financialisation-in-social-care

62 Vivek Kotecha, 'Plugging the leaks in the UK care home industry', Centre for Health and the Public Interest, November 2019, p. 10, https://chpi.org.uk/wp-content/uploads/2019/11/CHPI-PluggingTheLeaks-Nov19-FINAL.pdf

63 Sharvari Patwardhan, Matthew Sutton and Marcello Morciano, 'Effects of chain ownership and private equity financing on quality in the

English care home sector: retrospective observational study', *Age and Ageing*, volume 51, issue 12, December 2022, https://academic.oup.com/ageing/article/51/12/afac222/6936404

64 The King's Fund, 'Social care 360: workforce and carers', 13 March 2024, https://www.kingsfund.org.uk/insight-and-analysis/long-reads/social-care-360-workforce-carers#:~:text=Between%202021%2F22%20and%202022,fell%20from%20165%2C000%20to%20152%2C000.

65 Richard Wachman, 'Southern Cross's incurably flawed business model let down the vulnerable', *The Guardian*, 16 July 2011, https://www.theguardian.com/business/2011/jul/16/southern-cross-incurable-sick-business-model

66 Cristine Spolar, 'Britain's hard lessons from handing elder care over to private equity', *Fortune*, 27 September 2022, https://fortune.com/2022/09/27/uk-four-seasons-health-care-elder-care-private-equity/

67 E.g. National Audit Office, 'The adult social care market in England', 22 March 2021, https://www.nao.org.uk/wp-content/uploads/2021/03/The-adult-social-care-market-in-England.pdf

68 Anne West and Philip Noden, 'Nationalising and transforming the public funding of early years education (and care) in England 1996–2017', *LSE Research Online*, May 2018, http://eprints.lse.ac.uk/87947/1/West_Early%20Years%20Education_Accepted.pdf

69 Rachel Statham, Sam Freedman and Henry Parkes, 'Delivering a Childcare Guarantee', IPPR, December 2022, p. 25, https://www.ippr.org/articles/delivering-a-childcare-guarantee

70 Ibid., p. 18.

71 E.g. Neil Puffett, '"Austerity and underfunding" pushes nursery chain into liquidation', *Children and Young People Now*, 29 November 2019, https://www.cypnow.co.uk/news/article/austerity-and-underfunding-pushes-nursery-chain-into-liquidation

72 Bethan Staton, 'Private equity groups spot profit in UK's nurseries', *Financial Times*, 18 December 2022, https://www.ft.com/content/96bc7e0d-39e5-4a01-9c97-173dbe2b0e89

73 Children's Commissioner, 'Private provision in children's social care', November 2020, p. 13, https://assets.childrenscommissioner.gov.uk/wpuploads/2020/11/cco-private-provision-in-childrens-social-care.pdf

74 Michael Savage, Carmen Aguilar García and Pamela Duncan, 'Revealed: children's care homes flood into cheapest areas of England, not where

most needed', *The Observer*, 9 July 2023, https://www.theguardian.com/society/2023/jul/09/revealed-childrens-care-homes-flood-into-cheapest-areas-of-england-not-where-most-needed

75 Josh MacAllister, 'Independent review of children's social care', 23 May 2023, https://www.gov.uk/government/groups/independent-review-of-childrens-social-care

CHAPTER 4: DEMOCRACY BYPASS

1 David Mitchell, 'Who'd want to be an MP in a sorting office in Bristol?', *The Observer*, 17 April 2016, https://www.theguardian.com/commentisfree/2016/apr/17/david-mitchell-renovation-houses-parliament-palace-westminster-bristol-sorting-office

2 Though it could have been very different. The 1701 Act of Settlement included provision that once Queen Anne died the monarch's ministers could not be MPs, but it was repealed in 1705, and thus the legislature and executive became fused together into the modern Parliament.

3 Matthew Flinders and Alexandra Kelso, 'Mind the Gap: Political Analysis, Public Expectations and the Parliamentary Decline Thesis', *British Journal of Politics and International Relations* (2011), volume 13, number 2, pp.249–68.

4 Hollis, C., 'Can Parliament Survive? (London: Hollis & Carter, 1949); quoted in Flinders and Kelso, p. 9.

5 See summary in Meg Russell and Philip Cowley, 'The Policy Power of the Westminster Parliament: The "Parliamentary State" and the Empirical Evidence', *Governance*, volume 29, issue 1, January 2016, pp. 121–37.

6 Ibid.

7 Aubrey Allegretti, 'Sunak to scrap housebuilding targets after pressure from Tory MPs', *The Guardian*, 5 December 2022, https://www.theguardian.com/politics/2022/dec/05/sunak-backs-down-on-house building-targets-after-pressure-from-tory-mps

8 Interview with David Lidington.

9 Quoted in 'MPs' Outside Interests', Committee on Standards in Public Life, July 2018, p. 19.

10   Andrew C. Eggers and Jens Hainmueller, 'MPs for Sale? Returns to Office in Postwar British Politics', *American Political Science Review*, volume 103, number 4, November 2009.

11   'MPs' Outside Interests', p. 16.

12   Ibid., p. 28.

13   Colin Brown, 'Labour to end union backing of MPs', *The Independent*, 7 August 1995, https://www.independent.co.uk/news/labour-to-end-union-backing-of-mps-1595245.html

14   Erksine May, 'Normal days and hours of sitting and rising', last updated August 2021, https://erskinemay.parliament.uk/section/4613/normal-days-and-hours-of-sitting-and-rising/

15   Interview with David Lidington.

16   'MPs' Outside Interests', p. 20.

17   Ibid.

18   Isabel Hardman, *Why We Get the Wrong Politicians?* (Atlantic Books, 2018), location 1259 Kindle edition.

19   'MPs' Outside Interests', p. 28.

20   Ibid., p. 22.

21   Elise Uberoi et al, 'Women in Politics and Public Life', House of Commons Library, 6 March 2023, https://commonslibrary.parliament.uk/research-briefings/sn01250/

22   Elise Uberoi and Helena Carthew, 'Ethnic diversity in politics and public life', House of Commons Library, 2 October 2023, https://commonslibrary.parliament.uk/research-briefings/sn01156/

23   Peter Walker and Jessica Elgot, 'Tory defector says whips told him to back PM or lose school funds', *The Guardian*, 20 January 2022, https://www.theguardian.com/politics/2022/jan/20/ministers-attempting-blackmail-colleagues-who-might-oppose-pm-alleges-tory-mp-william-wragg-boris-johnson

24   Ibid.

25   Public Administration Select Committee, 'Too Many Ministers?', 11 March 2010, https://publications.parliament.uk/pa/cm200910/cmselect/cmpubadm/457/457.pdf

26   Quoted in ibid.

27   Ibid.

28   Ibid.

29 Lucinda Maer, 'Parliamentary Private Secretaries', House of Commons Library, 4 September 2017, p. 9, https://researchbriefings.files.parliament.uk/documents/SN04942/SN04942.pdf

30 Interview with Charlotte Leslie.

31 https://www.instituteforgovernment.org.uk/article/explainer/payroll-vote

32 MPs who were fighting to stop a 'no deal' Brexit had spotted the threat and passed a bill which required Parliament to be sitting on various dates, but left a five-week gap which Johnson tried to exploit. Had they not passed this legislation he could have tried for a longer prorogation.

33 Owen Bowcott, 'Gina Miller to continue "fight for democracy" after prorogation ruling', *The Guardian*, 6 September 2019, https://www.theguardian.com/politics/2019/sep/06/boris-johnson-prorogation-of-parliament-is-lawful-high-court-rules

34 Meg Russell and Lisa James, *The Parliamentary Battle over Brexit* (OUP, 2023), p. 112.

35 Ibid.

36 Ibid., p. 122.

37 Procedure Committee, 'Programming of Legislation', 7 July 2004, p. 5, https://publications.parliament.uk/pa/cm200304/cmselect/cmproced/325/325.pdf

38 Ibid., p. 8.

39 Hansard, 26 April 2023, https://hansard.parliament.uk/commons/2023-04-26/debates/5751EE9A-180E-48BA-A8CA-D51B230C1984/IllegalMigrationBill

40 David Lidington, 'Building a More United Kingdom: a Conservative Case for Constitutional Reform', *The Political Quarterly*, volume 94, issue 1, January/March 2023, pp. 16–25, https://onlinelibrary.wiley.com/doi/abs/10.1111/1467-923X.13233

41 Nicola Slawson, 'Boris Johnson faces legal action over peerage for billionaire Tory donor', *The Guardian*, 12 June 2021, https://www.theguardian.com/politics/2021/jun/12/boris-johnson-faces-legal-action-over-peerage-for-billionaire-tory-donor-peter-cruddas

42 Ross Kaniuk, 'Queen "asked to block Lebedev's peerage over security fears"', *The Times*, 26 June 2023, https://www.thetimes.co.uk/article/late-queen-was-asked-to-block-lebedev-s-peerage-wq3z2dnk7

43 Norman Fowler, 'The House of Lords is bloated. We need an inquiry into the peerages system', *The Guardian*, 23 December

2020, https://www.theguardian.com/commentisfree/2020/dec/23/
house-of-lords-peerages-appointments

44 Lord Speaker, 'Report of the Lord Speaker's committee on the size of the
House', 31 October 2017.

45 Alice Lilly, 'The Slow Death of Parliamentary Scrutiny', *The House*
magazine, 15 May 2023, https://www.politicshome.com/thehouse/
article/scrutiny-scarcity-parliament-commons-lords

46 Interview with Camilla Cavendish.

47 House of Lords website, 'Government defeats in the House of Lords',
last accessed 6 January 2024, https://www.parliament.uk/about/faqs/
house-of-lords-faqs/lords-govtdefeats/

48 UK Parliament website, 'The Parliament Act', https://www.parliament.
uk/about/how/laws/parliamentacts/

49 Anonymous interview with senior official in the Department for
Education.

50 House of Lords Delegated Powers and Regulatory Reform Committee,
'Democracy Denied? The urgent need to rebalance power between
Parliament and the Executive', 24 November 2021, https://publications.
parliament.uk/pa/ld5802/ldselect/lddelreg/106/106.pdf

51 House of Lords Secondary Legislation Scrutiny Committee,
'Government by Diktat: A call to return power to Parliament', 24
November 2021, https://committees.parliament.uk/publications/7941/
documents/82225/default/

52 House of Lords Delegated Powers and Regulatory Reform Committee,
'Special Report: Response to the Strathclyde Review', 23 March 2016, p.
16, https://www.regulation.org.uk/library/2016_HoL_delegated_powers_
etc_committee_HenryVIII_powers.pdf

53 Lord Judge, 'Ceding Power to the Executive; the Resurrection of Henry
VIII', transcript of speech given at King's College London on 12 April
2016, p. 8, https://www.regulation.org.uk/library/2016_Henry_VIII_
powers-Lord_Judge.pdf.

54 UK – Court of Appeal, 26 September 2009, EN (Serbia) v Secretary of
State for the Home Department & Anor [2009] EWCA Civ 630.

55 Hansard Society, 'Delegated legislation: the problems with the process',
November 2021, p. 10, https://www.hansardsociety.org.uk/publications/
reports/delegated-legislation-the-problems-with-the-process

56 Ibid., p. 11.

57 Tom de la Mare, 'Statutory Instruments: the Unseen Constitutional Crisis', Blackstone Chambers, 14 October 2020, https://www.blackstone chambers.com/news/statutory-instruments-unseen-constitutional-crisis/

58 Linklaters, 'Brexit SI Tracker', https://www.linklaters.com/en/insights/ thought-leadership/brexit/brexit-si-tracker

59 Greener UK, 'Issues identified in Defra EU exit statutory instruments', April 2021, https://greeneruk.org/sites/default/files/download/2021-04/ Issues_identified_in_Defra_EU_exit_statutory_instruments.pdf

60 Adam Wagner, *Emergency State* (Bodley Head, 2022), p. 49.

61 Ibid., p. 61.

62 Ibid., p. 161.

63 Ibid., p. 68.

64 Helen MacNamara, witness statement to the UK Covid-19 Inquiry, 9 October 2023, p. 68, https://covid19.public-inquiry.uk/wp-content/ uploads/2023/11/03103311/INQ000273841.pdf

65 Hannah White, *Held in Contempt: What's Wrong with the House of Commons?* (Manchester University Press, 2022), p. 25.

66 Ibid.

67 Hansard Society, p. 19.

68 David Allen Green, 'Telling the story of how the "serious disruption" public order statutory instrument was passed', *The Law and Policy Blog*, 14 June 2023, https://davidallengreen.com/2023/06/telling-the-story-of-how-the-serious-disruption-public-order-statutory-instrument-was-passed/

69 See e.g. Meg Russell, Hannah White, Lisa James, 'Rebuilding and renewing the constitution', Institute for Government and the Constitution Unit, pp. 13–16, https://www.instituteforgovernment.org. uk/sites/default/files/2023-07/rebuilding-and-renewing-the-constitution. pdf

70 Stephen Holden Bates, 'Is chairing Select Committees in the House of Commons really an "alternative career"?', Hansard Society, 5 January 2023, https://www.hansardsociety.org.uk/blog/is-chairing-select-committees-in-the-house-of-commons-really-an-alternative

NOTES

CHAPTER 5: ENEMIES OF THE PEOPLE

1 Lord Burnett of Maldon, 'Institutional independence and accountability of the judiciary', The Lionel Cohen Lecture, Hebrew University of Jerusalem, 30 May 2022, https://www.judiciary.uk/wp-content/uploads/2022/07/Cohen-Lecture-300522-1.pdf

2 Joshua Rozenberg, 'Emergency State', *A Lawyer Writes* . . . blog, 3 October 2022, https://rozenberg.substack.com/p/emergency-state

3 Jessica Leigh v The Commissioner Of Police Of The Metropolis [2022] EWHC 527 (Admin).

4 Haroon Siddique, 'Use of "VIP lane" to award Covid PPE contracts unlawful, high court rules', *The Guardian*, 12 January 2022, https://www.theguardian.com/politics/2022/jan/12/use-of-vip-lane-to-award-covid-ppe-contracts-unlawful-high-court-rules

5 Jonathan Jones, 'Government loses judicial review on Covid-19 Inquiry WhatsApps', Institute for Government, 6 July 2023, https://www.instituteforgovernment.org.uk/comment/government-loses-judicial-review-covid-inquiry-whatsapps

6 Dominic Casciani and Sean Seddon, 'Supreme Court rules Rwanda asylum policy unlawful', BBC News, 15 November 2023, https://www.bbc.co.uk/news/uk-67423745

7 E.g. https://www.thetimes.com/article/judges-block-uks-deportation-of-criminals-in-human-rights-test-case-960g0jh9jn0

8 E.g. Shiv Malik, 'Poundland case: government defeated again over back-to-work schemes', *The Guardian*, 30 October 2013, https://www.theguardian.com/business/2013/oct/30/poundland-case-government-defeated-work-schemes-duncan-smith

9 Rachel Sylvester, 'Blunkett accuses judges of damaging democracy', *The Telegraph*, 21 February 2003, https://www.telegraph.co.uk/news/uknews/1422661/Blunkett-accuses-judges-of-damaging-democracy.html

10 Nigel Morris, 'Reid attacks judges who hamper "life and death" terrorism battle', *The Independent*, 10 August 2006, https://www.independent.co.uk/news/uk/politics/reid-attacks-judges-who-hamper-life-and-death-terrorism-battle-411252.html; Alan Travis and Vikram Dodd, 'Reid warning to judges over control orders', *The Guardian*,

25 May 2007, https://www.theguardian.com/politics/2007/may/25/
uk.topstories3

11   Kit Heren, ' "Ignore the laws and put the planes in the air now": Tory
     fury after Supreme Court rules against Rwanda migrant plan', LBC
     News, 15 November 2023, https://www.lbc.co.uk/news/tory-fury-after-
     supreme-court-rwanda-ruling/

12   Joanna Dawson and Alexander Horne, 'Judicial Review: Government
     reforms', House of Commons Library, 7 August 2015, https://
     commonslibrary.parliament.uk/research-briefings/sn06616/

13   The Conservative Party Manifesto 2019, p. 48, https://cchq2019.
     webflow.io/our-plan

14   James Tapsfield, 'Ministers "could use legislation to strike out judicial
     rulings they don't like" under reforms being pushed by Boris Johnson',
     Daily Mail, 6 December 2021, https://www.dailymail.co.uk/news/article-
     10279363/Ministers-use-legislation-strike-judicial-rulings-dont-like.html

15   Judicial Independence Inquiry, 8 June 2022, https://www.icdr.co.uk/
     judicial-independence-inquiry

16   Judicial Institute at UCL, 'Judicial Attitudes Survey', Courts and
     Tribunals Judiciary, February 2021, https://www.judiciary.uk/guidance-
     and-resources/judicial-attitudes-survey/

17   Unlike many written constitutions, the American one does not expressly
     give the Supreme Court the right to overturn Congressional legislation
     but in the 1803 Marbury vs Madison case the Court took this power
     and has kept it since.

18   See Stephen Gardbaum, 'Separation of Powers and the Growth of
     Judicial Review in Established Democracies (or Why Has the Model
     of Legislative Supremacy Mostly Been Withdrawn From Sale?)', *The
     American Journal of Comparative Law*, volume 62, number 3 (summer
     2014), pp. 613–39, https://www.jstor.org/stable/43669514?saml_data=e
     yJzYW1sVG9rZW4iOiIwNzQ2YTlkZi0wZmY1LTRmMzItYjIwZi04
     ZWFjZjM1ZTliMDIiLCJpbnN0aXR1dGlvbklkcyI6WyIxOGVlZT
     JmYS1mODcxLTQwYTktODI4NS1mNTRlYzdhMDM4MjciXX0

19   Human Rights Act 1998.

20   Lord Neuberger, 'The Supreme Court and the Rule of Law', The
     Conkerton Lecture 2014, Liverpool Law Society, 9 October 2014, p. 6
     https://www.supremecourt.uk/docs/speech-141009-lord-neuberger.pdf

NOTES

21 Lord Hodge, 'The scope of judicial law-making in constitutional law and public law', Supreme Court, 27 October 2021, p. 14, https://www.supremecourt.uk/docs/judicial-law-making-in-constitutional-law-and-public-law-paper.pdf

22 Ibid., p. 26.

23 Ibid., pp. 13–14.

24 Ibid., p. 10.

25 Lord Dyson, 'Is Judicial Review a Threat to Democracy?', Judiciary of England and Wales, November 2015, p. 2, https://www.judiciary.uk/wp-content/uploads/2015/12/is-judicial-review-a-threat-to-democracy-mr.pdf

26 Jackson and others (Appellants) v. Her Majesty's Attorney General (Respondent) [2005] UKHL 56, p. 33, https://publications.parliament.uk/pa/ld200506/ldjudgmt/jd051013/jack.pdf. This case was heard by law lords in the House of Lords which, prior to the establishment of the Supreme Court in 2009, was the highest court.

27 Ibid., p. 47.

28 Ibid., p. 49.

29 R (Unison) vs Lord Chancellor, Trinity Term [2017] UKSC 51, https://www.supremecourt.uk/cases/docs/uksc-2015-0233-judgment.pdf

30 Jonathan Sumption, 'Judicial and Political Decision Making: The Uncertain Boundary', The F.A. Mann Lecture 2011, p. 17, https://www.studocu.com/en-gb/document/bpp-university/public-law/jonathan-sumption-qc-fa-mann-lecture-2011/9696580

31 Owen Bowcott, 'Covid measures will be seen as "monument of collective hysteria and folly" says ex-judge', The Guardian, 27 October 2020, https://www.theguardian.com/law/2020/oct/27/covid-measures-will-be-seen-as-monument-of-collective-hysteria-and-folly-says-ex-judge

32 For an overview of their core arguments see Richard Ekins, 'The Case for Reforming Judicial Review', Policy Exchange, 2020, https://policyexchange.org.uk/wp-content/uploads/2022/10/The-Case-for-Reforming-Judicial-Review.pdf

33 Paul Craig, 'Judicial Review, Methodology and Reform', Public Law, January 2022, p. 19, file:///C:/Users/sam26/Downloads/SSRN-id3875313%20(2).pdf

34 Bowcott, 27 October 2020.

35 Andrew Defty, 'Sense and sensibility: politicians, judges and the rise of judicial review', *Who Runs Britain?* blog, 14 December 2023, https://whorunsbritain.blogs.lincoln.ac.uk/2013/12/14/sense-and-sensibility-politicians-judges-and-the-rise-of-judicial-review/

36 Kate Malleson, 'Judicial reform: the emergence of the third branch of government', in Andrew McDonald (ed.), *Reinventing Britain: Constitutional Change under New Labour* (University of California Press, 2007), p. 139.

37 Owen Bowcott, Amelia Hill and Pamela Duncan, 'Revealed: legal aid cuts forcing parents to give up fight for children', *The Guardian*, 26 December 2018, https://www.theguardian.com/law/2018/dec/26/revealed-legal-aid-cuts-forcing-parents-to-give-up-fight-for-children

38 The Law Society, 'LASPO Act', 22 November 2023, https://www.lawsociety.org.uk/topics/legal-aid/laspo-act

39 Amelia Hill, 'How legal aid cuts filled family courts with bewildered litigants', *The Guardian*, 26 December 2018, https://www.theguardian.com/law/2018/dec/26/how-legal-aid-cuts-filled-family-courts-with-bewildered-litigants

40 Dr James Organ and Dr Jennifer Sigafoos, 'The impact of LASPO on routes to justice', Equality and Human Rights Commission Research report 118, September 2018, p. 27, https://www.equalityhumanrights.com/sites/default/files/the-impact-of-laspo-on-routes-to-justice-september-2018.pdf

41 Ibid., p. 14.

42 Amelia Hill.

43 Richard Oldershaw, 'Legal Update: Tackling family court delays', *Children and Young People Now*, 31 January 2023, https://www.cypnow.co.uk/features/article/legal-update-tackling-family-court-delays

44 E.g. see this article for the impact on housing: Chaminda Jayanetti, ' "The bailiffs will come at noon": desperation and devastation in England's housing courts', *The Observer*, 16 December 2023, https://www.theguardian.com/society/2023/dec/16/legal-aid-cuts-britain-housing-crisis-county-court-tenants-homes-lawyers

45 Joint Committee on Human Rights, 'The implications for access to justice of the Government's proposals to reform legal aid', 11 December 2013, https://publications.parliament.uk/pa/jt201314/jtselect/jtrights/100/10004.htm

46   Joint Committee on Human Rights, 'The implications for access to justice of the Government's proposals to reform judicial review', 9 April 2014, pp. 11–12, https://publications.parliament.uk/pa/jt201314/jtselect/jtrights/174/174.pdf

47   Owen Bowcott, 'Plans to restrict judicial review face further concessions', *The Guardian*, 13 January 2015, https://www.theguardian.com/law/2015/jan/13/plans-restrict-judicial-review-concessions-lords-chris-grayling

48   Owen Bowcott, 'Former top judge lambasts Grayling and Truss in memoir', *The Guardian*, 21 August 2019, https://www.theguardian.com/law/2019/aug/21/former-top-judge-lambasts-recent-ministers-in-memoir

49   Rajeev Syal and Owen Bowcott, 'Geoffrey Cox signals he would accept lead role in review of judiciary', *The Guardian*, 12 February 2020, https://www.theguardian.com/politics/2020/feb/12/geoffrey-cox-signals-would-accept-lead-role-review-judiciary

50   Anthony Seldon and Raymond Newell, *Johnson at 10: The Inside Story* (Atlantic, 2023)

51   Lisa O'Carroll, 'Government admits new Brexit bill "will break international law"', *The Guardian*, 8 September 2020, https://www.theguardian.com/politics/2020/sep/08/government-admits-new-brexit-bill-will-break-international-law

52   BBC News, 'Lord Keen: Senior law officer quits over Brexit bill row', 16 September 2020, https://www.bbc.co.uk/news/uk-scotland-scotland-politics-54179745

53   Owen Bowcott and Daniel Boffey, 'Amal Clooney quits UK envoy role over "lamentable" Brexit bill', *The Guardian*, 18 September 2020, https://www.theguardian.com/world/2020/sep/18/amal-clooney-quits-uk-envoy-role-over-lamentable-brexit-bill#:~:text=Amal%20Clooney%2C%20the%20high%2Dprofile,through%20the%20internal%20market%20bill.

54   All Party Parliamentary Group on Democracy and the Constitution, 'An Inquiry into the impact of the actions and rhetoric of the Executive since 2016 on the constitutional role of the Judiciary', 8 June 2022, p. 53, https://static1.squarespace.com/static/6033d6547502c200670fd98c/t/62a05b38f1b9b809f61853ef/1654676281940/SOPI+Report+FINAL.pdf

55   Owen Bowcott, 'Brexit strategy risks UK "dictatorship", says ex-president of supreme court', *The Guardian*, 7 October 2020, https://

www.theguardian.com/law/2020/oct/07/brexit-strategy-puts-uk-on-slippery-slope-to-tyranny-lawyers-told

56 Faulks Committee, 'The Independent Review of Administrative Law', p. 132, https://consult.justice.gov.uk/judicial-review-reform/judicial-review-proposals-for-reform/supporting_documents/IRALreport.pdf

57 Joshua Rozenberg, 'Faulks defends judicial review', *A Lawyer Writes . . .* blog, 23 March 2021, https://rozenberg.substack.com/p/faulks-defends-judicial-review

58 Owen Bowcott, 'What is judicial review and why doesn't the government like it?', *The Guardian*, 11 February 2020, https://www.theguardian.com/law/2020/feb/11/what-is-judicial-review-and-why-doesnt-the-government-like-it

59 The Law Society, 'Judicial review reform', 28 April 2022, https://www.lawsociety.org.uk/topics/human-rights/judicial-review-reform

60 Martina Bet, 'PM: "Liberal lawyers" will make Rwanda plan difficult but "we will get it done"', *The Independent*, 4 May 2022, https://www.independent.co.uk/news/uk/boris-johnson-rwanda-priti-patel-north-yorkshire-downing-street-b2071595.html

61 Faulks Committee, p. 131.

62 Malleson, p. 149.

63 Matthew Gill and Grant Dalton, 'Reforming Public Appointments', Institute for Government, August 2022, p. 5, https://www.institute forgovernment.org.uk/sites/default/files/publications/reforming-public-appointments.pdf

64 Michael Moran, 'The rise of the regulatory state in Britain', *Parliamentary Affairs*, volume 54, issue 1, January 2001, pp. 19–34, https://academic.oup.com/pa/article-abstract/54/1/19/1462525?redirectedFrom=PDF

65 Fraser Nelson, 'Gordon Brown's secret army could defeat the Coalition's welfare and education reforms', *The Telegraph*, 25 October 2012, https://www.telegraph.co.uk/news/politics/david-cameron/9633379/Gordon-Browns-secret-army-could-defeat-the-Coalitions-welfare-and-education-reforms.html

66 Michael Pinto-Duschinsky and Lynne Middleton, 'Reforming Public Appointments', Policy Exchange, 2013, p. 32, https://policyexchange.org.uk/wp-content/uploads/2016/09/reforming-public-appointments-1.pdf

NOTES

67 Gerry Grimstone, 'Better public appointments: review of the public appointments process', 11 March 2016, https://www.gov.uk/government/publications/better-public-appointments-review-of-the-public-appointments-process

68 Public Administration and Constitutional Affairs Committee, 'Better Public Appointments?: The Grimstone Review on Public Appointments', 28 June 2016, p. 3, https://publications.parliament.uk/pa/cm201617/cmselect/cmpubadm/495/495.pdf

69 Culture, Media and Sport Committee, 'Appointment of the Chair of the Charity Commission', 27 February 2018, https://publications.parliament.uk/pa/cm201719/cmselect/cmcumeds/509/50907.htm#_idTextAnchor017

70 Andy Martin, 'Is it time to abolish the Charity Commission?', *Firetail*, 25 February 2021

71 Patrick Butler, 'Commission chief tells charities not to be "captured" for politics', *The Guardian*, 4 February 2021, https://www.theguardian.com/society/2021/feb/04/commission-chief-tells-charities-not-to-be-captured-for-politics

72 Patrick Butler, 'Calls for rerun of selection process to find next head of Charity Commission', *The Guardian*, 20 December 2021, https://www.theguardian.com/society/2021/dec/20/calls-for-re-run-of-selection-process-to-find-next-head-of-charity-commission

73 Patrick Butler, '"Shambles": MPs attack appointment of Charity Commission chair', *The Guardian*, 11 January 2022, https://www.theguardian.com/society/2022/jan/11/shambles-mps-attack-appointment-of-charity-commission-chair

74 Alex Dean, 'Outgoing public appointments commissioner: "I've been concerned about the balance on panels"', *Prospect Magazine*, 30 September 2021, https://www.prospectmagazine.co.uk/politics/37987/outgoing-public-appointments-commissioner-ive-been-concerned-about-the-balance-on-panels

75 David Batty, 'Office for Students chair speaks at same event as denounced racist', *The Guardian*, 23 May 2022, https://www.theguardian.com/education/2022/may/23/office-for-students-chair-james-wharton-same-event-as-denounced-racist-zsolt-bayer

76 Dean.

77 *The Times*, 'Letters to the Editor', 19 November 2021, https://www.thetimes.co.uk/article/times-letters-levelling-up-agenda-and-the-u-turn-on-hs2-3g05sc07m

78 Sean Seddon, 'Richard Sharp: BBC chairman resigns over report into appointment', BBC News, 28 April 2023, https://www.bbc.co.uk/news/uk-65323077

79 Alan Rusbridger, 'Was there an attempt to "fix" who became head of Ofcom?', *Prospect Magazine*, 17 November 2023, https://www.prospectmagazine.co.uk/politics/63982/boris-johnson-nadine-dorries-ofcom

80 John Kingman, '5 Years of UKRI', transcript of speech given on 14 July 2021, https://www.thebritishacademy.ac.uk/documents/3372/Sir-John-Kingman-reflections-on-his-time-as-UKRI-Chair.pdf

CHAPTER 6: CIVIL WAR

1 Graham McCann, *A Very Courageous Decision: The Inside Story of Yes Minister* (Aurum, 2014), p. 175.

2 Graham McCann, 'Margaret Thatcher: sitcom star', British Comedy Guide, 21 February 2021, https://www.comedy.co.uk/features/comedy_chronicles/margaret-thatcher-sitcom-star/

3 Caroline Slocock, *People Like Us: Margaret Thatcher and Me* (Biteback Publishing, 2018) p. 172.

4 Pippa Crerar, 'At least 24 civil servants involved in complaints against Dominic Raab, say sources', *The Guardian*, 25 January 2023, https://www.theguardian.com/politics/2023/jan/25/dominic-raab-much-broader-inquiry-civil-servants-complaints

5 Adam Tolley, 'Investigation report to the Prime Minister', 21 April 2023, https://www.gov.uk/government/publications/investigation-report-to-the-prime-minister

6 Interview with anonymous civil servant.

7 Jane Croft, 'Revived Bill of Rights faces opposition in both houses of parliament', *Financial Times*, 30 November 2022, https://www.ft.com/content/e552daa6-d352-4dff-96ad-02a3a37c1ae7; Michael Cross, 'Raab rejects "flawed" UN criticism of Bill of Rights', *Law Society Gazette*, 23 August 2022, https://www.lawgazette.co.uk/law/raab-rejects-flawed-un-criticism-of-bill-of-rights/5113483.article

NOTES

8   PA Media, 'Philip Rutnam resignation: his full statement', 29 February 2020, https://www.theguardian.com/politics/2020/feb/29/philip-rutnam-resignation-his-full-statement

9   Sir Alex Allan, 'Findings of the Independent Adviser', 10 March 2021, https://assets.publishing.service.gov.uk/media/5fb7a21fd3bf7f573228a398/Findings_of_the_Independent_Adviser.pdf

10 BBC News, 'Philip Rutnam: £340k payout to official after Priti Patel bullying claims', 4 March 2021, https://www.bbc.co.uk/news/uk-politics-56281781

11 Dominic Cummings, 'Some thoughts on education and political priorities', https://dominiccummings.files.wordpress.com/2013/11/20130825-some-thoughts-on-education-and-political-priorities-version-2-final.pdf

12 Dominic Cummings, '"Two hands are a lot" — we're hiring data scientists, project managers, policy experts, assorted weirdos . . .' blogpost, 2 January 2020, https://dominiccummings.com/2020/01/02/two-hands-are-a-lot-were-hiring-data-scientists-project-managers-policy-experts-assorted-weirdos/

13 Martin Stanley, 'Fulton Report – Findings', blogpost, https://civilservant.org.uk/csr-fulton_report-findings.html

14 Martin Stanely, 'Civil Service History', blogpost, https://www.civilservant.org.uk/misc-history.html

15 See Michael Coolican, *No Tradesmen and No Women: The Origins of the British Civil Service* (Biteback Publishing, 2018), chapters 4–6.

16 The FDA, the union for senior civil servants, originally stood for 'First Division Association', though in 2000 they decided it didn't stand for anything.

17 Coolican, p. 162.

18 Ibid., p. 172.

19 Martin Stanley, 'The Fulton Report – Background', blogpost, https://civilservant.org.uk/csr-fulton_report-background.html

20 Martin Stanley, 'Civil Service Reform – Lord Maude Tries Again', blogpost, https://www.strategicreading.uk/2022/06/civil-service-reform-lord-maude-tries-again/

21 Lord Maude of Horsham, 'Independent Review of Governance and Accountability in the Civil Service', 13 November 2023, https://assets.publishing.service.gov.uk/media/6552350b8a2ed40013720d82/

Independent-Review-of-Governance-and-Accountability-in-the-Civil-Service-The-Rt-Hon-Lord-Maude-of-Horsham-Final-3.pdf

22 Martin Stanley, 'Civil service is poor, pompous and arrogant, say two former Permanent Secretaries', blogpost, 11 February 2023, https://ukcivilservant.substack.com/p/civil-service-is-poor-pompous-and

23 Ibid.

24 Peter Cardwell, *The Secret Life of Special Advisers* (Biteback Publishing, 2022), p. 26.

25 Ibid., p.35.

26 McCann, p. 298.

27 Interview with David Omand.

28 Anthony Seldon and Raymond Newell, *Johnson at 10: The Inside Story*, pp. 87–8.

29 Ibid., p. 296.

30 Interview with David Lidington.

31 Interview with Helen MacNamara.

32 Sam Blewett, 'Foreign office mandarin under fire for saying day after Brexit referendum: I voted Remain', *The Independent*, 11 September 2023, https://www.independent.co.uk/news/uk/home-news/brexit-referendum-simon-mcdonald-remain-b2409001.html

33 Interview with John Kingman.

34 House of Lords Select Committee on the Constitution, 'Permanent secretaries: their appointment and removal', 20 October 2023, p. 41, https://committees.parliament.uk/publications/41636/documents/206273/default/

35 Ibid., p. 20.

36 Ibid., p. 39.

37 Ibid., p. 34.

38 Interview with former permanent secretary.

39 Interview with senior Whitehall official.

40 Document published by the Covid Inquiry, https://covid19.public-inquiry.uk/wp-content/uploads/2023/12/06175412/INQ000303245_0001-0009.pdf

41 Michael Lewis, *The Fifth Risk: Undoing Democracy* (Penguin, 2019).

42 Werner Jann, 'Party time: exploring Germany's system of political civil servants', *Civil Service World*, 18 August 2021, https://www.

civilserviceworld.com/in-depth/article/party-time-exploring-germanys-system-of-political-civil-servants

43 Maude, 2023.

44 Alex Thomas, 'IfG response to the Maude review on civil service reform', Institute for Government, November 2023, https://www.instituteforgovernment.org.uk/sites/default/files/2023-11/maude-review-IfG-reponse.pdf

45 Jonathan Powell, *The New Machiavelli* (Vintage, 2011), p. 72.

46 Ibid., pp. 73–4.

CHAPTER 7: THE RANDOM ANNOUNCEMENT GENERATOR

1   David Foster Wallace, 'Up Simba', in *Consider the Lobster and Other Essays*, (Abacus, 2005), p. 162.

2   BBC News, 'Gove on new free schools figures', 5 September 2010, http://news.bbc.co.uk/1/hi/programmes/andrew_marr_show/8970305.stm

3   Interview with Camilla Cavendish.

4   Guido Fawkes blog, 'Liz Truss SPAD list', 13 September 2022, https://order-order.com/2022/09/13/liz-truss-spad-list/

5   Interview with Rupert Harrison.

6   A.J.P. Taylor, *English History 1914–1945* (Oxford University Press, 1965), p. 187.

7   J.M. McEwen, 'Lloyd George's Acquisition of the Daily Chronicle in 1918', *Journal of British Studies*, volume 22, number 1 (autumn, 1982), pp. 127–44, https://www.jstor.org/stable/175660

8   Carole Walker, *Lobby Life: Inside Westminster's Secret Society* (Elliot & Thompson, 2021), p. 16.

9   David Hendy, *The BBC: A People's History* (Profile Books, 2021), pp. 111–14.

10 Walker, p. 60.

11 Interview with Robin Butler.

12 Philip Webster, *Inside Story: Politics, Intrigue and Treachery from Thatcher to Brexit* (William Collins, 2016), location 671, Kindle edition.

13 Walker, p. 104.

14 Harold Evans, 'How Thatcher and Murdoch made their secret deal', *The Guardian*, 28 April 2015, https://www.theguardian.com/uk-news /2015/apr/28/how-margaret-thatcher-and-rupert-murdoch-made-secret-deal

15 Interview with Alastair Campbell.

16 Quoted in Cardwell, pp. 41–2.

17 Nicholas Jones, *Sultans of Spin: The Media and the New Labour Government* (Orion Books, 2000), p. 102.

18 Tim Shipman, ' "I've gone from being Churchill to a Nazi in a week": Clegg defends attack on Britain's "delusions of grandeur" over WWII', *Daily Mail*, 22 April 2010, https://www.dailymail.co.uk/news/election/ article-1267921/GENERAL-ELECTION-2010-Nick-Clegg-Nazi-slur-Britain.html

19 Interview with Nick Timothy.

20 Interview with former senior official at the DfE.

21 Damian McBride, *Power Trip: A Decade of Policy, Plots and Spin* (Biteback 2013), pp. 95–6.

22 Jill Rutter et al, 'Better Budgets', Institute for Government, 2017, p. 10, https://www.instituteforgovernment.org.uk/sites/default/files/publica tions/Better_Budgets_report_WEB.pdf

23 Interview with Rupert Harrison.

24 Interview with Giles Wilkes.

25 Interview with Robert Kramer.

26 Matthew Burton and Richard Tunnicliffe, 'Membership of political parties in Great Britain', House of Commons Library, 31 August 2022, https://commonslibrary.parliament.uk/research-briefings/sn05125/

27 Lauren Higgs, 'Lib Dem conference: Clegg unveils "catch-up" premium', *Children and Young People Now*, 26 September 2012, https://www. cypnow.co.uk/news/article/lib-dem-conference-clegg-unveils-catch-up-premium

28 Nicholas Watt and Patrick Wintour, 'Tories woo married couples with tax break', *The Guardian*, 28 September 2013, https://www.theguardian. com/politics/2013/sep/27/tory-tax-break-marriage-glue

29 Adam Forrest and Jon Stone, 'Rishi Sunak admits list of HS2 replacement projects just "illustrative" and not pledges', *The Independent*, 9 October 2023, https://www.independent.co.uk/news/uk/politics/hs2-rishi-sunak-cancel-pledges-metro-b2426729.html

30　Jill Rutter and William Knighton, 'Legislated Policy Targets', Institute for Government, 2012, https://www.instituteforgovernment.org.uk/sites/default/files/publications/Legislated%20policy%20targets%20final.pdf

31　Ibid.; Philip Loft and Philip Brien, 'The 0.7% aid target', House of Commons Library, 4 December 2023, https://commonslibrary.parliament.uk/research-briefings/sn03714/

32　Regulatory Policy Committee, 'Strikes (Minimum Service Levels) Bill: RPC Opinion (Red-rated)', 21 February 2023, https://www.gov.uk/government/publications/strikes-minimum-service-bill-rpc-opinion-red-rated

33　Joint Committee on Human Rights, 'Strikes Bill fails to meet human rights obligations', 6 March 2023, https://committees.parliament.uk/committee/93/human-rights-joint-committee/news/186524/strikes-bill-fails-to-meet-human-rights-obligations-jchr/

34　Rory Stewart, *How Not to Be a Politician* (Penguin Press, 2023), p. 156.

35　Ibid., p. 157.

36　Valentina Romei, 'UK public trust in political parties collapses to 12%', *Financial Times*, 1 March 2024, https://www.ft.com/content/c0b3a1d1-b887-4b67-ba0e-b6e745e1df7b

37　Interview with Gabriel Milland.

38　Mark Pack, 'The myth of Budget poll bounces', The Week in Polls, 10 March 2024, https://theweekinpolls.substack.com/p/the-myth-of-budget-poll-bounces

CHAPTER 8: HIGH SPEED CRASH

1　Chris York, 'Social media is "a plague on politics", says Tony Blair', *Huffington Post*, 13 September 2020, https://www.huffingtonpost.co.uk/entry/tony-blair-twitter_uk_5f5de4d9c5b62874bc1e2785

2　Interview with Ed Balls.

3　Interview with Paul Waugh.

4　Interview with Gabriel Milland.

5　Ibid.

6　Charlotte Tobitt and Aisha Majid, 'National press ABCs: The i and FT report steadiest circulations in November', *Press Gazette*, 19 December 2023, https://pressgazette.co.uk/media-audience-and-business-data/

media_metrics/most-popular-newspapers-uk-abc-monthly-circulation-figures-2/; *The Guardian*, 'ABCs: National daily newspaper circulation September 2010', 15 October 2010, https://www.theguardian.com/media/table/2010/oct/15/abcs-national-newspapers; Charlotte Tobitt, 'Who Reads the Sun?', *Press Gazette*, 5 July 2023, https://pressgazette.co.uk/media-audience-and-business-data/media_metrics/who-reads-the-sun-circulation-demographic/

7   Interview with Francis Elliott.

8   Interview with Paul Waugh.

9   Interview with Gabriel Milland.

10 Michael Blastland and Andrew Dilnot, 'Review of the impartiality of BBC coverage of taxation, public spending, government borrowing and debt', November 2022, p. 4.

11 Ibid., p. 18.

12 Interview with Paul Waugh.

13 YouGov, 'How the government is handling the issue of immigration in the UK', https://yougov.co.uk/topics/politics/trackers/how-the-government-is-handling-the-issue-of-immigration-in-the-uk

14 Interview with Gabriel Milland.

15 Daisy Stephens, 'PM refers to Telegraph as his "real boss", Dominic Cummings claims', LBC News, 20 July 2021, https://www.lbc.co.uk/news/boris-johnson-refers-telegraph-real-boss-dominic-cummings-claims/

16 Vanessa Thorpe, '"He wants to shape wider culture": Why Paul Marshall is turning from GB News to the Telegraph', *The Observer*, 30 September 2023, https://www.theguardian.com/media/2023/sep/30/why-paul-marshall-is-turning-from-gb-news-to-the-telegraph#:~:text=Mildness%20and%20integrity%20are%20not,the%20outset%2C%20temporarily%20took%20over

17 Interview with John McTernan.

18 Ibid.

19 Simon Reynolds, *Retromania: Pop Culture's Addiction to Its Own Past* (Faber and Faber, 2011), p. xi.

20 Box Office Mojo, 'Top Lifetime Grosses', https://www.boxofficemojo.com/chart/top_lifetime_gross/?area=XWW

21 Savannah Walsh, 'Which Netflix show was the most streamed of 2022? The ratings are in . . . ', *Glamour Magazine*, 27

January 2023, https://www.glamourmagazine.co.uk/article/
most-streamed-netflix-show-2022

22   Fergal Kinney, 'The retromania election', *New Statesman*, 31 July 2023,
https://www.newstatesman.com/comment/2023/07/the-retromania-
election

23   Reynolds, p. xiii.

24   Jordan King, 'Liz Truss wears "identical" outfit to Margaret Thatcher
at Tory leadership debate', *Metro*, 16 July 2022, https://metro.
co.uk/2022/07/16/liz-truss-wears-identical-outfit-to-margaret-thatcher-
at-tory-debate-17010566/

25   Nigel Lawson, 'Rishi Sunak is the only candidate who understands
Thatcherite economics', *The Telegraph*, 3 August 2022, https://
www.telegraph.co.uk/news/2022/08/03/rishi-sunak-candidate-who-
understands-thatcherite-economics/

26   Rowena Mason and Peter Walker, ' "Clause IV on steroids": Keir
Starmer says his Labour must go further than Blair', *The Guardian*, 12
May 2023, https://www.theguardian.com/politics/2023/may/12/
clause-iv-on-steroids-keir-starmer-says-his-labour-must-go-further-
than-blair

27   Kinney, 2023.

28   Daniel Johnson, 'A return to Margaret Thatcher's Right to Buy home
scheme will always be loathed by the Left – and loved by voters',
Daily Mail, 4 May 2022, https://www.dailymail.co.uk/debate/
article-10780065/Margaret-Thatchers-Right-Buy-home-scheme-hated-
Left-writes-DANIEL-JOHNSON.html; David Mellor, 'I saw how
Margaret Thatcher flashed her steel against the unions. Now Boris
Johnson must show his mettle', *Daily Mail*, 22 June 2022, https://
www.dailymail.co.uk/debate/article-10943479/DAVID-MELLOR-
saw-Margaret-Thatcher-flashed-steel-against-unions-Boris-mettle.html;
Henry Kissinger, 'Why there was only one Iron Lady', *Daily Mail*, 22
October 2022, https://www.dailymail.co.uk/debate/article-11344127/
HENRY-KISSINGER-Liz-Truss-saw-heir-Thatcher-one-Iron-Lady.
html; Andrew Pierce, 'Rishi Sunak should follow Margaret Thatcher
and defend using private health', *Daily Mail*, 10 January 2023, https://
www.dailymail.co.uk/debate/article-11616973/ANDREW-PIERCE-
Rishi-Sunak-follow-Margaret-Thatcher-defend-using-private-health.
html; Philip Johnston, 'We've blown Mrs Thatcher's legacy. Now Rishi

must confront the truth', *Daily Telegraph*, 3 October 2023, https://
www.telegraph.co.uk/news/2023/10/03/weve-blown-mrs-thatchers-
legacy-rishi-must-confront-truth/; Charles Hall, 'Britain needs bold
tax cuts to make Mrs Thatcher's shareholder democracy dream a
reality', *Daily Telegraph*, 19 August 2023, https://www.telegraph.
co.uk/business/2023/08/19/britain-needs-bold-tax-cuts-to-make-mrs-
thatchers-sharehold/; Charles Moore, 'Rishi Sunak hasn't yet grasped the
secret of how Mrs Thatcher inspired Britain to strive', *Daily Telegraph*,
20 January 2023, https://www.telegraph.co.uk/news/2023/01/20/
rishi-sunak-hasnt-yet-grasped-secret-how-mrs-thatcher-inspired/

29 Simon Heffer, 'No End of a Lesson: The Imitation Thatcherism of
Liz Truss', The Centre for Independent Studies, 14 December 2022,
https://www.cis.org.au/publication/no-end-of-a-lesson-the-imitation-
thatcherism-of-liz-truss/

30 Interview with Charlotte Leslie.

31 PA, 'Tory Candidate Condemns "Hate-Consumed" Anti-Fracking
Vandals Who Flooded Her Parents' Garden With 1,000 Litres Of
Oil', *Huffington Post*, 7 May 2015, https://www.huffingtonpost.
co.uk/2015/05/07/charlotte-leslie-fracking_n_7230090.html

32 Maya Oppenheim, 'Man who threatened to car-bomb female Labour
MPs jailed', *The Independent*, 18 June 2020, https://www.independent.
co.uk/news/uk/home-news/rakeem-malik-boris-johnson-jess-phillips-car-
bomb-labour-a9573946.html

33 Isabel Hardman, *Why We Get the Wrong Politicians*
(Atlantic Books, 2019), p. 165.

34 Ibid.

35 Tim Shipman, *No Way Out* (William Collins, 2024), p. 336.

36 Tim Durrant, Alice Lilly and Paeony Tingay, 'WhatsApp in
Government', Institute for Government, March 2022, pp. 5, 10, https://
www.instituteforgovernment.org.uk/sites/default/files/publications/
whatsapp-in-government.pdf

37 Esther Webber, 'The perils of Boris Johnson's government by WhatsApp',
18 June 2021, Politico.eu, https://www.politico.eu/article/dominic-
cummings-screenshots-reveal-boris-johnson-government-by-whatsapp/

38 UK Covid-19 Inquiry, 'Transcript of Module 2 Public Hearing on 3
October 2023', 3 October 2023, https://covid19.public-inquiry.
uk/documents/transcript-of-module-2-public-hearing-on-3-october-2023/

39 UK Covid-19 Inquiry, transcript of WhatsApp messages, https://covid19.public-inquiry.uk/wp-content/uploads/2023/10/18172614/INQ000102697_0033.pdf

40 Interview with anonymous civil servant.

41 Sarah Scrobie, 'Covid-19 and the deaths of care home residents', Nuffield Trust, 17 February 2021, https://www.nuffieldtrust.org.uk/news-item/covid-19-and-the-deaths-of-care-home-residents

42 Interview with anonymous civil servant.

43 Haroon Siddique, 'Use of "VIP lane" to award Covid PPE contracts unlawful, high court rules', *The Guardian*, 12 January 2022, https://www.theguardian.com/politics/2022/jan/12/use-of-vip-lane-to-award-covid-ppe-contracts-unlawful-high-court-rules

44 Gareth Iacobucci, 'Covid-19: Government writes off £10bn on unusable, overpriced, or undelivered PPE', *The British Medical Journal*, 3 February 2022, https://www.bmj.com/content/376/bmj.o296

45 Interview with Amy Gandon.

46 Interview with Robert Kramer.

47 Media Reform Coalition, 'Who Owns the UK Media?', October 2023, https://www.mediareform.org.uk/wp-content/uploads/2023/10/Who-Owns-the-UK-Media-2023.pdf

48 Alex Farber, 'Reach: local job cuts by Mirror owner threaten your right to know', *The Times*, 18 November 2023, https://www.thetimes.co.uk/article/reach-local-job-cuts-by-mirror-owner-threaten-your-right-to-know-d8m6cvrsh

49 William Hague, 'Death of local papers threatens democracy', *The Times*, 11 March 2024, https://www.thetimes.co.uk/article/ee898ead-dd42-47f7-ba0b-6c64edf6dc23?shareToken=64d7eb65b9edcd49af76a3f33c89e6f2

50 Joshi Herriman, 'Do we just have to shrug our shoulders?', *The Mill*, 17 March 2024, https://manchestermill.co.uk/p/do-we-just-have-to-shrug-our-shoulders

51 Aisha Majid, 'Most popular news sources in the UK: Tiktok overtakes BBC Radio 1 and Channel 5', *Press Gazette*, 20 July 2023, https://pressgazette.co.uk/media-audience-and-business-data/most-popular-news-sources-uk-tiktok-ofcom-news-consumption-survey/

52 Ibid.

53 Durrant, Lilly and Tingay (2022), pp. 16–23.

CONCLUSION: ENDING OUR CRISIS

1 Resolution Foundation, 'A pre-election Statement', 23 November 2023, https://www.resolutionfoundation.org/publications/a-pre-election-statement/; Joseph Rowntree Foundation, 'Flagship study finds a million children experienced destitution in the UK last year', 24 October 2023, https://www.jrf.org.uk/news/flagship-study-finds-a-million-children-experienced-destitution-in-the-uk-last-year; Department for Levelling Up, Housing and Communities, 'Statutory homelessness in England: financial year 2022–23', 13 October 2023, https://www.gov.uk/government/statistics/statutory-homelessness-in-england-financial-year-2022-23/statutory-homelessness-in-england-financial-year-2022-23; Office of Rail and Road, 'Passenger rail performance 1 July to 30 September 2023', 7 December 2023, https://dataportal.orr.gov.uk/media/1kdfjw4u/performance_stats_release_jul-sep-2023.pdf

2 Public Accounts Committee, 'Dismantled National Programme for IT in NHS: report published', 18 September 2023, https://committees.parliament.uk/committee/127/public-accounts-committee/news/181704/dismantled-national-programme-for-it-in-nhs-report-published/

3 For a more detailed version of this analysis see Sam Freedman and Rachel Wolf, 'The NHS productivity puzzle: Why has hospital activity not increased in line with funding and staffing?', Institute for Government, June 2023, https://www.instituteforgovernment.org.uk/publication/nhs-productivity

4 See e.g. Shelter, 'Building for our future: A vision for social housing', https://england.shelter.org.uk/support_us/campaigns/a_vision_for_social_housing

5 Dominic Cummings, 'Temporary location for statement in response to Sunday Times story', blogpost, 30 December 2023, https://dominiccummings.substack.com/p/1-on-bismarck-the-ultimate-practical

INDEX

academy schools programme 59–61, 71,
72–3, 87
Adonis, Andrew 35
adult social care services 76, 114–17,
122, 283
Aleena, Zara 102–3
Allan, Sir Alex 201
Amess, David 280
Amis, Kingsley 70
Ancona, Matthew d' 238
Anderson, Lee 270
anti-terrorism policies 165, 250
appointments
to House of Lords 144–7, 299
of judges 174, 184
of MPs to special roles 138–9
to public bodies 184–93
of senior civil servants 218–19, 220–2, 225
Armstrong, Robert 42
Armstrong, Sir William 1–2
Asquith, Herbert 42, 233
asylum seekers. *See* immigration policies
Atos 97–8, 106, 108–9, 110, 113
Attlee, Clement 4, 66, 206, 278
Attorney General role 178–80
Audit Commission abolition 74
austerity policies 16, 74–5, 107–8, 153, 218
Avanti West Coast 105

Baker, Kenneth 59, 245
Baldwin, Stanley 233–4, 270
Balls, Ed 45–6, 47–8, 55, 212–13, 214, 257–8

Balogh, Thomas 206
Barber, Michael 32–3, 35–6, 36–7, 46
Barnardo's 189
Barran, Diana 149
BBC
Chairman appointments 190–1
early years 234, 235
news services 237, 264–5, 267, 269–70,
271, 287
Beaverbrook, Lord 233–4
Beer, Stafford 229
Bercow, John 142
Bernstein, Howard 82–3, 85
Bevan, Aneurin 67
Big Society policy 38, 48, 74, 139
Birmingham City Council 291
Birmingham Prison 99
Birt, John 31, 55
Blair, Cherie 247
Blair, Tony
backbench MPs, relations with 129,
132, 138
Chancellor (Brown), relationship with
45, 46–7, 55, 247
contemporary Labour Party's nostalgia
for 275–6, 277, 278
counter-terrorism policies 165, 250
crony/donor appointments 145–6
devolution to UK national assemblies
65, 72
local government reforms 72–3, 81–2
Lord Chancellor's role reform 174–5

Blair, Tony – *cont.*
  media relations 30, 237–40, 258, 271–2
  outsourcing policies 106–7, 292–3
  Prime Minister's Office reforms 31–3,
    35–7, 57
  programme motions introduced by 142–4
  special advisers *See* Campbell, Alastair;
    Powell, Jonathan
Blears, Hazel 82
Blunkett, David 165, 173–4, 175
Boateng, Paul 134
Bogdanor, Vernon 6
Bolsonaro, Jair 287
Brand, Paul 265–6
Braverman, Suella 156, 179–81, 182, 267
Brexit
  civil service, impact on 208, 216–18
  governance crisis attributed in part to
    16, 52, 291–2
  'left behind' regions voting for 62
  legislation implementing 144, 147, 150,
    152, 153, 156, 158
  May's Brexit deal efforts 39, 140,
    141–2, 163–4, 178
  Northern Ireland Protocol controversy
    179–80, 182
  prorogation of Parliament (2019)
    140–1, 142, 158, 164, 178, 183
Brown, George 43
Brown, Gordon
  as Chancellor of the Exchequer 45–9,
    50–1, 55, 106–7, 212–13, 243–4, 247
  as Prime Minister 33, 55
  Prime Minister's Office of 24–5, 33
Buckland, Robert 180–1, 200
Burnett, Lord 163
Burnham, Andy 87
Busy Bees Nurseries 119
Butler, Sir Robin 2, 3, 235–6, 239

Cabinet Office
  Downing Street offices 42
  establishment 26, 42
  proposed relocation of No. 10 to 25,
    31–2, 55
  role change over time 27, 54

cabinet secretary role 209–10, 220–2, 225
Cable, Vince 245–6
Callaghan, James 28, 70, 211, 235, 278
Cameron, David
  austerity policies 16, 74–5, 107–8,
    153, 218
  Big Society policy 38, 48, 74, 139
  Chancellor (Osborne), relationship
    with 55
  civil service reforms 208, 218–19
  crony/donor appointments 146
  local government policies 38,
    73–5, 82
  media relations 240–1, 247–8
  Prime Minister's Office reforms
    33–4, 37–8
  public appointments system reforms
    186–8
  spending commitments 75, 250
  other mentions 145, 252, 259
Campbell, Alastair
  Blair, views on 30–1
  media communications management
    229, 237–8, 239–40, 255, 287
  public profile and political influence
    197, 212, 214
Capita 97–8, 106, 113
Carillion Plc collapse (2018) 93, 110–12
Case, Simon 201, 219, 220–2
Castle, Barbara 211
Cates, Miriam 269
Cavendish, Camilla 11, 147, 231
centralization of power. *See*
  hyper-centralization
Chancellor of the Exchequer role 41–2,
  44–8, 55. *See also* Treasury
Changing Places accessible toilets fund
  79–80
Charity Commission, appointments to
  188–90
chess tables installation fund 79
Chewing Gum Task Force fund 79
child poverty 249, 291
Childcare Act 2016 151
children's services 76, 93–5, 114,
  117–20, 122

INDEX

Churchill, Winston 26, 27, 128, 133, 211, 232, 233
Circle Health Group 99
city mayors. *See* regional authorities and city mayors
Civil Contingencies Act 2004 154
civil service. *See also* Treasury
  antagonism from ministers 10, 199–202, 212, 216–18, 261
  pressure from overwork 26, 208, 209–10, 283–5
  recruitment practices over time 202–9
  reform proposals 222–6, 299–300
  role usurpation by SPADs 212–16, 224
  senior officials, appointments and dismissals 52, 56, 201, 218–22, 225
  senior officials, resignations 17–18, 64, 198, 200–1, 217–18, 225, 239
  Yes Minister portrayal 195–7, 207, 210–11, 212
Clarke, Ken 45, 46, 48, 131, 238–9, 246, 281
cleaning services 97
Clegg, Nick 83, 146, 241, 247–8
Climate Change Act 2008 153
Clooney, Amal 179–80
combined local authorities. *See* regional authorities and city mayors
Commission for Smart Government 57
constitutional conventions 5–6, 9
Constitutional Reform Act 2005 174–5, 184
Cooper, Ellie 280
Cooper, Rosie 280
Coronavirus Act 2020 154, 155
Coulson, Andy 240
councils. *See* local government
counter-terrorism policies 165, 250
courts system. *See* judiciary
Covid-19 pandemic
  court cases arising from 158, 164
  government response, management style 58, 214, 221–2, 282–4

government response, Parliamentary scrutiny avoided 150, 154–6, 172, 173
media coverage 264, 265–6, 268–9
NHS procurement in 164, 283–4, 293
Partygate scandal 56, 265–6
Cowley, Philip 129
Cox, Geoffrey 178, 179
Cox, Jo 280
Craig, Paul 172
Crerar, Pippa 265–6
criminal justice policies
  counter-terrorism measures 165, 250
  'crackdown' announcements 253, 271–2
  generally 295
  prison services, private delivery 97, 98–9, 111, 112
  probation services private delivery 99–103
  sentencing 241, 253–4, 260–1
crisis cycles 2–5, 20
crony appointments.
  See appointments
Crossman, Richard 195–6
Cruddas, Peter 145
cultural nostalgia 272–3
culture war politics 189, 191
Cummings, Dominic
  civil service, frustrations with 201–2, 209, 210, 223
  executive dominance practised by 141, 156, 214, 220, 300–1
  media communications 81–2, 230–1
  other mentions 23, 25, 269

Dacre, Paul 190–1
Daily Mail, The
  circulation figures 262
  civil service opposition 225–6
  client journalism 240, 241, 268
  Dacre (editor), Ofcom appointment attempt 190–1
  early years 232, 233–4
  judicial review opposition 164, 175, 177
  nostalgia politics in headlines 276

Daily Mail, The – cont.
online version 268
political influence 260, 287
Daily Telegraph, The
client journalism 240, 252–3
nostalgia politics in headlines 276
online version 268
political influence 268–9, 287
prospective sale 270
Dale, Iain 258
Darling, Alistair 49, 55, 250
Davis, Sir Mick 146
Day, Robin 236
defence procurement 45–6, 75
Defoe, Daniel 11
delegated legislation, increasing use
150–7, 183
Delivery Unit of No. 10, Blair era 32–3,
34, 35–6, 36–7, 46
Deputy Prime Minister role 29
devolution
to local authorities *See* local government
in other countries 40, 62, 64–5
to regional authorities and city mayors
See regional authorities and city
mayors
to UK national assemblies 7, 65, 72
Disraeli, Benjamin 41
donor appointments. *See* appointments
Donoughue, Bernard 196, 212
Duterte, Rodrigo 287
Dyson, Lord 169–70, 178

economic crisis of 1970s 1–2, 28, 43
economic growth 44–6, 62–3, 277–8
Eden, Anthony 9, 235
education services
centralized control 38, 59–61,
70–1, 72–3
devolution need 87–8
media-focused policy announcements
229–31, 242, 245, 247–8
Office for Students, appointment to 190
outsourced school inspections 98
Schools Bill (2022) 149
sex education reviews 269

special educational needs provision 76
targets-based governance 37, 38–9
Treasury under-investment 53–4
Ekins, Richard 172
Elliott, Francis 232–3, 265
European Exchange Rate Mechanism
withdrawal (1993) 44
executive dominance. *See also* MPs;
Parliament
civil service undermined *See* civil service
Commons legislative scrutiny, efforts to
avoid 129–30, 140–4, 149–58,
163, 173
crony/donor appointments *See*
appointments
development over time 127–9
judicial review undermined *See* judicial
review
overview 8–10, 122–3, 129–30, 301–2
Prime Minister role *See* Prime Minister
pushback against rebellious MPs 130,
135–40
solutions 14, 158–61, 184, 222–6,
298–301

Falkender, Lady (Marcia Williams) 196,
206, 211
Faulks, Lord 180–1
'Fawkes, Guido' (Paul Staines) 258
fiscal rules of Treasury 48–51, 54–5,
107, 115
Flinders, Matthew 128
Foot, Michael 274
Four Seasons Healthcare 116–17
Fowler, Norman 146
Fraser, Orlando 189
French government 65
Fry, Stephen 258
fuel poverty legislation 249–50
Fulton Report on civil service recruitment
202–3, 206, 208, 223
funds for local regeneration 77–80, 136–7

G4S 97–8, 99, 101, 106, 112–13
Gandon, Amy 284
Gauke, David 253–4, 260, 261

GB News 270
German government 15, 223
Ghosh, Helen 47
Gibb, Nick 38–9
Gibb, Robbie 191
Gladstone, William 9, 41
global financial crisis (2007–8) 33, 49, 55, 293
Gove, Michael 54–5, 59, 86, 230, 245, 260–1
governance crisis
    dimensions of See executive dominance; hyper-centralization; media-focused politics
    as institutional failure 16–20, 295–7
    overview of 5–13, 291–5, 302–3
    whether unique to UK 15–16, 297
government departments
    in Cameron era 34
    competition for funding 17, 43, 44
    public services delivery by See hyper-centralization
    special advisers to 26
    Treasury oversight 33, 46–7, 48–50, 51, 53–5, 58
Grade, Michael 191
grant-maintained schools 71, 72–3
Grayling, Chris 100, 101, 175–6, 177–8
Greater Manchester
    economic productivity 62–3
    local government in 77–8, 82–3, 84, 85, 87
    Mill, The (online local newspaper) 286
Green, David Allen 157
Green, Philip 111
Grid (scheduled media communications) 229–32, 236, 238, 241–2, 251–2, 256, 302
Grimstone, Gerry 187–8

Hague, William 274, 286
Hailsham, Lord 5–6, 8, 128, 170
Haines, Joe 235
Hammond, Philip 56, 98, 244–5
Hancock, Matt 282–3
Hardman, Isabel 280

Harrison, Rupert 6–7, 83, 84, 89–90
Hayter, William 204
Healey, Denis 4–5
health service. See NHS (National Health Service)
Heath, Edward 1–2, 4, 27, 28, 129, 236
Heffer, Simon 277–8
Helm, Dieter 107
Hennessy, Peter 6, 27
Henry VIII powers 151
Heseltine, Michael 29, 83
Heywood, Jeremy 31, 32, 34, 35, 56, 209, 221
Heywood, Suzanne 31
Hickman, Tom 156
Hilton, Steve 33, 74
hospitals, private 98, 99
Houchen, Ben 84
House of Lords. See also Parliament
    Commons supremacy over 8, 148–9, 152, 153, 157
    constitutional role, increased significance 6, 10, 14, 144, 147–50, 301
    crony/donor appointments to 144–7, 299
    reform proposals 159, 299
housing, social 54–5, 69–70, 72, 294–5
Howe, Geoffrey 28
HS2 rail project 19, 248
Human Rights Act 1998 168, 172, 174
Hunt, Jeremy 39, 56, 160
Hunt, John 127
Hutton, Lord 239
hyper-centralization
    institutions of See Cabinet Office; Prime Minister's Office; Treasury
    local government diminution
        See local government
    of media announcements (the Grid) 229–32, 236, 238, 241–2, 251–2, 256, 302
    outsourcing to private sector
        See private sector delivery of public services
    short-termism concern 6–8, 18–19, 36, 51–2, 301–2

hyper-centralization – *cont.*
  solutions to 13–14, 56–8, 87–91,
    120–1, 186, 297–8, 302
  targets-based governance *See* targets-
    based governance

immigration policies
  generally 295
  Illegal Migration Bill (2023) 143–4,
    149–50, 250
  judicial review of 158, 164, 165, 167,
    181, 182
  media reporting on 266–7
  Rwanda, outsourcing to 164, 165, 167,
    181, 182, 267
  secondary legislation used for 152–3
Implementation Unit of Prime Minister's
  Office 34
Ingham, Bernard 197, 198, 236–7, 240
Institute for Government 56–7
International Monetary Fund bailout
  (1976) 4, 43, 68
Interserve 100–1, 112
Iraq War (2003-11) 36
Irvine, Derry 175

James, Lisa 141, 142
Janvrin, Robin 150
Jay, Antony 195–6
Johnson, Boris
  Brexit role *See* Brexit
  Chancellor (Sunak),
    relationship with 56
  civil service undermined by 201–2
  Covid-19 pandemic role *See* Covid-19
    pandemic
  crony/donor appointments
    145, 189–91, 299
  immigration policies 130, 181
  judicial review restrictions 179–82
  as Mayor of London 84
  media relations 130, 269
  personality and leadership style 16, 39,
    40, 179, 295–6
  Prime Minister's Office of 25
  senior civil servant dismissals 220–1

special adviser *See* Cummings, Dominic
  other mentions 35, 139, 160, 250
Jowett, Benjamin 204–5
Judge, Lord 151
judicial review
  access rules tightened 177–8, 181
  constitutional role 6, 9, 10,
    167–71, 301
  executive's attacks on 164–7, 173–4,
    178–83
  of immigration policies 158, 164, 165,
    167, 181, 182
  judicial appointments 174, 184
  judicial overreach concern 171–3, 183–4
  legal aid cutbacks 175–7
  Lord Chancellor role reform
    174–5, 177–8
  political campaigners' recourse to 163–4

Kelly, David 238
Kelso, Alexandra 128
Kempsell, Ross 145
Keynes, John Maynard 42–3
Kingman, John 53, 62, 85, 90,
  191–2, 217–18
King's Speech announcements 248–51
Kinney, Fergal 274, 275–6
Kinnock, Neil 27, 246, 274
Kipling, Rudyard 233–4
Kissock, Paul 52, 64
Kwarteng, Kwasi 52, 56, 245

Lamont, Norman 106
Lansley, Andrew 34, 39
Laws, David 97–8
Lawson, Nigel 28, 44–5, 275
Lebedev, Evgeny 145
legal aid cutbacks 175–7
legality principle 169
legislation. *See also* Parliament
  on immigration *See* immigration policies
  Parliamentary scrutiny,
    executive efforts to avoid 129–30,
      140–4, 149–58, 163, 173
  poor quality drafting 135, 144, 149–50,
    158, 252

secondary legislation, increasing use 150–7, 183

symbolic/performative 130, 149, 248–52

Leslie, Charlotte 139, 279–80

Letwin, Oliver 33–4

levelling up policy and funds 77–9, 86, 136–7

Lewis, Brandon 179

Lewis, Michael 222

Lidington, David 131, 133, 134, 144, 215–16

Littlejohn, Richard 11

Livingstone, Ken 69

Lloyd George, David 9, 26, 42, 66, 211, 232–3, 278

Lobby (media briefings in Parliament) 234–5, 236, 237, 262

lobbying 247

local government

autonomy restrained by central government 7, 61–3, 75–7, 80–1, 86–7, 89–90

bankruptcies 291

Cameron era policies and budget cuts 38, 73–5, 82

central government funding schemes 77–80

combined regional authorities See regional authorities and city mayors

early years of 65–7

education authorities, diminished role 38, 59–61, 70–1, 72–3

housing authorities, diminished role 69–70, 72, 294–5

outsourcing of operations See private sector delivery of public services

as solution to hyper-centralization 13–14, 87–91, 122, 186, 297–8, 302

Thatcher era reforms 29, 44, 67–72, 294

local media, decline of 285–6, 300

London

Covid lockdowns in 155

Docklands regeneration 83

economic productivity 62

local government in 67, 68–9, 84, 88, 120

probation service in 102–3

Lord Chancellor role 174–5, 177–8, 184

Lovegrove, Stephen 219–20, 221

Lowe, Robert 204–5

Lynn, Jonathan 195–6

McBride, Damian 243, 258

MacDonald, Ramsay 234

McDonald, Simon 217

Macmillan, Harold 4, 23, 27, 42, 278

MacNamara, Helen 17, 58, 155, 216–17

Macpherson, Nicholas 43, 44, 45, 47, 219

McTernan, John 270–1, 272

Maitland, Donald 236

Major, John 29–30, 105, 117–18, 132, 237–8, 240

Malleson, Kate 174–5, 183–4

Manchester. See Greater Manchester

Mare, Tom de la 153

Marshall, Paul 270

Maude, Francis 207–8, 218, 223–4

Maximus Inc. 109, 110

May, Theresa

Brexit deal efforts 39, 140, 141–2, 163–4, 178

Chancellor (Hammond), relationship with 56

Prime Minister's Office of 25

other mentions 139, 269

mayors. See regional authorities and city mayors

media relations of Prime Ministers

Baldwin 233–4

Blair and Brown 30, 237–40, 241, 243–4, 258, 271–2

Cameron 240–1, 247–8

Heath 236

Johnson 130, 269

Lloyd George and Churchill 26, 232–3

Major 30, 237–8, 240

Sunak 130, 269, 271

Thatcher 28–9, 236–7, 258

Truss 252–3, 275, 277

Wilson 235

media-focused politics. *See also* particular
  media outlets
  Budget briefings 242–6, 247, 255–6
  clichés and nostalgia 272–9
  development over time *See* media
    relations of Prime Ministers
  Grid (scheduled media communications)
    229–32, 236, 238, 241–2, 251–2,
    256, 302
  media industry changes, impact of 262,
    268–72, 285–7
  Ofcom, appointments to 190–1
  overview 10–12
  party conferences 246–8, 256
  political journalism, quality
    loss 261–7
  social media effects *See* social media
  solutions 14, 252–6, 285–9, 300
  symbolic/performative legislation 130,
    149, 248–52
members of Parliament. *See* MPs (members
  of Parliament)
Miliband, David 35
Mill, The (online local newspaper) 286
Milland, Gabriel 255, 259–60, 260–1,
    263–4, 268–9
Millar, Ronnie 23–4
Miller, Gina 163
miners' strikes 1–2, 274
Mitchell, David 127
Mitterrand, François 23
monarchy 6, 8
Montgomerie, Tim 270
Moran, Michael 185–6
Morgan, Sally 30
Morrison, Herbert 67
Mount, Ferdinand 25
MPs (members of Parliament). *See also*
    Parliament
  abused on social media 12, 279–81
  backbench rebellions 9, 129, 130,
    134–5, 142
  constituency work 132–3, 159
  as GB News presenters 270
  legislative work 14, 129–30,
    140–4, 149–58, 159–61, 298–9

  ministers, PPSs and other special roles
    9, 134, 137–9, 160, 186
  professionalization of role 131–4, 186
  public perception of 20, 127–8,
    130, 302
  social media use 258–60, 281–2
  whip system 9, 135–40
  women and minority group members
    134, 142–3, 280
Mullin, Chris 137
Murdoch, Iris 70
Murdoch, Rupert 237, 270, 272

National Trust 189
Nelson, Fraser 186–7
Nesta (think-tank) 57
Neuberger, Lord 180
New Labour. *See* Blair, Tony; Brown,
    Gordon
NHS (National Health Service)
  Cameron era reforms 34, 293
  in Covid-19 pandemic 164,
    283–4, 293
  current crises facing 5, 116, 291, 293–4
  foundation 66–7
  New Labour era reforms
    36, 292–3
  outsourcing to private hospitals 98, 99
  targets-based governance 37, 39, 292–3
  Treasury spending controls 53, 75,
    292, 293
No. 10 Downing Street. *See* Prime
    Minister's Office
Northcote–Trevelyan Report (1854)
    204–5, 206
Northern Ireland Protocol 179–80, 182
nostalgia, politics of 272–9
nursery care services 117–19

O'Donnell, Gus 39–40, 221, 237
Ofcom 190–1, 270, 288
Office for Students, appointment to 190
Office of Budget Responsibility 49, 50
Omand, David 213
Online Safety Act 2023 129–30
Osborne, George

departmental spending controls 48, 49, 55, 75

local authority budget cuts 38, 74–5

media relations 240–1, 244

on private sector contract awards 98

regional authorities encouraged by 83–4

other mentions 145

outsourcing. *See* private sector delivery of public services

over-centralization. *See* hyper-centralization

overseas aid legislation 250

Owen, Charlotte 145

Owen, Ed 213

Parliament. *See also* executive dominance; legislation; MPs

House of Lords *See* House of Lords

legislative scrutiny, executive efforts to avoid 129–30, 140–4, 149–58, 163, 173

media briefings from 234–5, 236, 237, 262

Prime Minister's Questions 27, 28, 40

programme motions 142–4

prorogation by Johnson (2019) 140–1, 142, 158, 164, 178, 183

reform proposals 14, 158–61, 298–9

select committees 160, 299, 302

sovereignty 168, 170–1, 173

televising of 11

Parliament Acts (1911 and 1949) 8, 148–9

parliamentary private secretaries (PPSs) 138

party conferences 246–8, 256

Patel, Priti 200–1, 217

Paxman, Jeremy 236

permanent secretaries, appointments and dismissals 52, 56, 201, 218–20, 225

Personal Independence Payment system 109–10

PFI (Private Finance Initiative) 106–7, 108, 114–15

Phillips, Jess 280

Pickles, Eric 38, 73–4

Pickston, Ampika 93–4, 114

Policy Unit of Prime Minister's Office 25, 27–8, 32, 34

poll tax 29, 71–2

Powell, Charles 198

Powell, Jonathan 24, 30, 138, 212, 224–5, 225–6

PPSs (parliamentary private secretaries) 138

PR (proportional representation) 297

Prescott, John 81, 82

Price, Lance 272

Prime Minister. *See also* Prime Minister's Office

media relations *See* media relations of Prime Ministers

powers 8–9, 17, 31–2, 40, 302

qualities desirable in 295–6

questions in Parliament to 27, 28, 40

role expansion over time 26–32, 39–40, 54

special advisers to (SPADs) 25–6, 197, 210–16, 224, 231

Prime Minister's Office (No. 10 Downing Street)

Blair era reforms 31–3, 35–7, 57

Cabinet Office proximity 42

Cameron era reforms 33–4, 37–8

cramped conditions 23–5, 41

Johnson era dysfunction 39, 58, 214, 221–2, 282–4

May era reform efforts 25, 39

media communications centre 11

reform proposals 57–8

Sunak era reform efforts 39

Treasury relations 46–8

principle of legality 169

prison services, private delivery 97, 98–9, 111, 112

private sector delivery of public services

accountability problem 8, 80–1, 97–8, 108–10, 121

austerity policies, impact on 107–8

cost inefficiency 93–5, 103

embedded practice/lack of true competition problem 103–4, 108–13

in New Labour era 73, 106–7, 292–3

private sector delivery – *cont.*
  private equity market's role 113–20
  public safety risk 98–103
  rationale for 95–7
  solutions to problems 121–2
  in Thatcher era 29, 69–70, 104–6
privatization of public utilities 67–8,
  105, 185
probation services, private delivery 99–103
programme motions 142–4
proportional representation (PR) 297
public bodies, appointments to 184–93
Public Order Act 2023 156–7
public service agreements of government
  departments 33, 46–7
public services. *See also* particular public
  services
  austerity policies affecting 16, 74–5,
    107–8, 153, 218
  centralized delivery *See*
    hyper-centralization
  civic delivery (Big Society policy) 38,
    48, 74, 139
  devolved regional delivery need 13–14,
    87–91
  private delivery *See* private sector delivery
    of public services
  under-investment in 51–3, 54–5
public utilities privatization 67–8,
  105, 185

quangos, appointments to 184–93

Raab, Dominic 175, 182, 199–200,
  215, 217
Reeves, Martin 85–6
regional authorities and city mayors. *See*
  also local government
  background to 81–4
  disparities between authorities 84–6, 88
  fiscal autonomy resisted by Treasury
    86–7, 89–90
  as solution to hyper-centralization
    13–14, 87–91, 122, 186, 297–8, 302
regulatory bodies, appointments
  to 184–93

Reid, John 165
Reynolds, Simon 272–3, 274
Riddell, Peter 190
Roney, Joanne 77–8
Rothermere, Lord 233–4, 288
Rothschild, Victor 1
Russell, Justin 213
Russell, Meg 141, 142
Rutnam, Philip 200–1
Rutter, Jill 238–9
Rwanda, asylum seeker transfer to 164,
  165, 167, 181, 182, 267
Rycroft, Philip 209

Scholar, Tom 52, 56, 201, 219, 221
schools. *See* education services
Schools Bill (2022) 149
secondary legislation, increasing use
  150–7, 183
Sedwill, Mark 201, 219–20
select committees of Parliament 160,
  299, 302
sentencing policies 241, 253–4, 260–1
Serco 97–8, 101, 106, 110, 112–13
Sharp, Dame Evelyn 195–6
short-termism 6–8, 18–19, 36, 51–2,
  301–2
skeleton bills 151–2, 183
Sky News 11, 237, 269
Slater, Jonathan 201, 208
Slocock, Caroline 198
Smith, Adam 16
social care services 76, 93–5, 114–17,
  119–20, 122, 283
social housing 54–5, 69–70, 72, 294–5
social media. *See also* media-focused politics
  abuse of MPs on 12, 279–81
  acceleration of news cycle 11–12,
    257–60, 262–3, 265–6
  decision-making on WhatsApp 281–5,
    288–9
  populist politicians on 287
  traditional news media replaced by 270,
    287–8
social welfare system 75, 108–10
Sodexo 100–1

Southern Cross Healthcare 116
Spanish flu pandemic (1918-20) 7
special advisers (SPADs) 25–6, 197, 210–16, 224, 231. *See also* particular SPADs
special educational needs services 76
spending control rules of Treasury 48–51, 54–5, 107, 115
Staines, Paul ('Guido Fawkes') 258
Starmer, Keir 271, 275–6
statutory instruments 152–7
Steward, George F. 234
Stewart, Rory 252–3
Steyn, Lord 170, 172
Stowell, Baroness 188–9
Strategy Unit of Prime Minister's Office 32, 34, 35, 36
Straw, Jack 211, 213
Street, Andy 84
Strikes (Minimum Service Levels) Act 250–1
Sullivan, David 93–4
Sumption, Lord 171–2, 173
Sun, The 237, 262, 272
Sunak, Rishi
  backbench rebellions against 129, 140
  as Chancellor of the Exchequer 56
  Cummings's advice to 300
  immigration policies 143–4, 149–50, 164, 165, 167, 182, 250
  media relations 130, 269, 271
  party conference speech (2023) 18–19, 248
  Prime Minister's Office of 39
  other mentions 35, 78, 145, 199, 276
Swift, Jonathan 11

Talk TV 270
Talyor, A. J. P. 233
targets-based governance
  in Cameron era 38–9, 74, 293
  in New Labour era 33, 37, 46–7, 73, 292–3
  problems generally 37, 249
10 Downing Street. *See* Prime Minister's Office

Thatcher, Margaret
  civil service, attitudes towards 196–8, 207, 211
  contemporary Tories' nostalgia for 274–5, 276–8
  economic policies 5, 277–8
  local government reforms 29, 44, 67–72, 294
  media relations 28–9, 236–7, 258
  outsourcing policies 29, 69–70, 104–6
  personality and leadership style 28–9, 33–4
  Prime Minister's Questions reform 27, 28
  special advisers 25, 28, 211–12
  other mentions 23, 129
The Thick of It 197–8, 257
Thomas, Alex 222
Thomas, John 150
Thomas, Martin 189
Times, The 232–3, 236, 237, 268
Timothy, Nick 25, 56, 241–2
Tinline, Phil 3
Tolley, Adam 199
Towns Fund 78–9
Treasury. *See also* civil service
  Budget, media briefings 242–6, 247, 255–6
  Chancellor of the Exchequer role 41–2, 44–8, 55
  culture of ('Treasury brain') 42, 51–4, 89, 293, 294
  economic growth policies 44–6, 277–8
  fiscal devolution resisted by 86–8, 89–90
  proposals to break up 55, 56, 57
  role expansion over time 41–8
  spending control rules 48–51, 54–5, 107, 115
  targets-based governance by *See* targets-based governance
  Whitehall offices 41, 42
Trevelyan, Sir Charles 205
Trump, Donald 15, 222, 287

Truss, Liz
  crony/donor appointments 145, 299
  energy support package 105
  as Lord Chancellor 175
  media relations 252–3, 275, 277
  'mini-budget' 245, 277
  senior civil servant dismissals 52, 56,
    201, 219–20, 221
  special advisers 26, 231
  other mentions 16, 23, 39, 149, 295–6
Tugendhat, Tom 160

United Kingdom Internal Market
  Bill (2020) 179–80
US government 9, 15, 40, 223

Vallance, Patrick 283
Vine, Sarah 11

Wagner, Adam 154
Wakeford, Christian 136
Walden, Brian 236–7
Wallace, David Foster 229
Wallace, Mark 103
Walpole, Robert 41, 159
Warner, Norman 213
Waugh, Paul 258–9, 263, 266
welfare benefits system 75, 108–10
West Midlands Combined Authority
  84, 85–6
Westlake, Sheridan 74

Wharton, James 190
WhatsApp, decision-making on
  281–5, 288–9
Whelan, Charlie 238, 239, 243
whip system 9, 135–40
White, Alan 109
White, Hannah 156
Whitehouse, Mary 197, 198
Wilkes, Giles 51, 245–6
William Tyndale Junior School,
  Islington 70
Williams, Marcia (Lady Falkender) 196,
  206, 211
Williamson, Gavin 190
Wilson, Harold
  civil service review 202–3, 206–7
  media relations 235
  Prime Minister's Office of 27–8
  special advisers 195–6, 206,
    211, 212
  Treasury, relationship with 43
  other mentions 1, 4
Wilson, Richard 31–2
work capability assessments, private
  delivery of 108–9
Working Links 101, 102, 112
Wragg, William 136–7
Wyatt, Woodrow 237

Yes Minister 195–7, 207,
  210–11, 212